South Asia
Post-Nehruvian Dynamics of Diplomacy

South Asia

Post-Nehruvian Dynamics of Diplomacy

Edited by

K.M. Sajad Ibrahim

Director, UGC-Nehru Studies Centre,
University of Kerala, Thiruvananthapuram

New Century Publications
New Delhi, India

NEW CENTURY PUBLICATIONS
4800/24, Bharat Ram Road,
Ansari Road, Daryaganj,
New Delhi - 110 002 (India)

Tel.: 011-2324 7798, 4358 7398, 6539 6605
Fax: 011-4101 7798
E-mail: indiatax@vsnl.com • info@newcenturypublications.com
www.newcenturypublications.com

Editorial office:
LG–7, Aakarshan Bhawan,
4754-57/23, Ansari Road, Daryaganj,
New Delhi - 110 002

Tel.: 011-4356 0919

First Published: **July 2013**

ISBN: **978-81-7708-355-2**

Published by New Century Publications and printed at Salasar Imaging Systems, New Delhi.

Designs: Patch Creative Unit, New Delhi.

PRINTED IN INDIA

About the Book

South Asia continues to be one of the most volatile regions of the world. Even though it has a common cultural background and shared political experience, many groups have been fiercely fighting, challenging the national governments and frustrating their nation-building efforts, such as in India, Pakistan, Nepal, Sri Lanka, Myanmar, and Bangladesh. The negative effects of ongoing ethnic conflicts, civil wars, communal and political violence, terrorism, counter-terrorism, religious extremism, militarization, violation of human rights, unresolved inter-state and intra-state conflicts, and subversive economic activities are more visible today than ever before.

In this context, the role of Jawaharlal Nehru to promote peace in South Asia deserves special attention. Apart from his careful handling of India's tumultuous domestic situation during the years immediately after Independence in 1947, Nehru's major contribution lies in the field of foreign policy of the country. However, post-Nehruvian era has witnessed dramatic changes in India's foreign policy, with South Asia emerging as a crisis region in the world.

This book contains 13 scholarly research papers which provide deep insights into divergent issues/concerns in South Asia in the background of Nehruvian vision of peace and co-operation in the region.

Editor's Profile

Dr. K.M. Sajad Ibrahim is the Director of UGC-Nehru Studies Centre, University of Kerala, Thiruvananthapuram. He is also Assistant Professor, Department of Political Science, University of Kerala. He is the recipient of Dr. Ramaswamy Mudaliar Gold Medal and Professor K.V. Nandan Menon Prize of University of Kerala (1990). He was International Visiting Fellow in US in 2008. He has contributed more than twenty research articles in reputed journals including *Economic and Political Weekly* and *India Quarterly*.

Dr. Sajad has made more than thirty presentations at various international and national seminars/conferences. His areas of research interest include West Asian Politics, Indian Muslims, Comparative Politics, and International Relations.

Contents

Contributors

G.P. Ramachandra	Former Professor and Director, School of International Relations, M.G. University, Kottayam.
W. Lawrence S. Prabhakar	Associate Professor, Department of Political Science, Madras Christian College, Chennai.
Maqbool Ahmed Siraj	Senior Executive Editor, Islamic Voice, Bangalore.
Joseph Antony	Associate Professor in Political Science, Fatima Mata National College, Kollam.
Sayed Abdul Muneem Pasha	Associate Professor, Department of Political Science, Jamia Millia Islamia, New Delhi.
Josukutty C.A.	Assistant Professor, Department of Political Science, University of Kerala, Karivattom, Thiruvananthapuram.
S.Y. Surendra Kumar	Assistant Professor, Department of Political Science, University of Bangalore.
Venkat Lokanathan	Assistant Professor, St. Joseph's Post-graduate Political Science Research Centre, St. Joseph's College, Bangalore.
Anil Kumar P.	Assistant Professor, Department of Political Science, Maharaja's College, Ernakulum, Kochi.
Khursheed Ahmad Wani	Research Scholar, UNESCO Madanjeet Singh Institute of South Asia Regional Co-operation, Pondicherry University, Puducherry.

South Asia

Shibu M.P.   Assistant Professor in Political Science, VTM NSS College, Dhanuvachapuram, Thiruvananthapuram.

Shyna V.V.   Research Scholar, UNESCO Madanjeet Singh Institute of South Asia Regional Cooperation, Pondicherry University, Puducherry.

Yaqoob Ul Hassan   Research Scholar, Department of Political Science, Jamia Millia Islamia, New Delhi.

Introduction

By

K.M. Sajad Ibrahim

South Asia continues to be one of the most volatile regions of the world. It is characterized by multi-ethnic societies with striking internal divisions along linguistic, regional, communal and sectarian lines, externally linked to one another across national boundaries. Even though it has a common cultural background and shared political experience, many groups have been fiercely fighting with each other, challenging the national governments and frustrating their nation-building efforts, such as in India, Pakistan, Nepal, Sri Lanka, Myanmar, and Bangladesh. The negative effects of ongoing ethnic conflicts, civil wars, ethnic cleansing, communal and political violence, terrorism, counter terrorism, religious extremism, militarization, gross and systematic violation of human rights, unresolved inter-state and intra-state conflicts, and subversive economic interests, etc., are visible today more than ever before in the region.

Home to one fifth of the world's population, this region is accountable for fifty percent of the world's illiterate and forty percent of the world's poor. This poverty stricken region faces the worst hit of innumerable adversities in terms of securing peace, and security. The extent of human deprivation in the region contrasts with the large armies, modern weapons and increasing defence budgets, arms race, and nuclear power struggle, which keep the region seething with growing unrest. The criminalisation of politics and corruption undermine the democratic principles of the electoral system.

South Asia has emerged as a regional entity in the international political system with the creation of SAARC but it failed to strengthen regional cohesiveness. Regional cooperation in South Asia cannot be said to have evolved into a complete bloc in terms of 'regionalism and economic integration' due mainly to the prevalence of conflict over the desire of peace and stability. Given the historical legacy and contemporary reality of endemic conflicts and mistrust in the region, the fact that the formal cooperation process in the region has survived recurrent setbacks is testimony of resilience of the organisation.

Undoubtedly, the intra-regional problems in South Asia are of such a vast magnitude that they demand not only a comprehensive understanding of regional specificities and particularities but also short and long-term modalities and mechanisms to manage the manifold nature of security perceptions and conflicts from a pragmatic perspective. South Asia has come into a sharp focus ever since India and Pakistan carried out multiple nuclear weapon tests in May 1998. The entire international community is seriously worried out over the disastrous consequences of nuclear South Asia.

The prolonged conflicts in Afghanistan, India's Northeast, Kashmir, Pakistan's Baluchistan and Nepal, substantiate the state's insecure control of territory, occupation, the pursuit of power and identity politics mobilization. These issues have gradually transformed into the politics of extremism in which the cause of justice, freedom and humanity have been destroyed.

There is no single factor or reason for the cause of conflict in South Asia. Rather, it is embroiled in many issues and provides a disappointing picture in every social, economic and political context. This is on account of the fact that South Asia is almost perpetually plagued by various inter and intra-state conflicts and crisis stemming from the insouciant approach of the ruling elite toward resolution of such problems which are based on narrow considerations of caste, religion, ethnicity, language, community, and the like. This damaged the national integrity and unity of the affected states.

Furthermore, South Asia is an area of tremendous political complexities. States like Pakistan and Bangladesh have been largely ruled by authoritarian military rulers. India, per se faces several unresolved issues that stem from internal as well as external sources. These include ethnicity, border disputes, separatist demands, terrorism and subversive activities, communal and religious tensions and so on. All these issues flout the basic ideals of nation building in India, that is, the ideals of democracy, secularism, socialism and federalism. In fact, the existence of these problems prevent India from becoming a 'nation' in a true sense of the term, which adversely affects the imperatives of order, welfare and legitimacy.

In Nepal, for example, the series of democratically elected government failed to bring any better result than the old royal regime as a result of widespread corruption and crisis of governance. The political fundamentalists like Maoists and mainstream political parties are posing major threat to democracy in Nepal. In addition to creating law and order problems, increased human rights violations and a heavy reliance on security forces have undermined the question of legitimacy of governance in Nepal. Moreover, the problem of civil violence in recent years has led to serious security issue than the problem of inter-state warfare in South Asia. India has been variously preoccupied with quelling separatists and religious conflicts, for the separatists, Mizoram, Assam, and Nagaland (Eastern India) for autonomy and in Gujarat, Mumbai, Karnataka and other parts have certain religious, ethnic, psychological and economic underpinnings.

South Asian nations, despite their apparent adherence to the ideal of nonalignment, have pursued extremely inconsonant foreign policies. Consequently, the major global powers have played their roles in aggravating the intra-regional cleavages of South Asia. Finally, India's overwhelming regional preponderance generates certain basic insecurities and sharp differences with its neighbourhood. All these aspects have created a multitude of problems for the South Asian region.

These problems collectively boil down to a crisis of legitimacy, welfare, and order in the affected area. The troubles in South Asia, its endemic tensions, mutual distrust and occasional hostilities are largely considered products of the contradictions of India's security perception with that of the rest of the countries of the area. India's neighbours perceive threats to their security coming primarily from India whereas India considers neighbours as an integral part of its own security system. The pre-eminence of India in the South Asian power configuration given its geography, demography, economy, and ecology is something about which neither India nor its neighbours can do nothing but accept. But the image of India in South Asia is that of a power that demands habitual obedience from its neighbours. Thus, the main theme of this doctrine is that South Asia is to be regarded as an Indian backyard.

India is placed in a unique position in South Asia. It is the only country in South Asia that shares borders with the rest of South Asian countries, whereas, none of them share common borders with each other. India also occupies a pre-eminent position in South Asia, unlike any to her country in the Southeast Asian region, in terms of the size of its population, natural resources, economy and industrial, military, and technological power. Nevertheless, Pakistan has a strategic value in comparison to India primarily because of its geographical proximity to the Gulf and Central Asian regions endowed with abundant energy and strategic resources.

Ruling leaders in South Asia have failed to address the mounting internal problems virtually on all fronts facing each country of the region. In this context, the name of Jawaharlal Nehru signifies special notice for his contribution as a statesman. Jawaharlal Nehru is considered to be the architect of modern India. Apart from his careful handling of India's tumultuous domestic situation in the years immediately after the Independence, Nehru's major contribution lies in the field of foreign policies.

In fact, Nehru determined India's international profile to a great degree in the post-Independence years, in his capacity as the foreign minister of India. Nehru saw war and violent insurgency from very close quarters as a freedom fighter, and he believed in neither. In his foreign policies, Nehru tried to guide India in such a way, so as to steer clear from any form of violence and militarism. He rightly believed that a newly decolonized nation must invest all its economic and logistic resources towards development and not defence and armament. Although many of his policies were not free from criticism, the values of democracy, non-alignment, and peace that Nehru upheld were significant.

However, post-Nehruvian era witnessed dramatic change in India's foreign policy and the South Asia emerged as one of the crisis regions in the world. In this context, it is imperative to enquire into the details of the causes which led to shift in India's foreign policy and the reasons for the violence and tensed relations among the states in South Asia, especially with India during the post-Nehruvian period.

The complex issues in South Asia are presented here through 13 scholarly articles with different perspectives. While examining the South Asian security scenario, it is very important to understand the policies and perceptions of West towards the South Asia, especially to India. G.P. Ramachandra in his paper, *India's External Environment and Threat Perceptions,* explores the threat posed by the West towards South Asia, particularly to India. According to him it is the western policies, aided by sections of our establishment, which pose the dangers. He narrates many incidents of western monkey business in the world affairs. As such, Ramachandra strongly believes that a western-ruled world would have catastrophic consequences for India and the south.

India is in the throes of a critical siege of violent asymmetric conflict in a South Asian region besieged by state-failure and economic fatigue. The paper, *Nuclear Proliferation Challenges and Asymmetric Conflicts in South Asia,* written by

W. Lawrence S. Prabhakar addresses four important matters: (a) India's critical security vulnerabilities and responses emergent from the worsening Afghanistan-Pakistan situation; (b) The consequences of a US retreat from Afghanistan and the Chinese assertive rise in the South Asian region; (c) critical imperatives and operational safeguards in India's nuclear security; (d) Future pathways of India in the region. He says that Nehru's vision of peace and development of the region has been reduced to perennial rounds of fratricidal conflict in the region with nuclear weapons in the backdrop. Lawrence S. Prabhakar remarks that India's development-disarmament narrative transformed into the growth-deterrence discourse—viewed as a paradigm shift of India's strategic locus.

Peace and development in South Asia presupposes a cogent vision for the region based on its historicity, resources, potential for economic development and its emergence as a cultural laboratory. Maqbool Ahmed Siraj in his paper, *Developing a Cogent Vision for Peace in South Asia*, narrates that the South Asian region has largely been hamstrung by petty rivalries, partisan concerns, communal competition, wars, arms race, irredentist tendencies and terrorism, notwithstanding ample perception among the leaders about the mutual benefits accruing from coming together and vulnerabilities in standing apart. He examines many issues affected by the countries in south Asia. For south Asian countries, Maqbool Siraj comments, the development goals are not easy to be met unless resources are diverted from defence and security apparatus which saps these economies and makes them the most attractive destination for western arms. He concludes his paper with the remark that only an insightful leadership can prepare the people to rise above their petty interests.

Joseph Antony in his paper, *China's South Asian Strategy in the 21st Century*, discusses the strategies of China to 'concircle' India. According to him, China tries to achieve this objective through its money, political and military power. But in its strategy to achieve a 'hegemonic' type of dominance in South Asia, the Indo-US relationship is a major stumbling block. Antony examines the South Asia with the policies of US and China, and its impact on India. He says that China is using their economic power, military muscle as well as global status to establish a strategic upper hand in the region. So these pro-China micro poles around India can create problems to India in a moment of crisis.

Pakistan occupies important status in South Asia after India. Sayed Abdul Muneem Pasha in his paper, *Islam and Governance Interplay: The Pakistan Experience,* examines the dilemmas of governance in Pakistan. He says that the dilemmas of governance in Pakistan are the consequences of political dysfunctionalism which itself is a product of military regimes. These dilemmas have to be located in the Pakistani polity instead of the Pakistani nation. Pasha believes that in the specific context of the Pakistani polity, it is high time now to bring a sense of priority in the Islamization process back into reckoning, by underlining the salience of equity, justice, and dignity in public life. He concludes that one of the consequences of military rule in Pakistan has been the increasing militarization of society, further reinforced by events emanating from external environment such as war on terror to which Pakistan has been drawn under circumstances beyond its control.

Josukutty C.A. in his paper, *Concords and Discords in Indo-Australia Relations,* brings out the significance of Indo-Australian relations within the framework of south Asian security. He says that the key factors that define and structure India-Australia relationship are its geographic location, resources, demography and its relationship with countries such as the US and China. The strategic partnership and common security threats that Australia is talking about is deceptive and a part of the US led western hegemonic machinations in the Asia-Pacific. According to Josukutty, Australia envisages a politico-strategic relationship of the multilateral alliance pattern with India. So he believes that entering into any sort of strategic and security alliance with Australia, beyond the economic realm, is detrimental to India's interest.

It is highly significant to note the paper, *China's Growing Influence in South Asia and India's Response,* written by S.Y. Surendra Kumar. He says that as the emerging powerful economic power, China is increasing its influence around the world and South Asia is no different. Surendra Kumar comments that China's Asia policy focussed more on Northeast and Southeast Asia region in the initial periods, however, in the recent times South Asia has also gained its importance in China's foreign policy since India began to look eastward, the former began to look southward to counter India's rise. He compares the Indian position in south Asia with China's influence in the region. In the final analysis, Surendra remarks that it is in the interest of both India and China to work towards a stable and manageable South Asia through cooperation, rather than involving in confrontation.

While analysing the South Asian security scenario, it is important to examine the role of the US, and its growing friendship with India. Venkat Lokanathan in his paper, *Emerging Indo-US Equations,* brings out the India's new friendship with the US by narrating the Nehruvian vision of India's foreign policy. Venkat explains the evolution of India's relation with the US and points out the common interest among them. He says that India's economic growth, its democratic stability, the increasing challenge from China and the unreliability of Pakistan meant that the United States could no longer afford to keep India out of its strategic global vision.

In the article, *China's Involvement in South Asia and India's Concerns,* Anil Kumar P. examines China's interest in South Asia during the Cold War and post-Cold War period. He narrates important relations between China and South Asian countries to establish his argument that China has important strategic interests and security concerns in this region. Therefore, China needs an approach to properly handle the relationship between it and South Asian countries in order to ensure its own strategic and security interests. According to Anil Kumar, India's growth as a major power and paradigm shift in India's foreign policy towards United States compelled China's involvement in South Asian region in an unprecedented manner. In the cold war period, the core of China's South Asian Policy was to keep the region away from any western influence, while in the post cold war period, the growth of India as a major power and cementing Indio-US relations changed the China's policy towards South Asia. Here Anil Kumar argues that China is focusing more on 'concirling' India with pro-China 'micropoles'.

Khursheed Ahmad Wani in his paper, *India and Pakistan in Afghanistan,* analyses both Pakistan and Indian interests in Afghanistan, particularly after 9/11 and how the two countries are trying to override the other. According to him, the situation demands that both India and Pakistan should make a treaty of peace, security and friendship with each other. The peace deal is very much necessary for the welfare of Afghanistan as well as South Asia. India and Pakistan's aim should be to prevent Afghanistan from once again becoming a source of terrorism. As such, Khursheed Wani remarks that both countries should understand the importance and each other's strength and role in international arena for the maintenance of security of the region. The strained relations will always give an opportunity to other countries to intervene in South Asia, that happened in past and that will happen in future, if the situation continues like this.

The social order mixed with religion is responsible for the current imbroglio in Pakistan. This argument is presented by Shibu M.P. in his paper, *Search for Public Sphere in the Radicalised Pakistan.* In Pakistan, the common perception amongst the academic think-tanks and strategic experts is that social order is maintained by Islamic laws and authority, backed by the use of force and reasonable threat of punishment, which is argued as a reflection of the Hobbesian method of maintaining a social order. Shibu discusses some prominent issues in Pakistan, as an outcome of Islamisation and radicalisation. The state failed to play an effective role in issues of increasing militancy and terrorist incidents, sectarian violence due to the unequal distribution of resources in provinces, unemployment and the recruitment of youth in terrorist organisations and the deteriorating human development indexes.

India's prominent status in South Asia is blamed for its big brother attitude towards neighbourhood. Shyna V.V. in her paper, *India's Role in South Asia,* tries to justify India's position by bringing our attention to various factors. According to her, India occupies a unique position in the South Asian region. By the virtue of its size, location and economic potential, India assumes a natural leadership role in the region. So it remains the biggest power in South Asia, and its significance in terms of how India sees itself and how others see it, is a key consideration for regional politics. Shyna's paper focuses on the regional interactions through the SAARC forum for ascertaining the degree of leadership or hegemony manifest in the policies of India and perceptions of other South Asian states.

Yaqoob Ul Hassan in his paper, *Af-Pak Region: A Major Challenge to Peace in South Asia,* examines the situation in Afghanistan and the policy of India and Pakistan in this direction. According to him, the growing militant commotion in Af-Pak border pose the number of key regional threats; the increase in major attacks against the coalition forces in Afghanistan, it will further destabilise the Pakistan, and it will add encumbrance to any political solution of Afghanistan. He comments that the portion of Pakistan-Afghanistan border continues to be home of the deadliest terrorists. The Pakistani failure to target Taliban after the Operation Enduring Freedom, when the Taliban leadership and top echelons fled to Pakistani tribal areas, had several deleterious consequences for years to come. The end game in Afghanistan needs a regional framework and number of national and regional approaches. Yaqoob Ul Hassan strongly believes that there should be dialogue between Pakistan and India on peaceful coexistence in Afghanistan.

Acknowledgements

I take this opportunity to place on record my deep gratitude and appreciation for all the contributors to this volume for their worthy contributions and co-operation. I extend my sincere thanks to University Grants Commission (UGC), New Delhi, for the financial support and UGC-Nehru Studies Centre, University of Kerala, for organizational support. Thanks are also due to my colleagues in the Department of Political Science, in particular Dr. Shaji Varkey and Josukutty C.A. for their unstinting support and help. Finally, I thank New Century Publications, New Delhi, for their co-operation at every stage of the publication of this work.

June 2013   **K.M. Sajad Ibrahim**
Thiruvananthapuram

1

India's External Environment and Threat Perceptions

G.P. Ramachandra

Our foreign policy perspective is badly confused about the dangers we face. China and Islamic terrorists are supposed to present grave dangers when the threat from China is zero and from Islamic terrorists almost zero. It is western policies, aided by sections of our establishment, which pose the dangers. The west, gripped by an economic crisis, cannot compete with China for energy and materials. Except for Germany and some north European countries, it is bankrupt. Even if the west could compete with China, the world lacks the resources to meet both western needs and the steadily growing Chinese demand for energy and raw materials. The western way of life is in danger and the west–primarily the US, Britain and France–is trying in desperation to grab the world's energy and raw material resources in the Middle East, Africa and Central Asia and subjugate and balkanize Russia and China by encirclement and the threat of nuclear strikes which China and Russia will not be able to deter owing to the installation of anti-missile defences around their perimeters.

The US in addition wants to preserve the dollar's role as the primary reserve currency, essential for its economic survival. The Arab Spring was instigated by the west to get a cover for this project. Libya has already been conquered and Syria and Iran are the current targets. India is being drawn-without the Indian government being fully aware of what is happening–into this deadly global campaign of conquest, encirclement and nuclear terror which can easily escalate into a world war or a nuclear war.

In a parallel development, Western and Israeli intelligence agencies have staged fake Islamist attacks in India. It was they and not the LeT, who were behind the shocking events of 26/11, which thwarted a possible thaw in Indo-Pakistan relations. Israeli intelligence again was behind the February 2012 attack on an Israeli embassy official in New Delhi. The intention was to curtail the close economic ties with Iran which India persisted in maintaining despite American pressure, so as to strangle Iran economically. India made the foolish decision to let the Mossad- the obvious suspect-investigate the crime. It has already fabricated proofs of Iranian involvement and this almost certainly will cause India to boycott Iran. The west has fearsome designs on India and the south generally in the economic sector. If it seizes the world's energy sources and destroys Chinese and Russian power, it can dictate terms to others.

Although the Sino-Indian border dispute has lasted over half-a century, it is totally unnecessary. The dispute concerns the western and eastern sectors. The land China is occupying in Aksai Chin was not administered by the British. The eastern sector which India is now occupying was not administered by Tibet, except for Tawang. (Maxwell, 1971) The obvious solution is to legitimize the status quo. This is what Chou Enlai proposed in the late 1950s and the offer is still open. This problem for India is that if it accepts the proposal, a misinformed public will regard it as appeasement. Moreover, the dispute keeps military expenditures high which is good business for arms lobbyists. Although the dispute is not settled, the Sino-Indian border is one of the most peaceful in the world. There has not been a fatality there for decades. Neither side has any intention of using force to settle the problem.

The notion that China is encircling India with naval bases is false. Much of China's imports and exports pass through the Indian Ocean and it is understandable that China should want ports of call for its ships. China is constructing ports, not bases, and these are commercial transactions.

There is, however, a danger that India could get drawn into the current NATO project of encircling China, cutting off its energy sources and threatening it with nuclear attack. This will result in a real threat from China to India. This western strategy is poorly understood in India. The west is now in economic decline, except for Germany and some north European countries. China, India and other BRICS are expanding, especially China. The implications for world power are obvious. It will shift from the west to China. Equally significant, China's growth poses a threat to the west's standard of living. China's intentions are peaceful. It wants to become a developed country. This, however, would require many times its present volume of imports of natural resources.

However, the Earth does not have the resources needed to raise 1.3 billion Chinese to the western living standard while maintaining the present standard of living of the west. China will prevail in a fair competition. The west–particularly the US, Britain and France–is following a policy of encirclement, denial of resources and nuclear terror meant to force China to capitulate. China's weakness is its dependence on distant countries for its energy and other needs. This is a critical weakness, because China, unlike the USA, cannot project its military power.

Russia is as much a target as China, because of its independent foreign policy and huge energy reserves, which the west wants to control. It is marked down for subjugation and balkanization. The west understands that control of the world's energy reserves, and the continuation of the energy trade in dollars and euros, is the key to world domination and the avoidance of an economic collapse.

The Arab Spring was not a spontaneous upsurge, any more than the previous colour revolutions in Europe and Asia were spontaneous. It was stirred up by the US, using agitators specially trained in Internet networking methods who exploited the huge discontent in these countries to spark off uprisings. It gave the west a pretext to intervene, using arguments like the right to protect civilians. The Arab Spring has not affected the west's position adversely so far. Dictators like Ben Ali and Mubarak were removed but the new Tunisian president is neo-liberal and pro-American while the pro-American army still dominates Egypt. A genuine popular uprising in Bahrain was brutally suppressed.

On the other hand, NATO effected a ruthless regime change in Libya. Although Libya is fragmenting, its oil reserves and gold deposits are now under western control. The conquest of Libya is a first step towards ousting China from Africa altogether. Already opportunities for intervention have been created in Nigeria, Uganda, Sudan and Mali, which the west will exploit. In Syria, an ally of Russia and Iran, death squads from abroad are murdering civilians. When the regime responds with force, the west says it is bombarding civilians and calls for intervention.

The west will invade Syria if diplomatic pressures do not work. The break-up of Syria however is only a step towards the next target=Iran. Iran has 10 percent of the world's energy reserves and an independent-minded regime. The west will not allow Iran to survive under its present regime and within its present boundaries. It must be broken up into several ethnic territorialities, and its energy reserves must come under western control. Since Iran supplies 20 percent of China's energy consumption, control of Iran will give the west a hold on China. The oil which China imports from the oil monarchies is already vulnerable to interdiction by the west which dominates the sea lanes China uses.

The west has imposed sanctions on Iran, using the bogus argument that it is developing nuclear weapons, the actual intention being to weaken the regime and have it overthrown from within. If sanctions do not work, the west will use force, with the use of nuclear weapons a real possibility. Central Asia, with its huge energy reserves and the energy–rich and cash rich Gulf monarchies (although they are currently trying to curry favour with the west) will also become targets. (Mahdi

Darius Nazemroaya, 2012; Engdahl, 2011; Petras, 2012; Corbett, 2012; Cartalucci, 2012; and Cartalucci, 2012)

NATO is concurrently pursuing a policy of nuclear terror towards Russia and China. The US, on the one hand, and China and Russia, on the other, presently have intercontinental ballistic missiles (ICBMs) capable of reaching the other's territory. Neither side can blackmail the other with the possibility of a nuclear strike, because it will itself be destroyed in a retaliatory strike. The US intends to deploy anti-missile missiles capable of intercepting Russian and Chinese ICBMs. If it acquires this capability, the Russian and Chinese nuclear deterrent will become useless, and both can be subjected to nuclear blackmail.

It is unclear just how efficient this screen will be but the US intends to create an apprehension in the minds of the Russians and Chinese. Theoretically, anti-missile missiles can be countered by increasing the number of attacking missiles but the problem is that ICBMs are expensive–much more expensive than the short-range missiles the US intends to deploy along the Russian and Chinese perimeters in the first phase of missile defence. (Rozoff, 2012)

The UPA government is probably not fully aware of Western intentions and the disastrous consequences for India and the South of a western-dominated world and it is led astray by the western media coverage. It has compromised with western policy to some extent. It did not oppose the NATO intervention in Libya. It broadly supports the NATO-Arab League intervention in Syria, apparently under the impression that the Assad regime is butchering civilians. Its policy on Iran is more nuanced. It has gone along with the unjustifiable UN sanctions on Iran but is unwilling to join in the subsequent unilateral sanctions imposed by the US, with a view to provoking regime change by causing unbearable suffering.

Iran is a valuable trade partner and Indo-Iranian trade has the potential to reach the equivalent of US$ 30 billion in a few years. More important, Iran is willing to accept payment in rupees for half of its oil exports to India. The greatest single obstacle to India's development is the need to acquire (in the face of northern trade barriers) dollars to pay for its burgeoning oil imports. Rupee payments are the answer to the problem. However, the US insists on the world's oil trade being in dollars. A move away from the dollar would be fatal to its supremacy. The invasions of Iraq and Libya were partly triggered by this consideration. The US intends to impose sanctions on India in July 2012 if it does not reduce imports from Iran. In the meantime, the Israeli Mossad staged a fake attack on an Israeli official in New Delhi. This attempt is being blamed on Iran to put pressure on the Indian government to sever economic ties with Iran on the ground that it is a promoter of international terrorism. This event will be examined in greater detail below.

NATO and the US are urging India to join in developing a global missile shield and India is studying the offer. (Anonymous, 2012 and Subramanian, 2011) If India accepts this offer, it would be the worst in a series of disastrous mistakes it has made regarding nuclear weapons. The first mistake was the decision to go nuclear. India has overwhelmingly superior conventional military power in relation to Pakistan. By opting for nuclear weapons and forcing Pakistan to do likewise, India has neutralized its own conventional military superiority and made the Kashmir crisis possible. India opted for nuclear weapons with China in mind.

However, China's nuclear capability was developed in response to American and Soviet threats and had nothing to do with India. Moreover, India is at a fatal geographical disadvantage in relation to China where nuclear weapons are concerned. China's major population centres are so far away that it is prohibitively expensive for India to target them; it has to develop and deploy the costly long-range Agni-V missile. On the other hand, China can easily target north Indian cities with inexpensive short-range missiles from bases in Qinghai, Xinjiang and Tibet.

What is a worse, Chinese warheads are much more destructive than ours. China has hydrogen bombs while we have only atom bombs, which have only a fraction of the destructive power of hydrogen bombs. India's atomic bomb missile force is not a credible deterrent to a hydrogen-bomb power and it is fortunate that China has no aggressive intentions towards India. India cannot develop the hydrogen bomb unless it does more testing but it has given up this right under the Indo-US nuclear accord. One purpose of the accord from the American point of view was to ensure that India would never develop hydrogen bombs, while Israel, a nation of less than one percent of India's population, has 200 to 400 hydrogen bombs.

The US now wants India to collaborate with NATO in the development of a global missile shield. Its intentions are obvious. It wants to complete the encirclement of China, to terrorize China with the prospect of a successful first strike, to unload costly weapons on India and defray the cost of developing them and to incorporate India firmly into the NATO camp (which would require the abandonment of everything Nehru stood for in foreign policy). It would be a fatal mistake for India to accept this offer. Anti-missile defences can be countered by increasing the number of attacking missiles. It would be very expensive for China to build more ICBMs capable of reaching the US to counter the missiles the US proposes to install in India and other surrounding countries.

However, India is presumably interested primarily in intercepting Chinese missiles trained on India. Here, the new American weapons are useless for the Chinese can easily increase the number of shorter-range missiles targeted on north Indian cities. These missiles are much cheaper than the American interceptors. There are already Chinese hydrogen bomb warheads targeted on Indian cities. Agni-V when it is fully deployed will ensure there will be many more of them. If India joins global missile defence there will be still more.

Indian media discussion of this subject is very brief and shows no understanding of the awful dangers India will face if it is inveigled into accepting the American offer. A missile shield will create the risk of an accidental nuclear war given the heightened suspicion on both sides that it will create.

An ominous new development is the ability of western and Israeli intelligence to manipulate Indian policies by staging fake terrorist attacks. One has to accept the fact that western and Israeli intelligence agencies are active in India, have successfully manipulated Indian policies in the past and are trying to do even now and that the Indian government, investigative agencies and media have failed miserably to present us with the truth. If these agencies are left unchecked, their ability to manipulate situations will increase. The official version of 26/11 holds that those terrible events were the work of ten Lashkar-e-Taiba terrorists who landed in Mumbai that same night in a hijacked fishing vessel. This version is in flagrant contradiction with information which appeared in the Indian and world media immediately after the attack but is no longer mentioned. The contradictions have to be accounted for if the official version is to be accepted but the media do not even draw attention to them.

An eyewitness told the *New Sunday Express* that the Nariman House drama began with two Israelis and four South Asians with rucksacks entering the building (and not with terrorists storming it as the official version says) whereupon two other South Asians rushed up with additional rucksacks for the four men and left in great haste. (Shivakumar, 2008) This implies Israeli involvement in the attacks. Once the official version appeared, neither the newspaper nor the author C. Shivakumar drew their readers' attention to the contradiction. A police officer who encountered the terrorists inside Nariman House on the night of 26 November and had an exchange of fire with them told the British newspaper *Guardian* said he was shocked to find they were white men. (Ramesh, 2008)

They were keeping Jews as hostages and were shooting at them when they tried to leave. Nariman House neighbours were confident they had seen some of the terrorists before and that they had even lived in Nariman House, although it was a hostel for Jews only. (Bavadam, 2009) Freelance journalist Arun Asthhana told CBC News of reports that a huge mass of ammunition, food and arms was stored at Nariman House and that some terrorists had lived there for up to 15 days. (Anonymous, 2008) Terrorists who were already living in Nariman House, a Jewish hostel, must have been Jews, not Islamists, even if some of them (although not all) were South Asian in appearance. All this suggests that Nariman House was a Mossad target, not a Lashkar target and the rabbi, his wife and other Jewish residents were killed to deflect suspicion.

Early reports indicated that white men were also involved in the attacks at the CST and the Leopold café The BBC reported on 27 November that Pappu Mishra, a café owner at the CST, saw two 'foreign-looking, fair-skinned' men enter the station and start shooting. It also reported that an Iraqi tourist stated that the two men he saw firing at the Leopold Café looked like foreigners and he thought one had blond hair. (Biswas, 2008) The attacks on the Taj, a sprawling, labyrinthine structure, and the Trident, a 21-storey building, were massive, coordinated affairs.

They required many more than a total of six attackers (the official version allows only four in the Taj and two at the Oberoi), and far more material than six men could bring in rucksacks. The material must have been stored earlier in the hotels. They required centres in the hotels from which the operation could be controlled. The attackers exhibited phenomenal knowledge of the buildings, particularly of the Taj–of entry and exit points, of strategic positions, the closed circuit TV control room, even of a hidden door. This surely required inside help and prior reconnaissance. Early reports fully supported these shocking conclusions.

The *Hindustan Times* reported on 28 December that two

terrorists had checked into the Taj into room 630 on 22 November. They received many visitors who bought bags probably filled with weapons and explosives. This would not have been possible without inside help. The commandos who engaged the terrorists told the *Times of India* and *Hindustan Times* that the terrorists had long military training. They showed phenomenal knowledge of the hotel interiors (even of a secret door) which implied prior reconnaissance and inside help. According to an NDTV report, an Indian man said 6-7 of the attackers were foreigners.

The official version allows only four attackers at the Taj, all of whom were Pakistanis, whom no Indian would call foreigners. Another report spoke of 15 terrorists holed up at the Oberoi and of nine being captured. (Dasgupta, 2008; *Hindustan Times,* 2009: 36-37, 39-40, 115-116) According to DNA news, security at the Taj, which had been stringent earlier, was relaxed at the time of the attack, leaving the Taj virtually undefended. Who was responsible for this decision and why? (Ramana, 2008)

According to Zeenews, there were several terrorists among the Taj trainee chefs. One had been there for ten months. (Anonymous, 2008) It should be possible to identify this person even now. Mr. P.R.S Oberoi, Chairman of the Oberoi Group dismissed reports that Trident staff were involved in the attack but acknowledged that the terrorists seemed to have reconnoitred the hotel well and were familiar with the layout. (Someshwar, 2008) A prior reconnaissance is fatal to the official version, which holds that the terrorists arrived the same evening by sea.

According to early media reports, the attackers could not have come by sea without the help of Dawood Ibrahim, the Karachi-based don who runs a smuggling empire in drugs, diesel and other commodities and is a long-time CIA asset. The Mumbai coast was tightly guarded but thanks to Dawood's clout with local authorities, his smuggling operations were not affected in the least even after 26/11.

(Balakrishnan, 2008; Balakrishnan, 2008; Balakrishnan, 2008) Initially, Dawood's name was first on India's list of suspects, but it subsequently disappeared from the list. The LeT was projected as the guilty party although according to reports from Pakistan, the LeT was banned after 9/11 and its affiliate the JUD is a charitable organization. (*Hindustan Times*, 2009: 151-153)

The attackers-who must have numbered dozens, not ten-probably, did not come that same night by sea. They were in place well before the attacks. The hijacking of the *Kuber* and the murder of its captain was a feint, meant to strengthen the version of terrorists coming by sea. But Dawood's infrastructure in Mumbai could have provided the local support the attackers needed.

The official version that LeT bosses directed the entire operation watching the attacks on their television sets and communicating with the attackers over their mobiles, is an insult to the intelligence. The transcripts of these conversations would have been forged by the foreign intelligence agencies who were foolishly allowed to participate in the investigation. (Anonymous, 2008:1; Anonymous, 2009:1; Anonymous, 2009:1 and Mushrif, 2009:237) Why could not an emerging giant like India have handled the investigation itself?

S.M. Mushrif, a former Maharashtra police chief, argues that most (although not all) of the attacks in India attributed to Islamists were the work of Hindu communal elements, operating independently of the BJP/RSS leadership, who have connections with the Intelligence Bureau and local investigative agencies and American and Israeli intelligence. (Mushrif, 2009, 79-100, 242, 251) The truth about these events, according to him, has been systematically distorted. Did foreign intelligence agencies, who are richly experienced in staging false flag attacks, find a similar tradition in India, and latch on to it and use it for their own purposes? Did Hemant Karkare discover these connections? The official version of his death is unsatisfactory. (R.H., 2008)

The FBI has arrested David Headley for being an LeT spy who did reconnaissance for the 26/11 attacks. He was a drugs trafficker who turned DEA informer and, according to the Americans, subsequently went rogue. (Rotella, 2011) This writer believes that his Mumbai reconnaissance was for the Americans. The 26/11 attacks aborted a promising Indo-Pakistani peace initiative over Kashmir. Israel and the US were able to unload weapons on India after the attack, and consolidate their strategic partnership with India. (Chossudovsky, 2008; Anonymous, 2009; Anonymous, 2009 and Datt)

The 13 February attack on an Israeli official's wife in New Delhi was a move by western and Israeli intelligence agencies in the current violent western drive for world hegemony. It was an attempt to change Indian policy towards Iran and it appears to be succeeding. On February 13, 2012, the wife of an Israeli official was injured in a car blast in New Delhi very close to the Prime Minister's residence. A motorcyclist tailed the vehicle, fixed a magnetic device to it when it stopped at a traffic light and escaped. On the same day police in Tbilisi, Georgia (a NATO ally) defused a device attached to an Israeli embassy car. The next day, a seemingly accidental explosion occurred in a house in Bangkok where three Iranians were staying. They left in a hurry.

All three were apprehended but one allegedly caused an explosion which resulted in the loss of his legs. Israel immediately accused Iran of being behind all three plots. It was true that the Mossad had used motorcyclists belonging to the MEK Iranian terrorist organization to assassinate Iranian nuclear scientists. However, it made absolutely no sense for Iran to stage revenge attacks in India and Thailand. Both countries were defying American sanctions by importing oil from Iran. Iran would be shooting itself in both feet if it did this. Terrorist attacks could result in a curtailment of Iran's trade with these countries, threatening it with economic disintegration. By the same token, the strategic gains for Israel and the US in such a curtailment would obviously be enormous. They had every reason to stage attacks which could be blamed falsely on Iran.

Gareth Porter argues (in an article which should have been republished in every major Indian newspaper) that the Delhi attack was not consistent with an Iranian or Hezbollah plot. (Porter, 2012) The bomb was low powered and did not contain iron filings, shrapnel or other items which would have made it deadly. It was affixed to the rear of the car where it would do the least damage to the Israeli and there was a gap of 40 seconds before it exploded giving her ample time to leave the car if she wished. Although she did not leave the car, she was only slightly injured and was able to walk to the embassy unaided. The car was severely damaged but from the fire the explosion caused, not from the explosion itself.

All this suggests that this was not an Iranian/Hezbollah revenge attack but an Israeli operation intended to drive India and Iran apart without causing serious injuries to the Israeli. The bombs in Tbilisi and Bangkok were totally different. The Tbilisi bomb was a grenade wrapped in a plastic bag fixed by tape to the underside of a car and was not a serious threat. The Bangkok bombs were deadly magnetic devices filled with shrapnel but Porter doubts that the Iranians concerned worked with the Iranian government or Hezbollah, since they were mixing with prostitutes. They were more likely to have been Mossad terrorist recruits (sacrificed by the Mossad when they became more useful in that role).

India's current policy is to maintain relations with Iran, a major trade partner and with Israel, a major arms supplier. This is understandable, considering that Iran is willing to receive payments for oil in rupees and barter and Indo-Iranian trade has the potential to reach US$ 30 billion by 2015 from the current US$ 13.7 billion but the policy will not be sustainable. This is because India made the disastrous decision to allow the Mossad–the obvious suspect–to participate in the probe. (Sharma, 2012:1) It was certain that it would fabricate evidence. By March 2012, the Delhi police claimed to have solved the case. They accused four Iranians of plotting the attack, with the help of a pro-Iranian Indian journalist, Syed Mohammed Ahmad Kazmi. Kazmi allegedly received money from them for his help.

The police provided incriminating email, mobile phone and account details to the court. Kazmi's family insisted that the payments came from relatives in the Gulf and could all be accounted for. Concerned citizens organized a conference in Delhi at which they maintained that Kazmi was a responsible citizen and that the Delhi police were acting under pressure from the US and Israel. (Anonymous, 2012:9) The fact is that once the Mossad was allowed to investigate the case, it was certain to fabricate evidence. A senior Israeli intelligence official said that India received "a great deal of assistance in the investigation from the United States and Israel". (Anonymous, 2012:9) What exactly was this assistance? One would expect it to be in with the international aspects of the case—the communication of the Iranian suspects with conspirators in Iran, Georgia and Thailand. It is necessary to take a closer look at this evidence and ascertain whether the Delhi Police Special Cell, which handled the case, have accepted it uncritically.

India is now under pressure from the US to reduce its oil imports from Iran. So far it has been unwilling to do so but thanks to this Israeli stunt it may not be able to maintain this position. The UPA government surely understands that the case is a Mossad fabrication but saying so would be too provocative. It will not provoke the US and Israel beyond a certain point. An easier course would be to go along with the version. Iran as a self-respecting power will not surrender innocent persons on the basis of fabricated evidence. This will result in an estrangement. In the changed atmosphere, India will reduce its oil imports from Iran citing the noble reason that it is a promoter of international terrorism. The humiliating real reason is that it dare not accuse Israel of faking the attack.

The plans for greatly expanded trade between the two countries will not materialize and the opportunity to pay for oil in rupees-so important for our development-will be lost and the western–Israeli strategic goal of starving Iran into submission will be advanced. If the 13 February operation does not succeed in breaking Indo-Iranian ties, the Mossad will stage more attacks.

The centre is now proposing to set up a National Counter Terrorism Centre. The states are objecting that it infringes on their rights. Equally important, since the central government is involving the Mossad in investigations in which it is fabricating evidence, the proposed centre will give the Mossad an all-India theatre for future frame-ups. P.R. Kumaraswamy of Jawaharlal Nehru University says inputs from Israel went into the formation of the National Counter-Terrorism Centre. Did the idea originate with Israel? He also says that Israel and India have been cooperating on counter-terrorism since the normalization of relations in 1992. (Kumaraswamy, 2012:8) What has been going on between the intelligence agencies of the two countries? Israel urged step up anti-terrorist cooperation on counter-terrorism between India and Israel after the 13 February attack. (Anonymous, 2012:9)

The February 13 Mossad stunt was a move in the policy of subjugating Iran, a precondition for a western global hegemony based on control of the world's natural resources especially petrochemical resources. A western dominated world would have catastrophic consequences for India and the south. The west will pursue predatory policies unrestrained by Chinese and Russian power.

It will complete its one way penetration of southern markets, without giving corresponding access to its own market. It will press for the removal of tariffs. It will dump subsidized agricultural and dairy products on Southern markets, in complete violation of the principles of free trade. It will secure access to retail, PSUs, banking (public and private), telecommunications, services, government procurement and pensions, without giving an equivalent. It is already seeking control of Indian agriculture by capturing the seeds market for GM seeds. The current India-EU negotiations, which the UPA government is conducting off stage, are a precursor of what will follow. (Singh, 2012) The UPA government is already willing to allow FDI in the retail sector, a move which will adversely affect 40 million people and the plan has been only temporarily shelved in the face of political opposition. Indian corporations support the plan.

The south will not be allowed to increase its consumption of oil and gas or coal in a western ruled world. Under present technology, it means that southern development will be frozen. Western desperation over access to increasingly contested oil and gas reserves is the main motive for the current global domination project. As for coal, the west is running out of this cheap fossil fuel and does not want the south to increase its use because of the comparative advantage it would give. The desire to restrict the south's use of oil, gas and coal is behind the global warming campaign, which amounts to one big lie. There is no satisfactory evidence for the claim that C_O2 emissions are overheating the planet. The evidence suggests that global warming and cooling succeed one another in natural cycles and that there has been no global warming phase in the last decade. (Johnston, 2010; Evans 2010; Rose 2012)

The western mass media are ignoring the evidence and regurgitating the lies of their climate establishment. The south, even China, is a victim of this hoax. India, China and other countries of the south have swallowed the global warming thesis but want the west to bear its fair share of the sacrifices required to combat the supposed warming while the west wants the south to bear the sacrifices in violation of the Kyoto Protocol. In a western-dominated world, the west will insist on a complete surrender by the south. The essential point is that western nations know very well that there is no threat to humanity from global warming and feel no pressure to make concessions for this reason. Southern delegations think there is a threat to humanity and might be pressured into making unilateral concessions to save humanity.

A western-dominated world carries with it the danger of the corporatization of agriculture on a global scale, with corporations like Monsanto taking over southern agriculture by monopolizing the seed sector where only GM seeds will be available. Evidence is accumulating that GM crops are harmful to animals, that they do not increase productivity over the long run, that they destroy local varieties, and that the glysophate used in Monsanto's Roundup herbicide, which must be used together with the seeds, is toxic to humans (causing among other things infertility and DNA damage) and induces the growth of monster weeds. GM seeds have been ineffective and costly in India, where farmers have been forced to buy them after the monopolization of seeds in certain crops.

The result, when the crops did not produce the desired yield and the farmers could not repay their loans, has been a tidal wave of agricultural suicides. (Engdahl, a 2009; Engdahl, b 2010; Margulis, 2010; Huber, 2010; P.M. Bhargava, 2011; Huff, 2012; Gucciardi, a 2012; Gucciardi, b 2012; Barrett, 2012 and Shrivastava, 2012) These disasters will be repeated on a global scale in a world where western power is unchecked. Far from recognizing the dangers posed by GM seeds, the UPA government is on the side of Monsanto. It plans to constitute a Biotechnology Regulatory of India (BRAI) which will centralize decision-making on GM seeds in a three member team. Anyone drawing attention to the dangers of GM seeds will be liable to punishment-a truly incredible provision which infringes the Constitution.

A western-ruled world will see pressure on the south to nuclearize its energy sector using plants supplied by western corporations, without any liability on the supplier in the event of a nuclear accident. American nuclear companies are liable to pay huge compensation in case of a nuclear accident. It is only fair that this model should be followed elsewhere in the world. The Indian bill limits supplier liability to ₹ 1,500 crore only. Foreign nuclear companies are unwilling to accept even this lower figure. Moreover, India has signed the Convention on Supplementary Compensation which disallows supplier liability and an international treaty will override a national law.

The west will argue that fossil fuels will bring on a climate catastrophe while nuclear power is safe. Not only is there no proof that fossil fuels have this effect but nuclear power is too dangerous, as the Fukushima disaster has shown. Nuclear fuel, whether active or spent has to be cooled continuously. Otherwise it will heat up and emit radiation. The cooling must go on for thousands of years, far beyond what any government can guarantee meaningfully. The destruction of the cooling system, as happened at Fukushima after the tsunami struck, will bring disaster. A reactor at Fukushima is still emitting radiation at a high level more than a year after the disaster and the robots used there for construction cannot work in this environment.

Another disaster seems to be brewing at Fukushima. Reactor number 4 at Fukushima has a collection of 1,535 spent fuel rods. The building housing the rods is listing. The likelihood of an earthquake striking the area in one to three years is very high. If the building collapses, not only will the rods heat up but it will affect 6,375 spent fuel rods in another building. The result will be a release of radiation on a scale never seen before and likely to threaten all life on earth. Tokyo will certainly have to be evacuated. (Washington's Blog, 2012) Germany has already decided to phase out its nuclear power industry after Fukushima. In fact, new nuclear power plants will probably not be built anywhere in Europe after Fukushima, particularly if a second disaster happens there. Public opinion will not allow it. But the nuclear power industry will look for alternative markets in the south, and will be backed by their governments, and in a western-ruled world the south will have to submit. Already foreign nuclear power corporations have the support of Indian atomic energy officials, politicians and corporations, despite what has happened at Fukushima. A western-ruled world would have catastrophic consequences for India and the south.

References

Balakrishnan, S. (2008), "Attack Enabled by D Gang-Cops," 28 November,
http://timesofindia.indiatimes.com/Mumbai/Attack_enabled_by_D_gang_Cops/articleshow/3766908.cms.

Balakrishnan, S. (2008), "Dawood Sitting Pretty in Karachi," 4 December,
http://timesofindia.indiatimes.com/Dawood_confident_Pak_establishment_wont_touch_him/articleshow/3789890.cms.

Balakrishnan, S. (2008), "Don of the Docks Goes Untouched," 11 December,
http://timesofindia.indiatimes.com/India/Don_of_the_docks_goes_untouched/articleshow/3821005.cms.

Barrett, Mike (2012), "Monsanto's Roundup is Causing DNA Damage," 30 March, http://naturalsociety.com/monsantos-roundup-is-causing-dna-damage.

Bavadam, Lyla (2009), "Chabad Encounter," *Frontline*, January 14: 34.

Bhargava, P.M. (2011), "Time not Ripe for Bt Brinjal," *New Indian Express* (Thiruvananthapuram) 14 January: 8.

Biswas, Soutik (2008), "Mumbai Attackers Create 'Killing Zone'," 27 November,
http://news.bbc.co.uk/2/low/south_asia/7752625.stm.

Cartalucci, Tony (2012), "West Seeks to Perpetuate Syrian Bloodbath," 2 April, http://www.prisonplanet.com/west-seeks-to-perpetuate-syrian-bloodbath.html.

Cartalucci, Tony b (2012): "NATO's Slow Genocide in Libya and Syria is Next," 20 April, http://www.prisonplanet.com/natos-slow-genocide-in-libya-syria-is-next.html

Chossudovsky, Michel (2008), "India's 9/11-Who was Behind the Mumbai attacks? Washington is Fostering Divisions between India and Pakistan," 29 November,
http://www.globalresearch.ca/index.php?context=va&aid=11217

Corbett, James (2012), "From Libya to Syria: 'War is a Racket, It Always Has Been," 14 April,
http://www.globalresearch.ca/index.php?context=va&aid=30295

Dasgupta, Devraj (2008), "Terrorists Seemed to be Sure of Taj Hotel

Terrain," 28 November
http://timesofindia.indiatimes.com/Terrorists_seemed_to_be_sur
e_of_Taj_hotel_terraih/articleshow/3770533.cms.

Datt, Gautam a (2009), "Budget brings Cheer to Defence," *New Indian Express* (Thiruvanathapuram) 17 February.

Datt, Gautam b (2009), "India to Buy Missiles from Israel," *New Indian Express* (Thiruvananthapuram) 25 March.

Datt, Gautam c (2009), "Israel Bags Yet Another Defence Deal," *New Indian Express* (Thiruvananthapuram) 7 April.

Engdahl, F. William a (2009), "A Moratorium on Genetically Modified (GMO) Foods," 22 May,
http://www.globalresearch.ca/index.php?context=va&aid=13701

Engdahl, F. William b (2010), "The GMO Catastrophe in the USA. A Lesson for the World," 18 August,
http://www.globalresearch.ca/index.php?context=va&aid=20675

Engdahl, F. William c (2011), "Arab Spring a Western Ploy to Control Eurasia," 2 November
http://www.prisonplanet.com/engdahl-arab-spring-a-western-ploy-to-control-eurasia.html.

Evans, David (2010), "Is the Western Climate Establishment Corrupt?," Science and Public Policy Institute Collaborative Paper, 8 November,
http://scienceandpublicpolicy.org/originals/western_climate_establishment_corrupt.html.

Gucciardi, Anthony a (2012), "Monsanto's Roundup is Killing Human Kidney Cells," 15 March,
http://naturalsociety.com/monsantos-roundup-biopesticide-is-killing-human-kidney-cells/

Gucciardi, Anthony b (2012), "Monsanto's GMO Seeds Contributing to Farmer Suicides Every 30 Minutes,", 4 April,
http://naturalsociety.com/monsantos-gmo-seeds-farmer-suicides-every-30-minutes/

Hindustan Times, 26/11: The Attack on Mumbai (2009), New Delhi: Hindustan Times/Penguin Books.

Huber, Don (2010), "Monsanto's Glyophosate: Impact on Human Health and Plant Life," 10 December,
http://www.globalresearch.ca/index.php?context=va&aid=22354

Huff, Ethan A. (2012), "Study: Roundup Diluted by 99.8 Percent Still Destroys Human DNA," 23 February,
http://www.prisonplanet.com/study-roundup-diluted-by-99-8-

percent-still-destroys-human-dna.html.

Johnston, Jason Scott (2010), "Global Warming Advocacy Science: A Cross Examination," University of Pennsylvania, Institute for Law and Economic Research, 1 May, http://papers.ssrn.com/sol3/papers.cfm?abstract_id=1612851.

Kumaraswamy, P.R. (2012), "Probe Blast with an Open Mind," *New Indian Express* (Thiruvananthapuram) 17 February: 8.

Margulis, Charles (2010), "Monsanto's Superweeds Come Home to Roost: 11 mn US Acres Infested," 27 October, http://foodfreedom.wordpress.com/2010/10/27/monsantos-superweeds-come-home-to-roost-11-mn-us-acres-infested/

Maxwell, Neville (1971), *India's China War*, Bombay: Jaico Publishing House.

Mushrif, S.M. (2009), *Who Killed Karkare? The Real Face of Terrorism in India*, New Delhi: Pharos.

Nazemroaya, Mahdi Darius (2012), "Confrontation between Military Blocs: The Eurasian 'Triple Alliance.' The Strategic Importance of Iran for Russia and China," 23 January, http://www.globalresearch.ca/PrintArticle.php?articleId=28790.

Petras, James (2012), "The Bloody Road to Damascus: The Triple Alliance's War on a Sovereign State," 10 March, http://www.globalresearch.ca/index.php?context=va&aid=29679.

Porter, Gareth (2012), "Who's Behind Anti-Israel Bomb Plots," 5 March, http://www.globalresearch.ca/index.php?context=va&aid=29611

R.H. (2008), "Who Killed Hemant Karkare?," 15 December, http://www.samarmagazine.org/archive/article.php?id=278.

Ramana, K.V. (2008), "Insider Whiff in Taj Attack," 3 December, http://www.dnaindia.com/ report.asp?newsid=1211083.

Ramesh, Randeep, Daniel Pepper, Thomas Bruce and Angela Balakrishnan (2008), "Indian Commandos Storm Mumbai Hotels," 27 November, http://www.guardian.co.uk/world/2008/nov/27/mumbai-terror-attacks-india4.

Rose, David (2012), "Forget Global Warming- It's Cycle 25 We need to Worry About," 29 January, http://www.dailymail.co.uk/sciencetech/article-2093264/Forget-global-warming--Cycle-25-need-worry-NASA-scientists-right-Thames-freezing-again.html.

Rotella, Sebastian (2011), "The American Behind India's 9/11-and How the U.S. Botched Chances to Stop Him," 22 November, http://www.propublica.org/article/david-headley-homegrown-terrorist

Rozoff, Rick (2012), "U.S. Furthers Reagan's Star War Plans with Global Nato," 21 April, http://globalresearch.ca/index.php?context=va&aid=26461

Sharma, Ritu (2012), "India Doing a Tightrope Walk," *New Indian Express* (Thiruvananthapuram) 16 February: 1.

Shivakumar, C. (2008), "Two Terrorists Have Escaped," *New Sunday Express* (Thiruvananthapuram) 14 December: 1.

Shrivastava, Arun (2012), "Weaponization of the Food System: Genetically Engineered Maize Threatens Nepal and the Himalayan Region," 24 April, http://www.globalresearch.ca/index.php?context=va&aid=30512

Singh, Kavaljit (2012), "India-EU Trade Agreement: Rethinking Free Trade Pact with Europe," 14 February, http://globalresearch.ca/index.php?context=va&aid=29278

Someshwar, Savera R. (2008), "Terrorists Will not Check In as Guests," 29 November, http://www.rediff.co.in/news/2008/nov/29mumterror-oberoi-says-no-terrorist-worked-as-staff.htm.

Subramanian, T.S. (2011), "India Studying NATO Offer on Joining Missile Programme," 7 October, http://www.globalresearch.ca/index.php?context=va&aid=26974

Washington's Blog (2012), "The Top Short-term Threat to Humanity: The Fuel Pools of Fukushima," 7 April http://www.prisonplanet.com/the-top-short-term-threat-to-humanity-the-fuel-pools-of-fukushima.html.

2

Nuclear Proliferation Challenges and Asymmetric Conflicts in South Asia

W. Lawrence S. Prabhakar

India contends a critical phase of its post-Independence existence with an alarming besiege of hostile states and violent non-state actors. The existential security predicament has emerged in an irony that features India's steady and solid economic growth and development. Despite the robustness of the economic and strategic macro-fundamentals, India is in the throes of a critical siege of violent asymmetric conflict in a South Asian region besieged by state-failure and economic fatigue. As US and allied strategic dilemmas vacillate in Afghanistan; a Pakistan in the throes of a new round of critical internal destabilization with a massive spurt in radicalization threatening to engulf the Afghanistan-Pakistan region and a China that exploits India's unsettled boundary issues; leveraging support to Pakistan all present India its double jeopardy.

The Asian region features a relentless pursuit of nuclear and missile proliferation in North Korea, Iran and Pakistan. All the three states have strong and enduring Chinese linkage and support that comes unquestionable despite the fact that these states strongly support violent non-state actors whose threats have a clear WMD dimension. Beijing's nuclear patronage to Pakistan with a civilian nuclear agreement, overriding all international procedural measures of transparency comes despite the fact that Pakistan faces critical internal instability is a clear Chinese reiteration to dent US influence in Pakistan and leverage Pakistan in the sustained challenge of India.

In the context of this critical situation, what are India's

options in the region and responses that it has to design? What would be the credibility of India's nuclear disarmament initiatives measures in the face of a zestful and abrasive Chinese nuclear and missile modernization? Are there convergences between India, US and China with regard to cooperate to secure from nuclear and WMD terrorism? What would be the convergences between India and the US in the Afghanistan-Pakistan region in the context of a post-US exit? What would be China's role in the region (given increased intransigence of China in Kashmir and Arunachal Pradesh) and how would India have to respond are critical imperatives that India needs to consider.

The paper would endeavour to examine: (a) India's critical security vulnerabilities and responses emergent from the worsening Afghanistan-Pakistan situation; (b) the consequences of a US retreat from Afghanistan and the Chinese assertive rise in the South Asian region; (c) critical Imperatives and operational safeguards in India's nuclear security; (d) future pathways of India in the region.

India stands at a critical threshold of its national existence; ever besieged by a turbulent regional and extended regional environment. Even as the country's economic growth and development is in good momentum, the discontents of its domestic situation is marked by a very sharp development divide with 40 percent of the country's population below the poverty line. Poverty and lopsided development is further complicated by its internal political and civic conflicts accentuated by growing threats and perils of terrorism that are internal and external-aided; insurgency that is thorough home bred bolstered by a ceaseless flow of small arms and light weapons. In its own admission, India finds itself in a default and deficit of governance in what it claims to be Naxalite territory or better known as "Red Corridor" territory.

Since the 1999 Kargil War emanating from the earlier and the continuing 'intifada' in Kashmir since 1989, India has been bled by a 'thousand cuts' in relentless asymmetric war by Pakistan's Inter Services Intelligence (ISI) and more in a concerted manner in 1999 by Pakistan's Northern Light Infantry's special operations in India's territory masquerading as the Jihadi ingress into India. India has been since been subject to a Pakistani-Chinese asymmetric pincer aggression with the territory of Kashmir been subject to a series of acupunctures that has paralyzed the Indian state, its people and its armed forces.

Amidst the encircling gloom, however, India's resilience has been robust with a dynamic economic growth and development sustained at 7-9 percent in the first decade of this century. With a vibrant democracy, exhibiting an amazing level of social, cultural, civic and political pluralism, India has been able to turn the tides of economic and social stagnation into growth, development and stability. However, the templates of growth and development have not been with equity and have sharply divided the nation into several segregations. The deepening economic divide, the increased levels of corruption and criminalization of society and politics has been most corrosive to the health of India's vibrant democracy. Assessing the critical security vulnerabilities and debating the appropriate responses is vital for the nation.

Nehru's Vision of Peace, Democracy and Development

Nehru envisioned India as the Beacon of Peace (within), champion of democracy and the harbinger of development in the region. His emphasis on the investments on development; the faith in the diplomacy for peace was most pronounced. Nehru envisioned the importance of Peace and Democracy as the pre-requisites for development that was equitable and just. India's foreign policy and its development approach reflected the imperatives for India's peaceful neighbourhood and walked the extra mile for its achievement. With Pakistan, Nehru was ever willing to resort to diplomacy even as it commenced its strategy of asymmetric conflict in 1948. With China, Nehru believed and affirmed the conviction of peace and stability and worked much to the mutual benefit and development of both states. Nehru's Nonalignment was a grand strategy of social economic development and a quest for a democratic order of international relations.

However, the vagaries and the realities began to shift from the optimism of Nehru's era to a strategic reality that India was soon swamped by a slew of regional conflicts propped by the Cold War and by Chinese aggression. Pakistan's continued resort to terrorism in Kashmir—resulted in the very defeat of Nehru's idea of popular consent. Conflict that Nehru wished away came back in fury haunting India in the region. Nehru's anticipation of a cooperative relationship with China and his willingness to engage Pakistan swayed to be a lethal China-Pakistan strategic relationship that subverted India's regional position. Nehru championed for nuclear energy; shunning nuclear power—but the reality has been that China and Pakistan propelled on the nuclear power quotient and has prodded India into the 'deterrence dynamic'.

India's Critical Security Vulnerabilities and Responses

Six critical security vulnerabilities stand out for India in the present situation and their perilous impact would have serious undermining consequences.

The unrelenting scourge of asymmetric conflict and religious extremism stand out to be India's most menacing threat. Even as the templates of asymmetric conflict of insurgencies, terrorism and political violence expand, the possible conflation between them is likely to increase. The Indian responses have been and continue to be predominantly in military responses even as social, civic, economic and political responses are experimented. The consequences of asymmetric conflict are tied to the polarizing religious extremism and the competitive sectarian politics in the country.

Catalyzing these conflicts are the complex social-economic and political strategies of democratic politics that is unmindful of the perilous impact. On the other, asymmetric conflict have also been aggravated responses to militarization of the Indian state and the flip effects of India's path of economic development that has come with several discontents. In the external context, asymmetric conflict and religious extremism have been conscious strategies of India's north-western neighbour, which seeks the continuing containment of India through symmetric and asymmetric means.

The quest for sustaining this pressure on India is even more evident as Pakistan seeks to manipulate Afghanistan; augmenting the sectarian forces to attrite the counter insurgency and counter terrorism measures of the International forces in Afghanistan and also undermine India's development initiatives in Afghanistan. India's contention with the unrelenting scourge of asymmetric conflict and religious extremism would continue in spite of its positive contribution to the stabilization of Afghanistan; since such stabilization measures are threatening the relevance of the brinkmanship of Pakistan's ISI and its allies the terrorist groups.

The consequences of failing states in India's neighbourhood with the double jeopardy of holding weapons of mass destruction and hosting terrorist groups emerges as a very powerful peril to India. Pakistan stands out in this category even as the toxic impact of sectarian fragmentation injures the country. The 'unholy grail' of terror, sectarian conflict and weapons of mass destruction have widely affected to the seismic fault-lines of Pakistan. With its state-sponsored WMD commerce and its networks, Pakistan has been the epicentre for WMD proliferation networks and the increasing tenuous grip of the regime on its internal matters. [1] The US interventionist presence in Pakistan has been a critical factor that has been double-edged aiding and hurting Pakistan. India is confronted by a cascade of regional insecurity in Bangladesh, Nepal and besides Sri Lanka where the post-conflict rehabilitation is increasingly turning to aid insurgency rather than its resolution.

The abrasiveness of Chinese hegemony and its destabilizing consequences for India is yet another critical security challenge and vulnerability. With all accents of cooperative relations with China explored by India and the paradigm, that economic interdependence would ameliorate the negative accents of competition and Chinese aggressiveness against India, yet, adversarial traits of China towards India prevails. With the apparent 'bonhomie' that India and China enjoy with secondary and tertiary levels of convergence on a variety of international and transnational issues, the persistence of the border/boundary disputes prevails even as China aggravates the Kashmir issue by its own contribution fuelling the fires in the entire dimension of conflicts. [2] Claims on Arunachal Pradesh as the southern end of Tibet and a range of covert operations including the shooting on Indian military aircraft, manipulating the Brahmaputra have been the malafide intentions of the Chinese against India. Leveraging the China-Pakistan strategic convergence, the Sino-Bangladesh, Sino-Nepal and Sino-Lankan relations have a clear Chinese intent to 'box' India in the region and apply its acupuncture on India.

The colossal impact of global economic slowdown and its impact on India and its growth is a crucial issue that confronts India. While India is able to maintain its robustness in its economic growth and development, the unmitigated consequences of the global economic crisis is likely to dent its performance. India's economic growth in its scope and pace is essential. There are, however, critical indices like the current account deficits and the national debt that have been expanding economic adjustments in the long run and the critical need for strategic stability are pivotal. [3] The secondary and tertiary consequences of asymmetric conflict on the country have to be properly accounted in perspective given its atrophying consequences.

The perilous consequence of inadvertent war in South Asia triggered by Kargil-type and Mumbai-type Low Intensity Conflicts is gaining credence even as Pakistan is on an assertive mode with unabated Chinese support. While China and Pakistan apparently condemn the attacks on India, yet, the Pakistani adventurism against India in the Kargil and Mumbai type assaults are 'useful tools' in its long-term destabilization of India. Chinese websites have also made mention about how India should be broken to a thousand pieces (and later withdrawn) are all indications of the clear intent-motivation of the Pakistani-Chinese aggressiveness against India. Should an inadvertent war be triggered the consequence management for India is likely to be far more complicated than what it had encountered in 1999 and 2008 when the US and international support has been unwavering.

With the US increasingly distracted and at times directionless, the incentives for Pakistan and China to resort to such tactics would be more emboldened. While China officially distances itself from Pakistan's 'unacceptable behaviour', yet, its covert solid support to Pakistan in the 2002 crisis and has extended its diplomatic and nuclear deterrence cover for Pakistan has been unequivocal. [4] Thus, the prospects of inadvertent war from Pakistani provocations have always remained at large.

The consequences of advertent nuclear accidents emanating from terrorism and safety issues are a critical concern for India. Even as India is now in a 'renaissance' of its nuclear power, the issues of nuclear safety and security is looming large. While India has the impeccable record and operational dexterity in safety and security of its civilian and strategic nuclear assets, the grim prospects of an orchestrated jihadi attacks on India's nuclear assets is not ruled out. Mumbai 26/11 was a soft-target opportunity of attack; what is possible and cannot be ruled out is a ramped up jihadi terrorist attack on any of India's nuclear installations. [5] The consequence of an attack or even an attempted attack would certainly be a dampener on India's quest for building nuclear power plants and its attempt to alleviate its energy deficits. Such an attack on India's critical infrastructure would be debilitating on India's economic profile with the intent to dent and corrode India's resilience.

While the critical security perils and vulnerabilities persist, India has been certainly tailoring its responses with a very wide spectrum. India has been building capabilities and capacities in defending its critical infrastructure. But critical gaps remain in its responses for three reasons: (a) While structural deficits have largely been not in terms of lack of institutions there have been grave problems of lateral linkages and force-multiplier synergies of institutional output; (b) The agency deficits have remained due to indifference of elite perceptions, attitudes towards the strategic issues compounded by the perennial bane of domestic politics that overrides strategic and security issues; (c) The response matrices have also been featured by a serious crisis in the lack of understanding on the evolving patterns of global, regional, theatre and national contexts of the evolving threats of asymmetric conflict.

India's response architecture has been compounded by the lack of appreciation and understanding of proactive evolution of the threat and the continued inhibition to respond. It is also evident in the failure in the right configuration of resources-operations matrices and resulted in the wastage of resources.

Chinese Assertive Rise in South Asia

South Asia and Central Asia are witnessing a flux of the strategic shifts that is coming after the first decade of the twenty-first century. With the 'War on Terror' being the defining construct, it saw the enactment of a 'new great game' played by the US-NATO with all its forward movement and basing in the region. The US aggressive quest saw a 'domino of regime changes' in Kabul and Baghdad in West Asia. Ten years into the region, the US-NATO was able to develop 'strategic depth' into the region within the proximity of Russia and China. On the one hand, it drove the Russians and Chinese closer and on the other, it reconfigured the theatre's geo-economic importance with a leverage of the region's potentially vast hydrocarbon energy resources to be in the hold of US-NATO.

It induced a power play, with China gaining advantage by its networking of the oil and natural gas pipelines using Russian networks and Chinese capital and had consolidated its grip. In the quest to build the regional cooperation, China had assiduously built the Shanghai Cooperation Organization with a clear economic-strategic objective with Russia and other partners. The Russian-Chinese partnership since July 2001 and the Shanghai Cooperation Organization are the effective bulwarks that secured China's geo-economic and geo-strategic interests. [6]

The United States in its complete 'reset' of its global role that was the strategic response of the Obama administration has undertaken a strategic review for the phased and complete withdrawal from Afghanistan. While the US efforts to stabilize Afghanistan has shown mixed results, the 'reset' decision of the Obama administration lacks a clear strategic desiderata of how this would secure the United States and more so the region that it wants to withdraw from. In reality, the pangs of the burdensome war operations in Afghanistan and Iraq had considerably drained the US resilience and the evident signs of disengagement emergent from its global fatigue are now setting on the US.

The complexities of US disengagement are fraught with several consequences that could be briefly analysed. First, the scope and timescale of US operational disengagement is going to be very difficult to define since arbitrary decisions of how stable the regime in Kabul is likely to be is a very tough factor to gauge. Secondly, the scope of US disengagement is likely to be replaced by either a strategic vacuum (which is mostly unlikely) or a Pakistan initiative that would see China emerging to be a power to reckon with in Afghanistan. China's interests are clearly geo-economic and its ability to extract the mineral treasure trove of Afghanistan estimated to be at US$ 3 trillion. Leaving aside the region for the US would save its blood and treasure, but the strategic opportunity costs would be equally higher even as the Taliban-Al-Qaeda-ISI triumvirate triumphs in the region.

The intractable challenge of Taliban and Pakistan's ISI would be most formidable as they emerge as the pivotal players in the region. This possible grim spectre leaves India at the receiving end of a blowback on India with a strategic vacuum too large to fill in left by the retreat of the US-NATO forces and the agglomeration of the Pakistani-Chinese strategic power that would be hostile to India's footprint in the region. In other words, what India was able to develop, as a 'development footprint' in Afghanistan would be simply erased by the Chinese-Pakistani pincer movement erasing India's new strategic depth and replacing it by their duo.

China's interest in Afghanistan's mineral resources estimated at US$ 3 trillion is quite evident. China would create a new geo-economic corridor that would lead it into a turbulent region. [7] Pakistan's facilitation and catalytic role for China is China's greatest asset even as China would be ready to step in. However, the moot point is whether China would deploy its armed forces for expeditionary and humanitarian operations and whether this westward expansion could check its own backyard problems in Xingjiang remains to be seen.

Thus, the plausibility of a Pakistani-ISI led Chinese presence would barter 'token development projects' in return for Afghanistan's resources would possibly be a new strategic reality, if the US decides its complete reset position. On the other hand, how much of US resilience in the region would remain in view of its growing economic difficulties at home and an indecisive executive President whose vision does not synchronize with the global and regional strategic realities.

India's critical dilemmas of its development footprint in Afghanistan thus increase with the gradual draw down of the hard power of the US-NATO military presence. While the credibility and resilience of the Afghan forces and police are growing thanks to the substantial infusion of capacity and aid, yet the ability to withstand the pincer inroads of the ISI and its allies in the Taliban and China would be difficult.

It is this fact of the relative drawdown of the US-NATO military power and the generic atrophy of the US will to engage, opens new uncertainties that are perilous from the Indian specs view. Therefore, the imperative lies in India to contend these strategic uncertainties and augment for a long drawn strategic plan perspective of what India should do in the wake of a resurgent Pakistani role in Afghanistan—a role in which China would throw its lot with Pakistan due to the dangling carrots of Afghanistan resources and the fact that Pakistan regains its 'strategic depth'.

Critical Imperatives in India's Nuclear Security

As the gathering storm unfolds in South Asia, India is situated in the epicentre of a dual-jeopardy of asymmetric conflict (only next to the West Asian region) that is gathering momentum from the resurgence of the Taliban and its hydra-headed allies. The gradual removal of the hard power of the US-NATO forces removes the deterrent and the ˉcritical stabilizing force in the region; opening the sluice gates for the rushing torrent of radical extremism and terrorism *par excellence*. It also jeopardizes Pakistan's regime and nuclear security due to the possible impact of the radicalization of the guardians of Pakistan's nuclear arsenal that might have inadvertent consequences of the possible compromise of the safeguards of its nuclear assets.

At the second level, India contends a heightened possibility of a Mumbai style nuclear or WMD terrorism attack- a possibility that cannot be ruled out. [8] The perils of a state-breakdown in Pakistan in view of escalating sectarian strife and the increased destabilization by the Taliban forces in Pakistan is a likely outcome in the event of the US-NATO military drawdown. Therefore, the imperatives of stabilization gains vital importance in which the compulsive roles of the US, NATO, Russia, China and India is evident. While the accents of cooperation and convergence would be most beneficial to India, China's expedient stand on Pakistan and its correlation to Afghanistan would have to be watched keenly. India thus contends three issues of vital significance in the calibration of its nuclear security.

The perils of nuclear terrorism stare at India even as the sectarian strife and the impetus of the Jihadi groups quest for the acquisition of WMD and the unfettered motivations to use them against India increases. India needs the comprehensive operational-technological and intelligence assets that would be able to track down the movement of such groups with the lethal cargo into India's soil. The imperative for India to invest in critical infrastructure security, enhanced intelligence and security coordination with all the powers US, NATO, Israel, Russia, China so to mitigate the threat and substantially be prepared for consequence management.

The challenges of the China-Pakistan nuclear cooperation and augmenting Pakistani nuclear arsenal is a clear and present danger to India. While certain convergences between India and China may work with regard to countering asymmetric threats with the WMD linkages, the prospect of state-to-state transfer of nuclear and missile technology from Beijing to Islamabad has gained heightened cooperation and coordination in the aftermath of the India-US Civil Nuclear Agreement. [9] China's readiness to assist Pakistan in the civilian nuclear area as a means to achieve energy sufficiency is however a loaded issue given the substantial scope of strategic cooperation between Islamabad and Beijing. The Chinese determination to maintain a level of India-Pakistan nuclear parity is quite evident. It also opens the covert horizontal proliferation of Beijing in the Pyongyang-Beijing-Islamabad-Teheran axis, with Beijing serving as the strategic bridge.

India's imperatives in strategic modernization thus gains momentum and critical importance. While, India's stand on nuclear disarmament is laudable, the scope of achieving regional disarmament is a super-myth. It is good for rhetorical value. Beijing's determination for strategic modernization of its nuclear and missile modernization and horizontal proliferation is quite evident. India is thus compelled to join the cascade of the nuclear arms race in the region.

India has striven to initiate global nuclear disarmament moves in its seven-point proposal: (a) reduction of the salience of nuclear weapons in national security strategy; (b) negotiation of an agreement on no-first use of nuclear weapons among nuclear weapon states; (c) negotiation of a universal and binding agreement on non-use of nuclear weapons against non-nuclear weapons; (d) negotiation of a convention on the complete prohibition of the use or threat of use of nuclear weapons; (e) negotiation of a nuclear convention prohibiting development, stockpiling and production of nuclear weapons; (f) moving towards a global, non-discriminatory and verifiable elimination of these weapons; (g) unequivocal commitment of all nuclear weapon states towards the goal of eventual elimination of nuclear weapons; (h) adoption of additional measures by nuclear weapon States to reduce risks, dangers and possibility of accidental use of these weapons. [10]

India has to hasten its strategic modernization of its deployed Triad so to achieve credibility, endurance and survivability in the face of the determined Chinese-Pakistani nuclear and missile modernization. India faces a new dimension of Chinese submarine launched ballistic missiles of the JL-2 from its *Jin* class SSBNs as well as Land attack Cruise Missiles with nuclear payloads capable of launched from its *Shang* class attack submarines. India's momentum with its Agni V and the follow-on missiles requires urgent imperatives. Similarly, India's survivable nuclear deterrent from the sea alone could guarantee India its nuclear insurance against the concerted Chinese-Pakistani nuclear compliance.

Future Pathways of India in the Region

India contends an unenviable position in the region. The double jeopardy of asymmetric conflict and nuclear proliferation including the dimension of its correlation with violent non-state actors has reached an epitome. The imperatives for nuclear security and safety of nuclear assets in the region are paramount. With the global nuclear summit and its initiatives have taken off well, the regional initiatives to secure fissile material and attribute its forensics is vital. The lethal combination of state-breakdown, ISI manipulation and the escalatory postures of radical extremist groups with WMD intentions increase the prospect of catastrophic attacks within Pakistan, India and in the wider region.

India needs to engage in multilateral diplomacy as well as operational synergies to secure the fissile material stocks in the region and the stabilization measures of Pakistan, which is the epicentre for sectarian conflict, relentless terrorism, and the exporting point of terrorism to the region. The continued presence of the US-NATO forces in the region seems inevitable. Announced withdrawals have only strengthened the Taliban-ISI convergence and have not contributed to the stability of the Afghanistan-Pakistan region. The combination of hard military power and the civilian development initiatives of India in Afghanistan would have to go a very long way.

The ambiguity of China with respect to Afghanistan is yet another issue; while China would like to secure its turbulent Xingjiang province; its interests in Afghanistan on the initiative of Pakistan would be different. A Pakistan-China convergence in Afghanistan would be detrimental to India. The imperative for India lies in how India and Russia could cooperate in Afghanistan and evolve parallel approaches of India-US-NATO engagements in stabilizing the regional insecurity as well ensuring nuclear safety and security measures.

India's engagement with Afghanistan needs to solid cement in the longer run with the evolution of a stable government in Kabul. The imperative for an Indian engagement in Afghanistan is necessary; but such an engagement would be possible as long as the regime in Kabul stays open to all regional powers and does not tilt towards Pakistan and be subject to the manipulations of the ISI.

While India's nuclear disarmament initiatives are most laudable, their relevance in the regional context would continue to remain questionable given the higher penchants for strategic modernization of China, Pakistan and the convergence of the two states in the region. Therefore, India's accents would be more towards security and safety aspects of nuclear weapons and arms control approaches rather than genuine disarmament measures.

India's quest for human security and development within the country and its emulation in the region is unquestionable; but the turbulent region that is increasingly conflict-ridden heightens various insecurities that renders inadvertent wars probable; asymmetric conflicts escalatory and nuclear proliferation inevitable.

In summation, what India needs to affirm is the following: (a) Sustain the momentum towards genuine disarmament initiatives at the global level; since regional level disarmament is out of question given the cascading effects of the Sino-Pakistani nuclear and missile build-up; (b) Invest and initiate human security and human development measures within the country as the country faces a monumental task of poverty alleviation and human development and at the same time maintain India's pace of commitments for human security and development for the economically weaker nations; (c) Reinforce credible deterrence as safety vault measure to ensure that the cascading impact of nuclear weapons and missile build-ups in India's turbulent neighbourhood do not adversely impact on India.

Nehru's vision of Peace and Development of the region has been reduced to perennial rounds of fratricidal conflict in the region with nuclear weapons in the backdrop. India's development-disarmament narrative transformed into the growth-deterrence discourse—viewed as a paradigm shift of India's strategic locus. While India enunciates the essence of equity and development; its ethos has been lost in the internal context due to the debilitating poverty of an overwhelming one-third of the populace. India's external aid diplomacy in Afghanistan, Bhutan, Nepal and in Africa reflects the accrual of regional influence of a rising power than the espousal of the Nehruvian vision.

The final grand solution to human ailments would come when the Messiah reigns in the Millennium on Earth. Human problems and challenges have gone perilous and complex that mere Nobel Peace Prize winning speeches cannot solve. Equity, peace and justice would finally prevail when the Messiah would reign on this Planet and the Universe in the Millennium. As it is written by Prophet Isaiah in the Holy Bible, "...And He shall judge among the nations, and shall rebuke many people: and they shall beat their Swords into Plowshares, and their Spears into Pruning hooks: Nation shall not lift up sword against nation, neither shall they learn war any more; "....Of the increase of His Government and Peace there shall be no end....". The Eternal Reign of The Messiah— Lord God of the Universe would give Planet Earth and the entire Universe; its Peace, Happiness, Equity, Justice with triumph of Good over the prevalent evil. The removal of the causal factors and the structural dimensions of human violence would be the final panacea to the elimination of nuclear armaments and the general armaments.

End Notes

1. World at Risk: The Report of the Commission on the Prevention of WMD Proliferation and Terrorism accessed at http://www.preventwmd.org/report/ on 18 Dec 2010.
2. Mohan Malik (2010), China unveils 'The Kashmir Card', *China Brief,* Volume 10, Issue 9, September 24 2010 accessed at http://www.jamestown.org/single/?no_cache=1 &tx_ ttnews percent5Btt_news percent5D=36915 on 18 December 2010.
3. Sanjaya Baru (2009), "India: Rising Through the Slowdown", in Ashley J. Tellis, Andrew Marble and Travis Tanner, *Strategic Asia 2009-10: Economic Meltdown and Geopolitical Stability* (Seattle, WA: National Bureau of Asian Research).

4. Mohan Malik (2009), "The China-Pakistan Nexus" in Wilson John (ed.), *Pakistan: The Struggle Within,* (Pearson Longman 2009), pp. 157-197.

5. S.R. Subramaniam (2009), "Combating nuclear terrorism in the age of nuclear renaissance: domestic implementation of international legal obligations in India", accessed at *International Journal of Nuclear Law,* 2009, Vol. 2, No. 3, pp. 251-263, 18 December 2010.

6. Mohan J. Malik (2006), Multilateralism Shanghaied in Articles July 14 2006 accessed at http://www.strategycenter.net/research/pubID.115/pub_detail.as p on 18 December 2010.

7. "Afghanistan claims mineral wealth is worth \$3 trillion" *The Telegraph* 17 June 2010 accessed at http://www.telegraph.co.uk/news/worldnews/asia/afghanistan/78 35657/Afghanistan-claims-mineral-wealth-is-worth-3trillion.html on 18 December 2010.

8. Ashley J. Tellis et al. (2009), "The Lessons of Mumbai" *RAND Occasional Paper* accessed at http://www.rand.org/pubs/occasional_papers/2009/RAND_OP2 49.pdf on 18 December 2010.

9. Jayashree Bajoria and Esther Pan (2010), The India-US Nuclear Deal, *Backgrounder*, New York: Council for Foreign Relations accessed at http://www.cfr.org/publication/9663/usindia_nuclear_deal.html on 18 December 2010.

10. Statement by Hamid Ali Rao, Ambassador and Permanent Representative of India to the Conference on Disarmament, February 28, 2008. www.mea.gov.in accessed at http://mea.gov.in/meaxpsite/speech/2008/09/16da01.pdf on 18 December 2010.

3

Developing a Cogent Vision for Peace in South Asia

Maqbool Ahmed Siraj

Any cogent vision for peace in South Asia should necessarily be premised with the realization that 'Geography binds the region and its people together while history and politics divide them.'

The South Asian region consisting of eight states, namely Afghanistan, Bhutan, Bangladesh, India, Nepal, Pakistan, Sri Lanka, and the Maldives, is one of the most ethnically and religiously diverse and conflict-ridden regions on the earth. Religious composition is just one way to describe the diversity. While every single country lays claim to being a nation-state, they are so only in terms of their Constitution. In reality, all of them are multinational states. India has more than 28 provinces, majority of them carved out on the basis of language, and are bound into a federal structure. Pakistan has four major ones while smaller ethnic entities within them are still struggling to get recognition. Sri Lanka has just returned from the brink of division on ethnic lines. Nepal and Bhutan have large Buddhist and Hindu minorities respectively.

Afghanistan may be 99 percent Muslim, but has sizeable Uzbek, Tajik and Shia population. Bangladesh has nearly 12 percent Hindu population besides its hill areas of Chittagong are inhabited with Buddhist tribes. While Hindus in India constitute 82 percent of its population, they are hierarchically divided into social classes or castes. Muslims of India and Pakistan have two major sects, Sunnis and Shias. Even otherwise they are far from being monolith. Hindu caste system has led them to identify themselves into *biradries* (fraternities) almost akin to Hindus. Madrassas, juristic schools and revivalist movements have ensured further sectarianization of Muslims all across the subcontinent. Buddhists and Jains too are equally infected.

Religion played the major role in carving out three states with Pakistan coming into existence on the basis of a demand for Homeland for Muslims of India. Emergence of Bangladesh though questioned the futility of such a basis, led to the creation of yet another and a third major nation, Bangladesh. However, not everyone is still convinced of the inefficacy of religion as glue for nationhood. Therefore, the Kashmir issue has been casting its shadow on Indo-Pak relations. This has spawned an arms race that saps the vitality of the economies of these two major nations, gives rise to militancy and feeds hatred between two major communities residing in the subcontinent.

In Afghanistan, the religion was used in global power and ideological struggle and made that nation a virtual battlefield for the last three decades. In short, religion and religious divide still retains a lot of disaster potential. Tribal loyalties incite a host of liberation movements in the North Eastern region of India and foment lawlessness in North-West of Pakistan.

Some Silver Lining

While religion, language and tribal loyalty have provided substance for nationalist struggles, casteist and sectarian differences have manifested themselves in social movements and political groupings. The era of globalization has added yet another ingredient to the friction and conflict i.e. corporatization. Usurpation of resources of the traditional communities by mining companies, dam builders and developers of SEZs is leading to dislocation of communities and impoverishment of masses. In short, too many traditional divisions, social differentiations and historical animosities together with economic crises and nationalist struggles have intersected each other leading to the creation of a tapestry of mosaics of crises that overlay the region. Nation-building efforts have therefore suffered considerably all across the region, and miserably in context to Pakistan, Afghanistan and Sri Lanka.

However, there are silver linings too. Classic failure of Ayodhya movement in binding together the majority community into a political vote bloc in India serves to indicate that the sway of faith-based, casteist, fundamentalist ideologies on people can be only short-lived alternatives for long-term and enduring ideologies based on peace, progress, prosperity, justice for all. Second, Pakistan's reconciliation with its geopolitical status as a South Asian nation (and thereby coming into existence of the SAARC in 1985) and moving away from ambition of allying with states west of it, has signalled dawn of the essential realization that destiny of all the people of the region lies in swimming, sailing and sinking together. [1] (It is useful to be reminded that Pakistan was a member of the US-led SEATO and CENTO and was a leading member of Regional Cooperation Development [RCD] with Iran and Turkey). The two developments signify a major reconciliation with the South Asian reality. These could be taken as defining moments in the history of the region that have powerfully endorsed their willingness to break with the fractious past.

However, forces seeking legitimacy in the name of religion and language still continue to fuel a thousand mutinies and sour the dream of peace and development in the region. But its rivers, resources, mountain ranges, climate and poverty bind them into a common entity. Himalayas in the north separate South Asia from the neighbouring states inhibited by Mongoloid racial strains and as an economic region.

Geography Binds Them

The Himalayas extending over a distance of 1,500 miles from east to west and ranging in width from 93 miles to 250 miles from north to south, have profoundly shaped the cultures of South Asia; many Himalayan peaks are sacred in Hinduism, Buddhism, and Sikhism. Some of the world's major river systems arise in the Himalayas, and their combined drainage basin is home to some three billion people (almost half of Earth's population) in 18 countries. The Himalayan range encompasses about 15,000 glaciers, which store about 12,000 cubic kilometre of freshwater. The 70 km. long Siachen Glacier at the India-Pakistan border is the second longest glacier in the world outside the polar region.

The higher regions of the Himalayas are snowbound throughout the year, in spite of their proximity to the tropics, and they form the sources for several large perennial rivers, most of which combine into two large river systems i.e., Indus River basin in Pakistan and Ganges-Brahmaputra basin in Bangladesh. Ten of largest rivers of Asia flow from the Himalayas and on them depends the livelihood of nearly one billion people. Besides, the Himalayas have profound impact on the climate in the South Asian region. It is precisely because of abundance of rivers and availability of water that South Asia could come to harbour such a vast mass of humanity.

A second factor affecting the climate and livelihood is June-September monsoon rising from the Arabian seas. The monsoon accounts for 80 percent of the rainfall in India and Pakistan. Indian agriculture (which accounts for 25 percent of the GDP and employs 70 percent of the population) is heavily dependent on the rains, for growing crops especially like cotton, rice, oilseeds and coarse grains. A delay of a few days in the arrival of the monsoon can badly affect the economy, as evidenced in the numerous droughts in India in the 1990s. The monsoon is widely welcomed and appreciated by city-dwellers as well, for it provides relief from the climax of summer heat in June. Similarly, nearly all rains in Pakistan and Bangladesh happen because of monsoons.

The twin factors shape the region's climate, seasons, soil conditions; determine crops and thereby food habits, clothing and lifestyles; provide a calendar for fairs, festivals, harvests, yatras, pilgrimages, marriages, shopping, educational schedule, et al. In short, whoever they may be, there cannot be an escape from a common destiny for the inhabitants of the region. But in the face of enormity of the human tragedy in the region, statement of all the above facts appears overindulgence with the pleasantries.

The grotesque irony cannot be simply wished away. Withdraw these two major life-sustaining sources from South Asia, and it will be a desert. With our cultures, rivers, temples, economies, forests and farms, so intricately entwined with these major features of geography, people of South Asia need to re-examine the concepts of nationhood yet again. It is time therefore to redefine the nationhood, not merely in terms of the millennia of shared history but also in terms of shared destiny.

Unnatural Division of India and Pakistan

India and Pakistan emerged as two major nation-states in 1947 but religious and cultural history still binds the people. Harappa, Moehnjodaro and Taxila, the cradles of ancient civilizations lie in Pakistan. Hindus from Punjab and Haryana still go to Katasraj near Islamabad for pilgrimage. Soudha Rajputs of Umarkot in Pakistan visit Jodhpur in hundreds of number to find matches for their girls. They are supposed not to marry their daughters in their own gotras and people from a different gotra are found only in Rajasthan. Sufi Peer from Multan Sufi Saqi Sarwar is still celebrated in Indian side of Punjab. Hundreds of Pakistanis come to visit Ajmer Shariff in India. Major monuments and institutions of Islamic learning of repute in the subcontinent, namely the Jama Masjid, Nadwatul Ulama, Darul Uloom Deoband, Taj Mahal, Lal Qila, Khuda Baksh Khan Library of Patna and Charminar are in India. Notwithstanding all these, the two countries today are two nation-states.

However, these historic relations urge more opportunities for people-to-people contact, visits, tourism, exploration of opportunities for seeking treatment and education, if not employment. Indian films are big draw in Pakistan and Pakistani cuisines, spices and garments are popular in India. Nobody denies the fact that roots of all languages spoken in India and Pakistan and Bangladesh go back to Sanskrit and are members of the Indo-Aryan family. Telemedicine networks between India and Pakistan can bring sizeable medical tourism revenue for India. In the final analysis if popular contacts are allowed to grow, mutual mistrust and demonization can come down.

Similarly, mutual dependence between India and Bangladesh has also been urging enhanced level of exchanges. For instance India has been seeking a transit route for trains and goods to access its far flung areas in the North Eastern states. Bangladesh has been seeking transit route through India for goods from Nepal. Flood control in Bangladesh requires construction of dams in Nepal, entailing tripartite arrangements for sharing of waters and hydel power thus generated in Nepal. [2]

Peace and a vision for peace in South Asia must begin with a stock-taking of the issues and problems faced by the huge mass of the humanity it harbours and resources and opportunities the region offers. This is one of the poorest, least literate and most malnourished ones of the world. The per capita income in South Asia is lower than that of any other region in the world with a share of the global income of only 1.3 percent and has 40 percent of poorest people in the world. Peace, progress and prosperity in South Asia is predicated upon understanding of how did the past events order and disorder, constrain and redefine the lines of emotions, intention, identity, territory, power, resource control, cultural expression and the universe of human relationships for particular ethnic or religious community. (HDI for regional countries: Afghanistan 172, India 134, Nepal 157, Pakistan 145, Bhutan 141, Sri Lanka 97, Maldives 109, Bangladesh 146,) [3] Per capita annual income in South Asian countries in

US$ in 2010: Afghanistan 1,000, Bangladesh 1,600, Bhutan 5,600, India 3,339, Nepal 1,250, Pakistan 2,789, Sri Lanka 5,103, the Maldives 5483. The per capita income for the US in 2010 was US$ 48,184.

Peace and development in South Asia pre-supposes a cogent vision for the region based on its historicity, resources, potential for economic development and its emergence as a cultural laboratory. In an environment dominated by despair and despondency, the SAARC has been the only ray of hope in this direction so far. But it has largely been hamstrung by petty rivalries, partisan concerns, communal competition, wars, arms race, irredentist tendencies and terrorism, notwithstanding ample perception among the leaders about the mutual benefits accruing from coming together and vulnerabilities in standing apart.

The region has witnessed three major intra-regional wars in 1948, 1965 and 1971 and a lesser military engagement at Kargil in 1999. Major conflicts in Kashmir and Sri Lanka have stemmed from perceived sense of injustice with ethnic segments even though attempts have been made to give it a communal and fundamentalist colour. Afghanistan has provided a chessboard for global power players who have tried both, to fan the fundamentalist fires and curb the same in their reincarnated war on terror.

What is evident is that the religion or religion-induced ideologies responsible for defining the nationhood in terms of religious affiliation have served to be the major diversionary issues taking away attention and resources from more substantial concerns like livelihood, sustainable progress, educational and technological development, employment generation, ecology, environmental degradation, etc. It calls for creative tackling of the issue whereby the people and the regional states could come to terms with their current boundaries and ethnic composition. Education and media will be two important tools in this direction.

Intra-regional cooperation in writing of regional history,

textbooks, and homogenizing the curriculum in terms of espousing a common South Asian identity with tolerance for diversity and hospitality towards others cultures will hold the key. [4] There are no quick-fixes as solutions. Roots of all kinds of chauvinisms go deep among the people and the soil of South Asia. The regional leaders, political parties, ideologues, environmentalists, ecologists, sociologists, educators, media-persons, economists, agricultural scientists, climatologists, and political scientists are the ones who understand the need for a common charter of priorities more than the others.

Europe could envision its shared destiny the hard way and is grappling with the new vision on a day to day basis. Those nation-states could live down their historic hostilities after two World Wars. The way forward for the South Asia is much more cumbersome for it is a minefield of more stubborn elements of faiths, cultures, languages, scripts, resources, rivalries of the past and overall prejudices that accept no erasures. Evidently, it is easier said than done.

With survival and progress in South Asia having so great stakes in peace and mutual trust, the task begins with identifying sources of tension and conflict. A Kashmir, an Eelam or Gorkhaland may be just symptoms. May be a hundred incipient rebellions brewing just underneath the surface. No war pacts or no-first-use treaties could come later. A sustained effort must be launched by professional (the ones mentioned above and list could be longer) to deemphasize the factors that make us nation-states. In context of nation-building this may sound like a disastrous recipe. But it must be recognized that narrowly defined nationalisms have wrought more disasters for nations than positive efforts at building them as we have seen them in Europe.

Nationhood in its narrower sense could also be a larger kind of tribalism, hence the need to envision common destinies more than as well as rather than shared pasts. South Asia requires some kind of a vision to march forward, rise above its petty rivalries, reinvigorate its human material to build a future for itself and regenerate a spirit of live, and let live. Import of Wahhabi fundamentalist ideology from the West Asia and aggressive cultural nationalism as espoused by the Hindutva forces, have both wreaked havoc. While religion is talked about loudly in South Asia, values espoused by all faith, have the weakest hold on its politicians and people alike. (Transparency Index shows that the SAARC countries have high public sector corruption: India 3.1, Pakistan 2.5, Nepal 2.2, Bangladesh 2.7, Bhutan 5.7, Afghanistan 1.5, Maldives NA. Compare it with: US 7.1, China 3.6, Japan 8, New Zealand 9.5, Denmark 9.4 on the Corruption Perception Index 2011 compiled by Transparency International for countries where 10 is for least corrupt and 1 for the most corrupt) [5]

A quick look at the following facts:

1. Share of defence to Central Government's expenditure in India's budget is 13.29 percent. [6]

2. Pakistan's defence budget 2011 has number three standing in the National Budget at Rs. 495 billion (18 percent) after debt servicing at Rs. 1034 billion (37 percent) and general public services at Rs. 626 billion (23 percent). [7]

3. India has been the world's biggest importer of weapons over the past five years, with Asian countries making up four of the top five, according to a new report from Swedish think tank SIPRI. "India received nine percent of the volume of international arms transfers during 2006-10, with Russian deliveries accounting for 82 percent of Indian arms imports", it said. [8]

4. 93 percent catchment area of rivers in Bangladesh lies outside its borders. Even if the country does not receive an inch of rainfall, it could witness floods over one-third area of its territory. [9]

5. India has a rapidly growing appetite for hydrocarbons to sustain its 8 percent annual growth rate and Iran is one of India's leading suppliers. Currently, India imports over 70 percent of its requirement of oil and natural gas. Of this, 12 percent comes from Iran. India's energy relations with

Iran extend well beyond the Iran-Pakistan-India (IPI) gas pipeline, which the US opposes. [10]

6. The Sethusamundram Project between India and Sri Lanka will allow India a navigable route around its Peninsula with a reduction of 350 nautical miles of distance and will allow its ships to remain near to the coast all along. [11]

The above facts or realities merely reflect the spectrum of bottlenecks, prospects, challenges and opportunities in mutual cooperation (or lack of it). A shared destiny for the people of the region therefore, cannot be overemphasized.

Issues and problems are just one aspect. We need to look at another aspect too. The region has a rich bio-diversity and is hospitable to all kinds of crops, cattle, wildlife, and faiths, religions, martial arts and has been an incubator of ideas since millennia. The region could therefore serve as a cultural laboratory. The people are extremely talented and intelligent. For want of incentives, the region witnesses massive brain drain, flight of talents and migration of labour. An effort should be mounted to retain the talents and priority should be given to set up manufacturing industries rather than service economies in order to provide employment to more people.

There is no gainsaying that some of the members of the SAARC groupings are the states with lowest per capital income, lowest literacy, high malnourishment, farthest from the Millennium Development Goals (MDGs), high infant and maternal mortality, or to say lowest on Human Development Index (HDI). Any vision for the region must include improvement of HDI through increased access to food, health and education, ensuring food security and employment, enhancement of rate of growth, lowering of disparities, etc. The development goals are not easy to be met unless resources are diverted from defence and security apparatus which saps these economies and makes them the most attractive destination for western arms. The agenda is therefore clear:

1. Defusing regional tensions, conflicts.

2. Special attention to resolve long festering issues such as

Kashmir's status, ensuring equality and cultural rights of Tamils in Sri Lanka and Chakma tribals in Bangladesh. Priority should be given to restoration of civil liberties, withdrawal of security forces from civilian habitation. It does not require merely political will but a willingness to avoid judging issue on the basis of national prestige and accepting solution capable of delivering enduring peace without heartburn.

3. Total elimination of possibilities of war by espousing of respect for each other's territory and existing borders.

4. Stamping out sources of terrorism. Role of Non-state actors such as private militias and chauvinist forces should be probed and checked.

5. Gradual slashing of defence budgets.

6. Keeping the arm manufacturers at bay.

7. Increasing awareness of commonalities rather than differences. There should be attempt to deemphasize ethno-religious differences and promotion of interdependence under the wide canvas of common destiny.

8. Relaxing curbs on travel for students, scholars, artists, pilgrims.

9. Curbing zealots, hate-mongers and importers of divisive ideologies and strengthening democratic forces in the region and frequent assertion of the rule of law. Curbing all such tendencies that seek to radicalize the youth and divert the popular attention from the path of shared destiny.

10. Encouragement to celebration of diversity and cultural exchange.

11. Guarantee for protection of religious places and cultural property as they have existed since antiquity.

12. Protection of civil and cultural rights of religious and linguistic minorities and avoid using them as political footballs.

13. Promotion of inter-university tournaments, tours and debates.

14. Establishment of a SAARC Human Rights Commission.

15. Creation of a Law Commission whereby all laws within the region could be humanized. (If Blasphemy Law in Pakistan is misused against minorities, anti cow slaughter laws are misused to harass Muslims in India)
16. Establishment of South Asian Studies departments and SAARC chairs in at least 10 universities across the eight nations.
17. Efforts to write objective history of South Asia.
18. Removal of element of hate from the textbooks and common resolve to inculcate the values of peace, justice, tolerance, hospitality, generosity, truthfulness, transparency etc among the younger generation.
19. Establishment of a SAARC news agency with focus on development news.
20. Establishment of a SAARC Radio news outfit.
21. Making of such films that promote harmony in the region with celebration of diversity.
22. A joint initiative to afforest Himalayan slopes, cleanse the polluted rivers, control floods, set up cyclone, tsunami, earthquake and locust warning systems, checking carbon emission, checking pirates at sea, stop human trafficking, prevent over fishing of the seas in economic zones of the oceans around, exchange criminals and innocent intruders, audit polls, checking propaganda by media, attempts at communalizing politics, etc.
23. Setting up bilateral trade commissions to exchange goods and services produced within the region, relaxing the trade barrier and reducing tariffs,
24. Establishment of Scientific bodies for exchange of information on crops, latest agri-technologies etc.
25. Improvement of rail network, boosting intra-regional traffic, tourism and pilgrimages. Reviving the plan for Trans-Asia rail network.

One realizes that all this is easier said than done. But a beginning has to be made. Europe envisioned itself as a formidable economic group towards 1980 which became a reality with European Union coming up in 1993 following Maastricht Treaty. [12] The road ahead is long and cumbersome. Prejudices are stubborn. Biases are deeply entrenched. Everyone is an ardent devotee of his/her own religious faith and shibboleths. Only a visioned leadership can prepare the people to rise above their petty interests.

End Notes

1. Maqbool Ahmed Siraj (2008), Religion and the Arts, in Richard Kearney (ed.), *India a Laboratory of Inter Religious Experiment,* Brill, Leiden, The Netherlands.
2. Farooq Sobhan (ed.), (2005), *Dynamics of Bangladesh-India Relations,* Dhaka: Bangladesh Enterprises Institute, The University Press Ltd.
3. http://hdr.undp.org/en.
4. Textbooks and history lesson in India and Pakistan reinforce religious orientation of their respective nationhood. Pakistani history books begin their lesson from the advent of Muhammad bin Qasim in Sind. In India we have seen constant deemphasizing of medieval history which was dominated by Delhi sultanate and Mughal rule. Sunil Sethi of India Today found that the Urdu Primer in a Pakistani school had the picture of a fierce-looking Sikh as pictorial support for Urdu word *Zalim* (oppressor). Incidentally, the picture appeared over the Urdu alphabet *zoe.*
5. http://cpi.transparency.org/cpi2011/results.
6. http://www.idsa.in/idsacomments/IndiasDefenceBudget2011-12_lkbehera_070311.
7. http://www.opinion-maker.org/2011/09/pakistan-fudging-defence-budget.
8. http://www.thelocal.se/32570/20110314.
9. Toufiq A. Siddiqui and Shirin Tahir-Kheli (eds.), (2004), *Water Needs in South Asia*, Hawaii: GEE-21, Honolulu.
10. http://www.deccanherald.com/content/229625/indias-tough-choices-over-iran.html.
11. http://en.wikipedia.org/wiki/Sethusamudram_Shipping_Canal_Project.
12. http://en.wikipedia.org/wiki/European_Union.

4

China's South Asian Strategy in the 21st Century

Joseph Antony

The post-Cold War world offers new avenues of challenges and opportunities to the powers that be in the global scenario. This makes every part of the world crucial for the global actors. At this juncture, with the emergence of China and India as the new economic power houses of the world, Asia has entered into the limelight of international community. This is unprecedented in the modern history of Asia. A statesman like Henry Kissinger equates the emergence of China, India and Japan with the situation which shaped the European balance of power during the 19th century. (Kissinger, 2008) The 9/11, the regime change and the subsequent unfolding events in Iraq, the looming crisis in Iran, terrorism infected Pakistan, and crisis in Syria etc. make Asia a virtual flashpoint. Moreover, economically and politically, Asia appears poised to determine the new world order. So, with the world's fastest-growing markets, fastest-rising military expenditures, and most serious hotspots (including the epicentre of international terrorism) Asia holds the key to the future global order. (Chellaney, 2010:13)

In Asia, the nuclearization of India and Pakistan, presence of Taliban–Al-Qaeda elements in Afghanistan, and the strategically significant Indian Ocean has made South Asia a high profile area. Scholars like B.M. Jain (2011) describe South Asia as "New South Asia" due to some drastic developments occurred in this region. He states that "the new South Asia apparently differs from the old South Asia of the Cold War era both from the domestic and external points of view. The new South Asia has witnessed unprecedented political changes. Monarchy in Nepal has been replaced by a republican state. Pakistan has witnessed the return to a democratic regime. Bhutan has become a parliamentary democracy. Maldives has witnessed a peaceful transformation. Sri Lanka has also heralded a new political era. (Jain, 2011:9-10) These crucial aspects have prompted external powers like the US and China to concentrate their attention on South Asia.

This study aims at understanding the Chinese policy towards South Asia in the post-Cold War era. And this study focuses on the Chinese strategy to prevent India from gaining an upper hand in South Asia, its home ground. It is an analysis of Chinese attempt to contain and encircle, or "concircle" India. China tries to achieve this objective through its money, political and military power. But in its strategy to achieve a 'hegemonic' type of dominance in South Asia, the Indo-US relationship, according to China, is a major stumbling block. So this paper is structured in a manner in which it firstly surveys the US forays into South Asia by strengthening Indo-US friendship. Secondly, it analyses the Chinese attempts to contain and encircle India by befriending the South Asian nations by hook or crook.

US Strategy in Asia

For many reasons, Asia has been a region to reckon with in the international landscape. It was also a playground of the Super Powers during the cold war period. The disappearance of the Soviet Union, however, did not change that situation radically. It is only an absence of one actor. As was stated, although the United States is a vast ocean away from Asia, it is one of the most critical factor in the Asian and the global security order. (Rajagopalan, 2009:1-2) But according to Chintamani Mahapatra (2005:156), the global reach and a robust military presence in Asia eminently qualify the United States to be an Asian power. The US authorities are also categorical in declaring their strategic interest in Asia. Former

US Defence Secretary Robert Gates reiterated this stand at the Shangi-La Dialogue 2008: "The United States is a Pacific nation with an enduring role in Asia. We welcome Asia's rise...I want to convey to you with confidence that any future US administration's Asia security policy is going to be grounded in the fact that the United States remains a nation with strong and enduring interests in this region. (Gates, 2008)

More recently at the Shangri-La Dialogue 2012, Leon Panetta, Secretary of Defense of the United States, explained a new defence strategy of Washington for the Asia-Pacific region. According to Panetta, "In the 21st century, the United States recognizes that our prosperity and our security depends even more on the Asia-Pacific region. After all, this region is home to some of the world's fastest growing economies: China, India, and Indonesia to mention a few. At the same time, Asia-Pacific contains the world's largest populations, and the world's largest militaries. Defence spending in Asia is projected by the IISS (International Institute for Strategic Studies), to surpass that of Europe this year, and there is no doubt that it will continue to increase in the future.

Given these trends, President Obama has stated the United States will play a larger role in this region over the decades to come. This effort will draw on the strengths of the entire United States government. We take on this role not as a distant power, but as part of the Pacific family of nations. Our goal is to work closely with all of the nations of this region to confront common challenges and to promote peace, prosperity, and security for all nations in the Asia-Pacific region." (Panetta, 2012) So, Asia is significant for the US, not only because of its geopolitical reasons, economic, military and political aspects have also made it important.

US in South Asia

India makes the South Asian region significant for all nations around the world. The emergence of India as a result of its new economic policies by the end of the 20th century has made India a power to reckon with in the region. The changes in the global political settings have also brought some role to India. This has made the global as well as regional actors to look at India with interest. "So after considerable soul searching, the US administration has recognized that its larger strategic interests require a resumption of its previous efforts at engaging India in the region. The efforts it has made in this direction include the waiving of sanctions imposed after the tests; the willingness on the part of the President to visit the region after a gap of more than 20 years; a restoration of US support for multilateral economic development programs; and a willingness to discuss the resuscitation of previous initiatives relating to strategic cooperation, depending on the proliferation choices made by both India and Pakistan." (Tellis, 2001:236)

US-India Relations and China

Some scholars believe that the India-US relationship is emerging as one of the three bilateral relationships that will shape Asia and perhaps define global politics in the decades ahead. (Sirohi and Saran, 2012) It was the end of the Cold War which paved the way for the new opening in the Indo-US relations. Strobe Talbott, (2004) one of the architects of the new opening in Indo-US relations stated, "the dissolution of the Soviet Union created an opening for the Clinton administration to free the United States' relations with South Asia from the strictures and distortions of the Cold War. The 1998 detonation of nuclear devices, the Kargil war between India and Pakistan, the 9/11 incident, the US intervention in Afghanistan etc. have hastened the strengthening of Indo-US relationship. Clinton administration took great pains to forge a good relation between the two nations. George Bush Jr. worked upon that base.

The words of Condoleezza Rice will be revealing with regard to the development of a new Indo-US relations: "Throughout the spring of 2001, we began to put the infrastructure into place for a transformation in US-India relations. The two countries launched the first political military dialogue in April 2002. Moreover, the Indian navy began a six month joint escort mission with the US fleet in the Malacca Strait, one of the busiest maritime trade routes in the world." (Rice, 2011:129) The Next Steps in Strategic Partnership (NSSP) 2004, the Civilian Nuclear Agreement, the US help at the IAEA and NSG, etc., are the milestones followed in the cementing of Indo-US relationships. (Malone, 2011:169-170) India and the US have succeeded in forging a strategic relationship which was absent throughout its history. Indo-US economic, trade, military relations are growing. The military exercises codenamed "Malabar" are sending the right signals of an emerging military relation. The Naval cooperation between India and the US reflects the long-term strategic relationship between the two countries. The two Navies have, over the years, collaborated over a wide spectrum of activities and exercises to advance the maritime partnership. "Malabar Exercise 2012' was the 16th in the series of structured bilateral exercises since 1992 that have steadily grown in scope and complexity. (*The Hindu*, 2012)

China Factor in the Indo-US Relations

Although the dramatic developments after the collapse of the Soviet Union had prompted many nations, including India, to cross the rubicon, Richard J. Ellings (2009) has presented how China became a cementing factor in the development of a strong US-India strategic relationship. He states, "The interests of United States with regard to China are critical, as China has assumed a central role in the global economy and seems to be the only power with the potential in the next few decades to challenge the existing order and American pre-eminence... America's interests in India are not simply derivative of its concerns with China. They derive as well from the nation's extensive global interests. America needs allies in the war on terror and partners for protecting the Indian Ocean and sea lines of communications (SLOCs). It needs collaborators to halt proliferation of weapons of mass destruction (WMD) and their delivery systems, and it desires new centres of economic growth to accelerate international prosperity.

To further stabilize the international system, it desires to bolster existing democracies and to encourage additional, preferably democratic, centres of power. From the US perspective, India is a long overdue strategic collaborator for a variety of very good reasons." (Ellings, 2009:301-302)

The statements and declarations of the leaders of American administration as well as well meaning scholars have clearly brought to the fore the Chinese factor in the emerging Indo-US relations. Writing in 2000, Condoleezza Rice argued that the USA should pay close attention to India as 'an element in China's calculation', suggesting a degree of regional rivalry that the USA might have the potential to exploit in its favour. (Rice, 2000)

Moreover, there was an attempt to institutionalize the anti-China mechanism through an 'Asian NATO' or an 'Arc of Democracy.' Since 2003 there have been serious discussions between the US and India about a possible Asian NATO in which India, Japan, Vietnam, South Korea, Philippines, Indonesia and Malaysia could be important nodes in the overall project of containing China. (Vanaik. 2008) A study made by Strategic Study Institute bluntly spells out the US thinking behind having an Asian NATO. "What's in it for the United States?

For one, the proposed security system is principally an in-region solution for dealing with two of the biggest international security threats—an over-ambitious China and the spread of Talibanised Islam. Second, this scheme being entirely indigenous, there is none of the odium that attends on US troops deployed locally as in South Korea and Japan…and finally, it in no way precludes the presence in the extended region of the US armed forces or limits US military initiatives." (Blank, 2005)

Chinese Position in the World

An awareness about the Chinese perception about the global scenario is essential to understand its strategic moves in South Asia. In the National Defence White Paper it says that, "world peace and development are faced with multiple difficulties and challenges. Struggles for strategic resources, strategic locations and strategic dominance have intensified. Meanwhile, hegemonism and power politics still exist, regional turmoil keeps spilling over, hotspot issues are increasing, and local conflicts and wars keep emerging. (China, 2008) China still considers the United States as a threat to its security. It also considers the US as the most powerful nation in the world. It holds the largest and strongest military force in the world. It is still a global power with the entire wherewithal. It is only a fact that China remains a decade behind the US in military force projection, battlefield management, and blue-water and space warfare capabilities. Not only is the United States likely to remain the most powerful country in the first half of this century, but China still has a long way to go to catch up in military, economic, and soft power. (Nye Jr., 2011)

China in Asia

China is more than an Asian power as it is marching forward to become a global power. So no nation in Asia can ignore China. China is located in a strategic place in Asia. Its western region opens to Central Asia, south opens to South Asia. Its border with Russia connects with Eurasia. And China itself is part of East Asia. "Beijing views South Asian countries as "neighbours" with whom it is especially important to have friendly, cooperative ties both to increase China's own economic and political influence and to lessen the ability of potentially hostile powers (currently the US) to injure China's interests." (Garver, 2005: 1)

Moreover, the military presence of the United States in Afghanistan, the new found bonhomie between India and the United States have forced China to make some strategic moves in South Asia. "China's broad objective in South Asia is to expand multi-dimensional cooperative relations with all the countries of that region. 'Multi-dimensional' signifies military ties as well as more innocuous political and economic cooperation. "All" means both India and India's smaller neighbours: Pakistan, Myanmar, Nepal, Sri Lanka, Bangladesh, Bhutan, and the Maldives." (Garver, 2005:1)

Chinese View of Indo-US Relations

"Chinese analysts are deeply sceptical of the new, far closer, far broader India-US relationship that emerged, starting with the Jaswant Singh-Strobe Talbott talks during the second half of 1998. Beijing suspects that a US desire to contain or balance China, to limit its rise and the expansion of its power, are key US motives behind the growing India-US strategic partnership. China's friendship diplomacy seeks to counter perceived US efforts to manoeuvre India into participation in nefarious American 'anti-China schemes'. This partially explains the 'strategic and cooperative partnership for peace and prosperity' agreed to by Wen Jiabao and Manmohan Singh in April *2005*." (Garver, 2005:4)

Strategic Significance of South Asia

South Asia's geographic location, midway between the oil rich Middle East and the South East Asian regions, lends it strategic importance. South Asia borders most of China's sensitive southern boundary. This gives China the strategic option of opening direct access through South Asia to the international sea lanes of Indian Ocean. The Indian Ocean region has always been the scene of power play between Russia, the US and the West, and the theocratic Islamic states because 75 percent of global merchant shipping passes through it. (Hariharan, 2008)

According to Ye Hailin, "only after 21st century, the relationship of China and South Asia has been significantly changed. For the first time in the history, China participates in the regional issues very positively and massively. China's policy vis-à-vis South Asia was redefined, the relationship between two sides were enlarged, deepened and reorganized. Someone cheers up to the new perspective of China-South Asia relationship, and someone complains publicly or privately, but it is unquestionably that China has been a crucial external partner of South Asia and would play more and more important role in the stage of South Asia." (Hailin)

China and South Asia are linked by land and water, mountains and rivers. Mountains pass through and major rivers flow down to China and South Asia from the Tibet Autonomous Region (TAR) of China. The region has a growing economy of over 1.5 billion people in different stages of economic and social development. Its huge, young population represents an enormous and untapped market for Chinese goods. Major political, economic and social problems within and between South Asian nations offer fertile ground for increasing China's influence through political, military and economic means. The region has considerable natural resources including coal, iron ore, natural gas and oil waiting to be fully exploited. (Hariharan, 2008)

Chinese South Asian Strategy

The Chinese South Asian strategy is part of its grand strategy of becoming a global power. (Saha, 2010) The present Chinese activities are aimed at ensuring the current pace of development going unaffected. The recent White Papers published by China highlight that strategy. China's sixth White Paper on Defence, 2009 declares Beijing's desire to advance its military capabilities from "strategic counter-attacks" (2004 White Paper) to "strategic projection operations." It highlights China's capability to deploy warships in "distant waters" or to engage its air force in long-range "strategic projection operations." It also declares China will "gradually develop its capabilities of conducting cooperation in distant waters and countering non-traditional security threats." Beijing's recent decision to dispatch three warships to support international efforts to curb piracy in the Gulf of Aden suggests a marked strengthening of China's naval capabilities as a result of over two decades of sustained efforts. (Kumar, 2009)

Chinese national security and development are the top priority of the leadership. China is also aiming to quadruple its per capita GDP by 2020 from the per capita attained in 2000. This would imply an average annual economic growth of 7.2 percent till 2020. In order to attain this, China will have to keep meeting the enormous appetite of its manufacturing economy for raw material and energy resources. (Hariharan, 2008) Conscious of these imperatives, China's international relations are developing on twin tracks: gaining sources of raw material across the globe, and increasing its strategic power projection.

Chinese Strategy towards South Asian Nations

India: No nation can ignore the sensitivity of India when they plan to engage any South Asian nations. Almost all nations, except one, shares borders with India. This provides India with a geopolitical hold all over the South Asian region. It is supported by its large population, vast area, its economic prowess, cultural bonds, and of course, military power. This gives India the role of a leader in South Asia.

Naturally, as part of its South Asian strategy, China has been engaged in the process of normalization of Sino-Indian relations. Now, China has become the largest trade partner of India by surpassing the US. The bilateral trade has crossed US$ 70 billion last year. As part of solving the border dispute, the Special Representatives have already made 15 rounds of talks. India and China are also holding joint military exercises. Recently, both nations have decided to resume joint military exercises after a gap of four years. (*BBC*, 2012) Moreover, both nations are members in many multilateral organisations which stand for the protection of the interests of the third world nations. India and China are also cooperating in global forums for the protection of the developing nations. Keep India in good humour while befriending others in South Asia is the policy of China.

Pakistan: China has cultivated an all weather friendship with Pakistan. They have long-standing strategic ties starting from 1956. China is the largest defence supplier to Pakistan. (Curtis and Scissors, 2012) China transferred equipment and technology to Pakistan's nuclear weapons and ballistic missile programs throughout the 1980s and 1990s, enhancing Pakistan's strength in the South Asian strategic balance. Stephen Cohen, an expert on the Indian and Pakistani militaries, describes China as pursuing a classic balance of power by supporting Pakistan in a relationship that mirrors the relationship between the U.S. and Israel. (Curtis, 2008)

China's support to Pakistan's overt and covert nuclear programme is a common knowledge in international politics. Now China is all set to construct the Chasma-3 and Chasma-4, nuclear reactors, in Pakistan in direct contravention of its non-proliferation commitments. (Yogesh, 2011) According to Subhash Kapila, Chinese designs here were not to contribute to Pakistan's defence capabilities or deterrence but to once again strategically de-stabilise India's security. (Kapila) The two countries have a vision for Pakistani nuclear energy to 2030, at which time they expect four new 320 MWe reactors and as many as seven 1000 MWe units to be in operation. China National Nuclear Company has been the main contractor at Chasnupp, sourcing main components like steam generators and steam turbines from Chinese firms. China also supplies nuclear fuel for the units. (World Nuclear News, 2008)

Besides the fast growing economic cooperation between these two old friends, their traditional politics and security links are also getting closer during the new millennium. From March 6 to 13, 2007, the Chinese navy task group participated in the naval exercises held in the Arabian Sea off Pakistan, which is the first time for Chinese navy force to participate in the multinational naval exercises. And before this, the "Friendship-2006" China-Pakistan joint anti-terrorism exercise was initiated on December 11th concluded on December 19th in the hilly area of northern Pakistan's Abbottabad. (Hailin) Last November, China and Pakistan held their two-week-long Joint Military Exercise in Jehlum city, in Punjab province. (*CNTV*, 2011) Recently, *India Today* reported on January 4, that a secret report prepared by the government's joint intelligence committee has confirmed India's worst fears— China is planning a military base in FATA or the Northern areas in Pakistan. (Ghazali, 2012)

Gwadar Port: China is also helping Pakistan develop a deep-sea port at the naval base at Gwadar in Pakistan's province of Baluchistan on the Arabian Sea. The port would allow China to secure oil and gas supplies from the Persian Gulf and project power in the Indian Ocean. China financed 80 percent of the US$ 250 million for completion of the first phase of the project and reportedly is funding most of the second phase of the project as well. (Curtis, 2008) Overlooking the Strait of Hormuz, the port is a declared defence area by Pakistan. It is supposed to host a large oil terminal, but can easily double as naval berthing facility, with the Jinnah Naval base nearby. (Roy, 2009) With the construction of Gwadar naval base in Pakistan (400 km. east of the Strait of Hormuz), China plans to restrict the movement of Indian Navy in the Arabian Sea.

The strategically important Gwadar will also reinforce Pakistan's Karachi naval base against India. (Kumar, 2009) Gwadar port is situated in a strategic location amid South Asia, Central Asia and the Middle East. The port lies near the Straits of Hormuz, through which about 20 percent of the world's oil is transported. (Washington Times, 2007) Located at the entrance of the Gulf and about 460 kilometres from Karachi, Gwadar has had immense geo-strategic significance on many accounts. The Chinese interest in Gwadar is not just economic and energy supplies related rather it is much, much more. It is of immense interest to its Navy—as a port of call, as a refuelling halt and as a listening and watch tower to monitor developments in the Gulf—particularly the movements of the US Navy. (Raman)

Sri Lanka: The bilateral relationship between China and Sri Lanka is marriage of convenience. China wants to expand political and security ties with the countries of the South Asia-Indian Ocean region to ensure the safety of Chinese sea lines of communication across the Indian Ocean. Sri Lanka, for its part, needs Chinese assistance—especially military aid. The US and India have curtailed military supplies to Sri Lanka because of human rights concerns, and Chinese aid to Sri Lanka comes with no strings attached. (Curtis, 2008)

In the case of Sri Lanka, China has been particularly attracted by that country's vantage location in the centre of the Indian Ocean—a crucial international passageway for trade and oil. Hambantota—the billion-dollar port Chinese engineers are now building on Sri Lanka's southeast—is the latest 'pearl' in China's strategy to control vital sea-lanes of communication between the Indian and Pacific Oceans by assembling a 'string of pearls' in the form of listening posts, special naval arrangements and access to ports. China indeed has aggressively moved in recent years to build ports in the Indian Ocean rim, including in Pakistan, Bangladesh and Myanmar. Besides eyeing Pakistan's Chinese-built port-cum-naval base of Gwadar as a possible anchor for its navy, Beijing has sought naval and commercial links with the Maldives, Seychelles, Mauritius and Madagascar. However, none of the port-building projects it has bagged in recent years can match the strategic value of Hambantota, which sits astride the great trade arteries. (Chellaney, 2009)

The significance of Hambantota to China lies in its proximity to India's south coast and on the fact that it provides Beijing with presence midway in the Indian Ocean. The Indian Ocean is a critical waterway for global trade and commerce. Half the world's containerized freight, a third of its bulk cargo and two-thirds of its oil shipments travels through the Indian Ocean. It provides major sea routes connecting Africa, the

Middle East, South Asia and East Asia with Europe and the Americas and is home to several critical chokepoints such as the Strait of Hormuz and the Strait of Malacca. The Hambantota Development Zone, which the Chinese will help build, will include a container port, a bunkering system, an oil refinery, an airport and other facilities. It is expected to cost about US$ 1 billion and the Chinese are said to be financing more than 85 percent of the project. (Ramachandran, 2007) The Chinese are also involved in building a US$ 60 billion stretch of highway that leads to the northeast area of the island and are funding the development of a coal power plant that they hope will generate 20 gigawatts by the year 2020. (Shoemaker, 2008)

Beijing began selling larger quantities of arms, and dramatically boosted its aid fivefold in 2008 to almost US$ 1 billion to emerge as Sri Lanka's largest donor. Beijing even got its ally Pakistan actively involved in Sri Lanka. With Chinese encouragement, Pakistan—despite its own faltering economy and rising Islamist challenge—has boosted its annual military assistance loans to Sri Lanka to nearly US$ 100 million while supplying Chinese-origin small arms and training Sri Lankan air force personnel in precision guided attacks. (Chellaney, 2009)

Bangladesh: The nation which owes India a lot for its birth too comes under the grips of China. For China, Bangladesh is a doorway into India's turbulent north-eastern region, including the Indian state of Arunachal Pradesh, to which China lays territorial claims. China prizes Bangladesh for its immense natural gas reserves which rival those of Indonesia. Bangladesh's geographic proximity with Myanmar makes these reserves accessible to China. India's access to Myanmar's gas reserves also hinges on Dhaka's willingness to allow a passage for laying a gas pipeline—a fact not lost on Beijing. (Niazi, 2005)

Both nations are also raising the level of trade. Total trade between China and Bangladesh was around US$ 3.5 billion in

2007, up about 8.5 percent from the previous year. China is an important source of military hardware for Bangladesh and increasingly is investing in Bangladesh's garment sector. With natural gas deposits in Bangladesh estimated at between 32 trillion and 80 trillion cubic feet, Bangladesh has gained strategic importance for both China and India as a potential source of energy. Apart from that, Bangladesh turned down India's proposal for a tri-nation gas pipeline with Burma. (Curtis, 2008)

Taking advantage of a sharp downturn in India's relations with Bangladesh over issues ranging from illegal immigration to Islamist terrorism, transit and trade, Beijing has upgraded its ties with Dhaka to gain naval access to the Chittagong port, to establish a road link with Bangladesh via Myanmar and to acquire Dhaka's immense natural gas reserves. (Malik)

Chinese naval activities in Bangladesh have significantly increased in recent times. With China's active collaboration, Bangladesh conducted in 2009 its maiden missile launch of a Chinese land attack anti-ship cruise missile C-802A from the Jianghu-class 1,500-ton F-18 Osman frigate in the Bay of Bengal. With the modernization of Chittagong naval port in Bangladesh, China intends to deter the movement of India navy in the Bay of Bengal. (Kumar, 2009) Bangladesh's Armed Forces today are predominantly equipped with Chinese military hardware. (Malik)

Nepal: Nepal occupies a strategic location along the Himalayan foothills dividing China and India. It has strong historical and cultural links with India. But, China, the northern neighbour of Nepal, was wise enough to fishing in troubled waters both during and after the monarchy. China provided military supplies to Nepalese King Gyanendra before he stepped down in 2005 while India and the U.S. were restricting their military assistance in an effort to promote political reconciliation within the country. (Curtis, 2008)

Unlike Bangladesh, Nepal has little energy potential to tempt Beijing, but its strategic location between China and

India makes it just as important. China wants the new ruler to stay clear of any foreign (Indian or the U.S.) influence that could make trouble in Tibet. To further the goal of status quo in Tibet, China is integrating Nepal into the Tibetan economy, and laying a highway that will connect the two. (Niazi, 2005)

Maldives: The island nation, Maldives also finds the favour of Chinese administration. To complete the "arc of influence" in South Asia, China is determined to enhance military and economic co-operation with the tiny but strategic Maldives. (Kumar, 2006) For that, China is planning to develop a submarine base at Marao in Maldives to counter the Indian navy's southern command. (Kumar, 2009)

Given China's known interest in developing bases around the Indian Ocean littoral, a Chinese base in Maldives would not be surprising. Although China claims that its bases are only for securing energy supplies to feed its growing economy, Indian experts perceive the Chinese base in Maldives as motivated by Beijing's determination to contain and encircle India, and thereby limit the growing influence of the Indian Navy in the region. The Marao base deal was finalized after two years of negotiations when Chinese Prime minister Zhu Rongzi visited Male in May 2001. Pakistan apparently, was instrumental in 'persuading' the Maldives to lease the island to the Chinese. The island will be operational in 2010. Once Marao comes up as the new Chinese 'pearl', Beijing's power projection in the Indian Ocean would be augmented. (*India Reacts*)

Bhutan: After Pakistan, Bangladesh, Bhutan, Nepal, the Maldives, and Sri Lanka, Beijing is skilfully employing economic and military means to Bhutan to draw it into China's orbit. The Chinese military's recent incursions and road construction activity in Bhutanese territory are aimed at coercing the tiny Himalayan kingdom to end its protectorate relationship with India and move into China's orbit "if Bhutan desires peace and development with the world's fastest growing superpower." (Malik)

Afghanistan: Afghanistan became the 8th member of SAARC during the Fourteenth SAARC Summit held in New Delhi on 3-4 April, 2007. China does not have a close relationship with Afghanistan. But it is trying its level best to develop strong relation with it. The major problem China fears is the intrusion of terrorists from Afghanistan. So, after years of standing in the background, Beijing is starting to show signs of closer engagement with its strife-torn neighbour in a bid to ward off disaster. Armed Uighur separatists, fighting for the independence of China's mainly Muslim Xinjiang region, which abuts Afghanistan and Pakistan, are believed to have set up camps in North Waziristan. The first priority of the Chinese will be to prevent the encroachments of the separatist elements. Stability in the tribal regions is of utmost national security importance to China. (*Christian Science Monitor,* 2012) China is waiting in the wings for the withdrawal of the NATO forces from Afghanistan to play its game in the South Asian region.

South Asia witnesses a triangular power play between the United States, India and China. For the US, as part of its global game plan, it is trying to forge a close relation with India in South Asia. Although the United States has more goals to be protected in South Asia in collaboration with India and Pakistan, China reduces it into single agenda—anti-China. The US has to keep its global superiority. India is the lord of the South Asian ring. Any encroachment on its backyard will be life and death issue for India. It is a fact that the relation of India with its South Asian neighbours are not in good taste. As a nation which is emerging into global status, China wishes to establish good contact with the friends in the region. All three nations want to project their power in the region.

It is a fact that China has succeeded in forging good relations with almost all South Asian nations. China is using their economic power, military muscle as well as global status to establish a strategic upper hand in the region. These pro-China micro poles around India can create problems to India in a moment of crisis. The port facilities acquired in Gwadar, Hambantota, Chittagong, etc. provide China a foothold into the land of India. India has to carefully plan a strategy to counter the moves made by China by taking the South Asian neighbours into confidence. A country which is keeping its eye on the high tables of global politics should try to make the small nations to pro-India micro poles, that too in a peaceful manner.

References

BBC (2012), "India and China to hold Joint Military Exercises," 4 September, at
http://www.bbc.co.uk/news/world-asia-india-19473365.

Blank, Stephen J. (2005), *Natural Allies? Regional Security in Asia and Prospects for Indo-American Strategic Cooperation*, Strategic Studies Institute of the US Army War College, at http://www.strategicstudiesinstitute.army.mil/pdffiles/pub626.pd

Chellaney, Brahma (2010), *Asian Juggernaut: The Rise of China, India and Japan*, New York: HarperCollins Publishers.

Chellaney, Brahma (2009), "China Fuels Sri Lankan War", *The Japan Times,* March 4.

China (2008), *National Defence White Paper*,
http://www.china-defense-mashup.com/? p=2456&page=30).

Christian Science Monitor (2012), "Why China is likely to get more involved in Afghanistan," 6 June, at
http://www.csmonitor.com/World/Asia-Pacific/2012/0606/Why-China-is-likely-to-get-more-involved-in-Afghanistan.

CNTV (2011), "Pakistan-China joint exercise concludes," 26 November, at
http://english.cntv.cn/program/newsupdate/20111126/102521.sh.

Curtis, Lisa and Scissors, Derek (2012), The Limits of the Pakistan-China Alliance, January 19, at
http://www.heritage.org/research/reports/2012/01/the-limits-of-the-pakistan-china-alliance.

Curtis, Lisa (2008), "US-India Relations: The China Factor," No. 2209, November 25, at
http://www.heritage.org/research/asiaandthepacific/upload/bg_2209.pdf.

Ellings, Richard J. (2009), "The Context and Purposes of US-India Strategic Cooperation" in Ayres, Alyssa and Mohan, C. Raja (eds.), *Power Realignments in Asia: China, India, and the United States*, New Delhi: Sage Publications.

Garver, John W. (2005), "China's South Asian Interests and Policies," at
https://uscc.gov/hearings/2005hearings/written_testimonies/05_07_21_22wrts/garver_john_wrts.

Gates, Robert (2008): "Challenges to Stability in the Asia-Pacific", at
http://www.iiss.org/conferences/the-shangri-ladialogue/plenary-session-speeches-2008/first-plenary-session-challenges-to-stability-in-the-asia-pacific/first-plenary-session-the-hon-robert-gates/.

Ghazali, Abdus Sattar (2012), "Growing Sino-Pakistan Military Ties Ring Alarm Bells In India", *Countercurrents.org*, 12 January at
http://www.countercurrents.org/ ghazali120112.htm.

Hailin, Ye, "China and South Asian Relations in a New Perspective," at http://iaps.cass.cn/ english/articles/showcontent.asp?id=1118.

Hariharan, R. (2008), "China's Influence in India's Neighbourhood-Part 1," C3S Paper No.200, August 12 at
http://www.c3sindia.org/strategicissues/305.

India Reacts, "Gayoom fears UK coup in Maldives", at
http://www.indiareacts.com/
nati2.asp?recno=3236&ctg=Defence.

Jain, B.M. (2011), *India in the New South Asia: Strategic, Military and Economic Concerns in the Age of Nuclear Diplomacy*, New Delhi, Viva Books.

Joseph S. Nye Jr. (2011), "China's Rise Doesn't Mean War…" in Chinese Strategy in South Asia, *Foreign Policy*, January/February at
http://www.foreignpolicy.com/articles/2011/01/02/
unconventional_wisdom?page=0,3.

Joshi, Yogesh (2011), "Understanding U.S. Policy on China-Pakistan Nuclear Deal," *World Politics Review*, 15 April.

Kapila, Subhash, "South Asia and China's Policy Record: An Analysis," http://www.southasiaanalysis.org/ percent5Cpapers4 percent5Cpaper387.html.

Kissinger, Henry A. (2008), "The Three Revolutions," *The Washington Post,* 7 April, at
http:/www.henryakissinger.com/articles/wp040708.html.

Kumar, Amit (2006): "China's Rise and its Impact on Asia: China's Growing Influence in Sri Lanka: Implications for India, *Institute for Peace and Conflict Studies*, 26 July.

Kumar, Sanjay (2009), "China's Naval Strategy: Implications for India," No. 2823, 2 March, at http://www.ipcs.org/article_details.php?articleNo=282Mahapatr a, *Chintamani* (2005): "The United States and the Asian Powers" in Sharma, R.R. (ed.), *India and Emerging Asia*, New Delhi: Sage Publications.

Malik, Mohan, "China's Strategy of Containing India", at http://www.pinr.com/ report.php?ac=view report&report_id=434

Malone, David M. (2011), *Does the Elephant Dance?: Contemporary Indian Foreign Policy*, New Delhi: Oxford University Press.

Niazi, Tarique (2005), "China's March on South Asia," 26 April, at http://www.asiamedia.ucla.edu/article.asp?parentid=23468.

Panetta, Leon (2012), "The US Rebalance Towards the Asia-Pacific," at *http://www.iiss.org/ conferences/the-shangri-la-dialogue/shangri-la-dialogue-2012/speeches/first-plenary-session/leon-panetta/.*

Rajagopalan, Rajeswari Pillai (2009), *Uncertain Eagle: US Military Strategy in Asia*, New Delhi: Rupa & Co.

Ramachandran, Sudha (2007), "China Moves into India's Backyard," Asia Times, 13 March, at http://www.tamilnation.org/intframe/indian_ocean/070313china _india.htm.

Raman, B. "Gwadar, Hambantota and Sitwe: China's Strategic Triangle," Paper No. 2158, http://www.southasiaanalysis.org/ percent5Cpapers22 percent5Cpaper2158.html

Rice, Condoleezza (2000), "Promoting the National Interest," *Foreign Affairs*, 79/1, January/February.

Rice, Condoleezza (2011), *No Higher Honour: A Memoir of My Years in Washington*, London: Simon & Schuster.

Roy, Bhaskar (2009), "Synthesis and Art of China's Security Perception–Part II," Paper No.3071, 26 February, at http://www.southasiaanalysis.org/percent5Cpapers31percent5Cp aper 3071.html.

Saha, Brigadier Subrata (2010), *China's Grand Strategy: From Confucius to Contemporary*, U.S. Army War College, Carlisle Barracks, PA 17013-5050 at http://www.dtic.mil/cgi-bin/GetTRDoc?AD=ADA518303

Shoemaker, Krik M (2008), "China in Sri Lanka," 7 May at

www.isn.ethz.ch/isn/Communities-and
partners/partners/Detail/?lng=en&id=88330.

Sirohi, Seema and Saran, Samir (2012), "Looking Beyond the Honeymoon", *The Hindu*, 29 September.

Talbott, Strobe (2004: 7), *Engaging India: Diplomacy, Democracy and the Bomb*, New Delhi: Viking.

Tellis, Ashley J. (2001), "The Changing Political-Military Environment in South Asia," in *The United States and Asia: Toward a New U.S. Strategy and Force Structure*, California: RAND Corporation.

Vanaik, Achin (2008), "Post-Cold War Indian Foreign Policy", *Seminar,* January at
http://india-seminar.com/cd8899/cd_frame8899.html.

Washington Times (2007), "China funds big deep-sea port in Pakistan," 25 May 2007 at
http://washingtontimes.com/news/2007/may/25/20070525-104503-5670r/?page=3.

World Nuclear News (2008): "China Develops South Asian Relationships," 28 April, at http://www.world-nuclear-news.org/NP-China_develops_south_Asian_relationships 2804081.html.

5

Islam and Governance Interplay:
The Pakistan Experience

Sayed Abdul Muneem Pasha

Pakistan's avowed adhesion to Islam as its overarching and organising principle of its public sphere provides an example to test the nature of interplay between Islam and governance. Pakistan's self-conscious cultivation of an Islamic identity has brought it into the international arena for ill or good effects. From its very inception, it has sought to binarize itself from an all-pervading Indian impact on the subcontinent. Pakistan, unlike India, has constitutionally designated itself as an Islamic republic bestowing upon Islam the status of the official religion.

However, it took nearly a decade for Pakistan to bring out a constitution in 1956. Since then, a series of constitutions were brought to the fore to inform the life of its citizens. The political experiments that took place in Pakistan in the form of military usurpations of power have led to consequences that were not forethought by its constitutional makers. Mohammad Ali Jinnah, the founder of the state, did not envisage that the military would, one day, become the defining force of polity. Successive regimes of Pakistan, not excluding some of the civilian dispensations, have trampled upon Islam, causing unaccountable, baneful consequences in their wake. In this context, it is not out of place to mention that the military regime of Zia-ul-Haq has played a major role in bringing about the negative image of Islam onto the fore.

His Hudood Ordinances have, in particular, tarnished the image of Pakistan in the most negative fashion. Instead of focusing on the ameliorative aspects of Islam such as justice, freedom, equality, poverty alleviation, most of the military regimes addressed themselves to control society authoritatively. General Pervez Musharraf is also not far away from the Zia effect, even though, the problems that the former was confronted with, are altogether distinct from the latter. This paper argues that the dilemmas of governance in Pakistan are the consequences of political dysfunctionalism which itself is a product of military regimes. These dilemmas have to be located in the Pakistani polity instead of the Pakistani nation.

Among members of contemporary international community, Pakistan evokes varied responses ranging from extreme negativity to passive acquiescence. Its actual behavioural and empirical patterns encompassing social, political, economic, foreign policy and other cognate realms have a lot to do with this external reaction. Unlike India, the fact of its birth in 1947 was hardly noticed by policy community much less the other sectors of international society. It had to start everything from scratch. The most formidable task that confronted its founding fathers was the question of the infant nation's identity. Islam provided a natural anchor to this identity problematique, with all its subsequent and attendant dilemmas.

Of late, a scholar of repute, SaadiaToor, has underlined the salience of the latter in her latest work titled, *The State of Islam: Culture and Cold War Politics in Pakistan*. She asserts that the forms of Islam deployed in Pakistan were neither consistent nor permanent as the organizing ideology of the nation-state, and the meaning of religion has been deeply contested, from the Left and from the Right, at every stage of the nation's development. Rather than a story of the nation moving along a trajectory of increasing degrees of religious puritanism, Saadia shows that the national elites in Pakistan has selectively deployed different variants of Islam in order to organize public sentiment against their antagonists: Bengali speakers, religious and national minorities, women, and the left. The relationship that emerges between Pakistan and Islam in Saadia's account is one in which the narrative of the rise of a particularly vicious form of militant Islam is best understood in the context of Pakistan's role as a frontline state in Afghanistan during the Cold War, and the vacuum created by the evisceration of the political left inside Pakistan through coercion under the sign of Islam. [1]

Pakistan's entry into the comity of nations in contemporary times was inauspicious, as Afghanistan tried in vain to block its membership into the United Nations General Assembly. Akin to any developing economy, Pakistan is afflicted with illiteracy, poverty, disease, and other ailments. When it started its independent career in 1947, it did so with a view to enabling its people to chalk out their individual and collective lives in accordance with the principles and tenets of Islam, emanating from the *Quran* and the *Hadith*. Successive Pakistani regimes sought to enshrine these principles into its constitutions. The latter contained within themselves systems of governance on the basis of which the governments of the day were expected to carry out their obligations. They contained provisions delimiting the powers and functions of the principal organs of the government, namely the executive, the legislature, and judiciary.

The political history of Pakistan has been witnessing an alternation of civilian and military governments, disturbing the normal course of political stability that one identifies in any mature polity. The incorporation and pre-eminence of army in the political system of Pakistan constitutes one of its baneful practices, giving rise, more often than not, to governance crisis, besides exacerbating tension between India and Pakistan. The dilemmas of governance are further vitiated with the cooption, by external powers, particularly the United States of America, of the military for reasons of geo-strategy. Shashi Tharoor, in his latest work titled *PaxIndica: India and the World of the 21st Century,* has poignantly brought out the pitfalls for Pakistan if it continues to rely upon terrorism as a state policy towards India. The ill effects of this policy on the domestic front of Pakistan are clearly visible to any keen observer. The situation is all the more deplorable in view of the fact that some state entities in Pakistan are organically related to some extremist networks thereby giving rise to governance crises. [2]

In the sphere foreign policy, Pakistan's obsessive Indo-centricism has diverted its precious material and manpower resources away from its pressing socio-economic allocations. It perceived India as its formidable security threat. The excessive budgetary allocations that it earmarked for defence at the cost of social sector, is explained, in justificatory terms, by this looming danger. This has resulted in a distorted human development index resulting in what may be called ill-governance or degovernance. However, this did not stop the successive Pakistani foreign policy makers to invoke Islam in order to obtain material, strategic, and political benefits from the Arab world. To a very large extent, they have achieved success in this regard. [3]

This serves as a typical example of a statecraft wherein religion has been instrumentalized and ideologized to serve the mundane purposes of a state and society. In the Pakistani foreign policy design Islam constitutes a significant component. This need not be viewed as a pernicious practice. History has been a witness to the use of democracy and liberalism in the realm of foreign policy of some European states including, in contemporary times, the United States of America. During the Cold War era, the then contending super powers employed the binary ideologies of democracy and socialism to attract the nascent countries of the developing world.

The instrumentalisation of Islam at the hands of political authorities in Pakistan is predominantly geared towards obtaining regime legitimacy, contrary to addressing issues germane to public welfare. Islam is used more for purposes of deterrence than for amelioration. Signifying the former, the *hudood* [4] laws promulgated during the regime of Zia-ul-Haq, can be cited as an example. Rights-promoting and enhancing ameliorative Islamic measures are not prioritized, bringing to the fore the crisis of governance, because Islam as a marker of identity in Pakistan is universally recognized. In the Islamic statecraft model of Pakistan, the benign and the malign effects of its use are very evident. The latter have manifested when the *hudood* laws are applied to women. In response, the women rose up in opposition under the banner of Women's Action Front.

Dilemmas of governance in any society are normally polity-generated. All forms of political regime, not excluding liberal democracies, are afflicted with them. The more the divergence and distance between polity and society, the more the dilemmas of governance. In the case of Pakistan, such dilemmas are exacerbated with the seizure of power by the military. Transparency International lists Pakistan as one of the most corrupt countries in the world. Pakistan has a weak tax basis. A grossly inefficient taxation system with only a fraction of the population paying taxes means that the government has a permanent fiscal deficit. [5]

The necessary administrative mechanism and the concomitant political will to pluck and bring justice to tax evaders are found wanting. Such a state of affairs gives rise to corruption. In this connection it will not be out of place here to underline the salience of civil society in redressing the evils of corruption in the Pakistani milieu. Fortunately, a galore of voluntary and non-governmental agencies has been at work in the country in this direction. It is of interest to note here that some religious forces are also engaged in mitigating the evils of corruption in the Pakistani state by emphasizing the importance of probity in public life, as gleaned from the scriptural sources. Incorruptibility or integrity in public life is considered as a religious obligation.

Zia-ul-Haq's Islamization programme affecting all walks of life gave birth to Sunni-Shia schism in the wake of its implementation. Pakistani Shias, through their successful agitational politics, got themselves excluded from the purview of the *Zakat* Ordinance effected during his regime. They sought to, and in turn accepted by the regime; govern themselves by their Jafari School of Jurisprudence pertaining to, among other things, Zakat payment. In this successful endeavour, Pakistani Shias obtained moral and political support from no less a person than the architect of the Islamic Revolution in Iran, Ayatollah Khomeini. The Zakat episode undoubtedly brings to the fore the international ramifications of Zia's Islamization measures. In this context, it is not out of place to hazard a comparison between these two personalities: Ayatollah Khomeini and Zia-ul-Haq.

The former was the leader of a revolution which was rooted in Islamic ethos and was bottom-up in nature; the latter got to Pakistan's helm of affairs through a military coup, and his Islamization effort was top-down in character. In the Islamization project of Pakistan under the regime of Zia-ul-Haq, the iniquitousness of Iran and Saudi Arabia in the political and ideological landscape of Pakistan is observable. Both of them have their respective cohorts in Pakistan. The contending visions represented by these two states are being tested on the Pakistani soil. They are proxies of the respective Islamic outfits indigenous to Pakistan. Such a reality is progressively paving the way for a rise of sectarianism in the country. In a heterogeneous country like Pakistan, sectarianism is the last thing that it can ill afford. It has so far eaten into the vitals of Pakistani polity and society.

In the realm of governance, mediated through the instrumentality of Islam as represented by the state, sectarianism is capable of banishing everything that is progressive and creative. It is high time for the Pakistani political managers to arrive at a common denominator, for the sake of governance, leading to a socio-political-theological conspectus. Fortunately, the country is blessed with a plethora of intellectual, technological and scientific manpower necessary to bring about such a vaunted conspectus. Of course, differences of opinion on matters of theology are endorsed in Islamic tradition. They are considered as God's grace on

Ummah (the universal community of believers).

However, one has to be very wary of allowing these differences metamorphose into irreconcilable contradictions. Pakistani polity can, at this moment, ill afford such a possibility. Pakistan requires a model of governance, intermediated by the ethos of Islam, to progressively inform and address the grievances of the populace at large. Regrettably, it has not till date done anything germane to this even after the passage of six decades of independent existence. The predominance of civilian component in the polity of a state is a necessary condition for a viable system of governance. As the history of Pakistan tells us in unambiguous terms that three-fourths of its career is spent under military tutelage which has given rise to authoritarianism. The latter has, more often than not, obliterated the significance of transparency, rule of law, fundamental human rights, constitutionalism, and so on.

Further, authoritarianism has trampled upon various constitutions functioning under different civilian dispensations. For any system of governance, adherence to constitution and rule of law besides other assorted axioms, are a necessary requirement. The Pakistani experience has, under the military rule, consistently disregarded these valued principles, resulting in the degradation of the lives of the Pakistani people. In this connection, it is very necessary to emphasize the importance of jihad, understood in terms of a movement to ameliorate the state- of- life situation of the Pakistani society. Such a role assigned to it will serve the function of a greater jihad, aimed at cleansing the virus of corruption and other ills from the Pakistani socio-political bodies. The purview of greater jihad can also be extended to other areas of the Pakistani life.

Prior to Zia-ul-Haq, Zulfiqar Ali Bhutto, for reasons of political expediency, got a legislative measure endorsed by the National Assembly to the effect that the Ahmadias were kept off the purview of Islam; they could not identify themselves as Muslims; their places of worship were not mosques. Their status was reduced to that of a non-Muslim minority in Pakistan. The question of Ahmadias in Pakistan also came upfront in the whirlwind of Pakistan's identity politics spearheaded by Jamaat-e-Islami of Maulana Abul Ala Maududi in the 1950s.

The nature of *Sharia* application in Pakistan has more to do with punitive justice and less to do with amelioration. Notions and concepts germane to the latter such as human rights, human development, human security, and human dignity are kept off the *Sharia* purview. The essence of Islamic governance in fact lies in these universal human values. Even though these concepts are sophisticatedly couched in modern terminology, the substance contained in them is not at all alien both to the Islamic *weltanschauung* and epistemology. [6] In any *Sharia*-centric Islamic polity, policy makers need to establish a fine balance between retributive justice and ameliorative justice. To attempt to overemphasize one at the price of the other does not yield sustainable, positive results. The Pakistan experience till date points only to the application of retributive *Sharia*. There is an urgent need to create those favourable socio-economic conditions in the lives of the Pakistani people which may bridge polity-society-divergence, characterizing public life today.

In the case of Pakistan, the need for a social conspectus between polity and society cannot be gainsaid. Further, the aforesaid needs to be juxtaposed to the reigning phenomenon of globalization understood in terms of ushering in the era of good governance: the notion of accountability, transparency, efficiency, adherence to the rule of law, probity in public life, and so on. Intrinsically, Islam is sufficiently comfortable with these axioms. The crux of the dilemma lies in translating these values into real social life. It is also required on the part of the policy community to internalize them and convert them into public policies.

Again, the Pakistani reality in this regard is off the ideal. Under these adverse circumstances, the emergence of a wise statesmanship is the need of the hour. In this regard, it is also necessary to highlight that the tenets of governance can also be adapted to any theologico-philosophical systems. In the case of Pakistan, the latter is encapsulated by Islam. Pakistan, through the employment of Islamic idiom and practice, can bring about a novel model of governance. The strict compartmentalization of the public and the private spheres–a primal definition of secularism–may not serve as a guide to society. A holistic perspective which integrates human affairs is capable of addressing and finding solutions to a myriad of dilemmas engulfing the Pakistani society. [7]

In the context of Pakistan, the interplay between Islam and governance is vividly reflected in the application of controversial blasphemy laws, creating international furore. The application, in fact misapplication, of such laws against religious minorities and women has sullied the image of Pakistan in the international community. Pakistan's adherence to some internal covenants and human rights on the one hand, and its simultaneous adhesion to domestically enacted legislative measures on the other, has apparently created a rift between the two. It is a tight rope on which Pakistan has to tread skilfully. Pakistan has to reconcile its assumption of *Sharia* obligations domestically with its international obligations emanating from its ratification of international human rights treaties. The persistence of contradictions between the two may not augur well for the image of Pakistan. Reflecting the sensitivities and feelings of the Pakistani nation, its constitution unambiguously stipulates that *Sharia* reigns supreme over it, and not the *vice versa*. To the extent of compatibility between *Sharia* and international human rights law, no legal crisis ensues. In the case of incompatibility, the question of legal allegiance to which one of the two, comes to the fore.

The current chaos which has taken Pakistan into its vortex is caused, *inter alia*, by its approach towards terrorism. Its alignment with the United States to obliterate terrorism following 9/11, has led to unintended consequences, one of which is the increasing radicalization and concomitant militarization of society.

The Army's role towards this predicament cannot be gainsaid. The Inter Services Intelligence (ISI) certainly comes to the fore when issues of terrorism, foreign policy and other allied ones are taken cognizance of. The vilificational descriptions of Pakistan by its hostile forces as a rogue, terrorist, failing, and failed state are more a function of incomprehension on their part than a reasoned attempt to squarely come to grips with the reality of the Pakistani nation. Pakistan does not sit well with Turkey and Malaysia as the exemplificative examples of the successful marriage of faith (Islam) and democracy in the Muslim world.

Of late, Turkey is being cited as an inspiration for Arab countries in West Asia presently undergoing a societal transformation towards democracy and freedom. Both Egypt and Tunisia have thrown out their authoritarian regimes. In Yemen, through a democratic election, the sitting president Abdullah Saleh, is replaced by his deputy. In the case of Pakistan, the cohabitation of Islam and democracy is yet to take place. The accumulated experience since 1947 has resulted only in separating Islam from democracy. Be that as it may, the Orientalist discourse on Islam–democracy relationship has been falsified by recent changes.

In the specific context of the Pakistani polity, it is high time now to bring a sense of priority in the Islamization process back into reckoning, by underlining the salience of equity, justice, and dignity in public life. So far, as this presentation has highlighted, the premium has been on retributive justice.

This alone will not suffice. Further, Pakistani polity has to firmly anchor itself in the ethos of Pakistani society rooted in its firm conviction in Islam. Perceptions of Islam held by unrepresentative regimes, if they do not conform to those held by the broad populace, may only succeed in keeping polity away from society. The need of the hour in Pakistan is to affect a synergy between polity and society. Pakistani polity has to undergo a great deal of qualitative change if Pakistani society is to secure a dignified and humane space in the country.

Further, governance in the context of Pakistan has to grapple with the changing nature of civil-military relations. Pakistan's polity has been bedevilled by this phenomenon. Military's supremacy over civilian forces tends to lead to governance crises as the history of Pakistan unambiguously demonstrates. One of the consequences of military rule in Pakistan has been the increasing militarization of society, further reinforced by events emanating from external environment such as war on terror to which Pakistan has been drawn under circumstances beyond its control. The targeting of alleged terrorists by the American forces stationed in Pakistan indicates the severity of the crises engulfing Pakistan. Such acts on the part of America have negatively affected the power of sovereignty exercised by Pakistan on its own territory and citizens.

End Notes

1. Saadia Toor (2011), *The State of Islam: Culture and Cold War Politics in Pakistan*, London: Pluto Press, p. 252.
2. For Details, see Shashi Tharoor (2012), *PaxIndica: India and the World of the 21ˢᵗ Century*, New Delhi: Penguin Books India Pvt. Ltd., pp. 27-82.
3. For Details, see S.A.M. Pasha (2005), *Islam in Pakistan's Foreign Policy*, New Delhi: Global Media Publications, p. 256.
4. For details, see, Rahat Imran (2005), 'Legal Injustices: The Zina Huudood Ordinanace of Pakistan and Its Implications for Women', *Journal of International Women's Studies*, 2, November.
5. Victoria Schofield (2011), "Pakistan: 2011," *The Round Table*, Oxfordshire 100, 417, December.
6. For details, see S. A. M. Pasha (2011), 'Conceptualizing Human Rights in Islam', in *Human Rights and Social Security: Perspectives, Issues and Challenges*, in Anisur Rahman (ed.)

New Delhi: Manak Publications, pp.104-119.
7. For details see, Humeira Iqtidar and David Gilmartin (2011), 'Secularism and the State in Pakistan', *Modern Asian Studies,* 45, 3.

6

Concords and Discords in Indo-Australia Relations

Josukutty C.A.

The relationship between India and Australia greatly impact the politics of South Asia, South East Asia and the Indian Ocean regions. Unlike the Cold War era, the post-Cold War period has been witnessing a growing convergence and synergy of shared values, interests and threat perceptions between India and Australia. At the same time there are a number of fundamental discords that question the rationality and durability of the growing engagement. The key factors that define and structure India-Australia relationship are its geographic location, resources, demography and its relationship with countries such as the US and China. Till the end of Second World War, Australia's foreign policy was driven by Britain, and during Cold War and thereafter, it has been under the US spell.

The rise of China as the pre-eminent power in the Asia-Pacific has placed Australia in a sort of predicament in balancing its relationship towards China and the US. Obviously, it finds a synergy with India in working out its hedging strategy towards China in the company of the US. The ideas of democracy, human rights, rule of law, prospects of economic ties, common security threats such as piracy and terrorism, and the proposed Asian security architecture provide a platform for India and Australia to work together. On the other hand there is a long list of irritants such as attack on Indian students, inconsistent positions on nuclear policy and uranium sale, the China factor and above all the political and cultural dissimilarities that have time and again troubled the relationship. The paper looks at these points of convergences and divergences in the bilateral relationship in the context of the current developments in international politics.

Introduction

Historically, India and Australia are two lonely powers in the global system. Despite their stable democratic systems and multicultural character, the relationship vacillated from hostility to indifference to moderate friendship. Australia has been an ardent Anglo-Saxon ally and an appendage of the United States. The politics of Cold War equations and its bend towards China and Pakistan on many issues and India's NAM based idealism and broad neglect of East-Asia and Asia-Pacific kept them disinterested players towards each other. Australia never figured in the Indian scheme of things. Practically, there was too little trade and politics between these two countries for long. This 'denial mode' on both sides continued till the early 1990s. The end of Cold War, opening up of Indian economy, improvement in Indo-US relationship and a rising Asia set the stage for warming up the relationship. But India's second nuclear test in 1998 distanced them once again. Australia's refusal to supply uranium to India and its strong anti-India stand on NPT began to evaporate the progress achieved.

However, the compulsions of the emerging realities of global politics, particularly the rising economic and political significance of Asia, the growing significance of Indian economy and the nature of global common problems like, maritime security and piracy, freedom of navigation, terrorism and global warming bought in opportunities for wide range of collaborative ventures. The key to this growing relationship is the common security threats and challenges both these countries face in the context of the emerging geo-political scenario in the Indo-Pacific. At the same the relationship is marred by a high degree of dilemma, ambiguity and unreliability. The major argument of the paper is that there are

certain fundamental discords in the Indo-Australian relations
that retards a strategic partnership between the two.

Historical Backdrop

India and Australia belonged to the same land mass called
Gondwana until 160 million years ago when they got drifted
away to their present geometrical locations due to glaciations
around 20,000 years ago. (Reddy, 2008:159-160) Many
geographical and life form features ranging from fauna and
flora to climatic conditions and ethno- linguistic features of
the natives link the relationship to time immemorial.
(Devahuti, 1976:76-78) In modern times, India and Australia
connections are traced back to the commercial ties started by
the Campell family with India in1790. (Devahuti, 1976:76-78)
Australia's first shipments of coal were to Bengal in 1799,
from Newcastle. For the next half a century, Australia's most
immediate and direct links were with India rather than London,
as bureaucrats, merchants, chaplains and judges, moved
between the two colonies. By 1840, a ship was leaving Sydney
for India roughly in every four days. It was a major source of
food and provisions for the young colony.

On India's Independence in 1947, when the Labour
government was in power, Australian approach was
sympathetic to India. But ideological and ego clashes between
two great leaders of the time—Nehru and Menzies—evolved into
an indifferent relationship in the early period. India was
lukewarm to the regional security proposal by Australia in
1947 itself and was unhappy over Australia's pro-Pak attitude.
(Mediansky, 1971:27) Australia never figured in India's view
of Asia and the world from the very beginning. Divergent
world views based on NAM for India and alliance politics for
Australia were the basic reasons for this lack of interest in
Australia. (Kuruppu and Henry, 2000:28-32) Ideologically,
they drifted in opposite directions—India against military
alliances and bloc politics and Australia an ardent bloc builder
and follower of the capitalist Camp. The Cold War equations

further distanced these countries to opposite tracks in world politics. The end of Cold War and the new equations in world politics, have not brought the expected warmth in the relationship as it is marred by attack on Indian students and the inconsistency over the supply of uranium to India. But these irritants are, apparently, being replaced by a host of new found commonalties that are emphasized as the bases of growing strategic convergence.

New Found Commonalities

India and Australia have lot of commonalities by virtue of their shared values, interests and goals, opportunities and the threats that confront them in the Asia/Indo-Pacific region. India is a model democracy in the developing world and Australia is a one of the best run democracies in the world. They are strong, vibrant, secular and multi-cultural, economic and political systems with a free press and an independent judiciary. The values and principles of rule of law, human rights and liberalism constitute the bases of governmental and societal organization in these countries. A strong and influential Indian diaspora and a contingent of Indian students in Australia are significant factors in the growing co-operation. Common interests and goals include a regional order based on freedom of navigation, free and open commerce, tackling issues of global commons, and above all, stability and security in Asia.

The gradual build up of security threats such as, conflicting maritime claims, piracy, transnational and home grown terrorism, nuclear proliferation, missile defence system and maritime trade security demand greater strategic collaboration. To realize these objectives India and Australia have been working together in multilateral mechanisms such as the G-20, Commonwealth, IOR-ARC, ASEAN Regional Forum, Asia Pacific Partnership on Climate and Clean Development, and have participated in the East Asia Summits and as members of the Five Interested Parties (FIP) in the

WTO. Australia is an important player in APEC and supports India's membership of the organisation. In 2008, Australia became an observer in the SAARC and Australia supports India's candidature in an expanded UN Security Council.

Growing Economic Ties

Economic collaboration between India and Australia has been flourishing since the 1990s, rather unaffected by the political happenings. The bilateral trade between Australia and India had doubled in the last six years and the trade is expected to reach US$ 40 billion by 2015. (The Hindu, 2012) India is Australia's third-largest export market and its fifth-largest trading partner. Australia is India's sixth largest trading partner. The share of Australia in India's imports is 3.5 percent and Australia exported about 8.1 percent of its total exports to India and imported around 0.9 percent of its total imports from India. (Nabeel A., 2011) Australia can play a significant role in meeting India's energy requirements. In the words of Australian Trade Commissioner, "…With the surge in mutual trading, the trade figure is all set to reach ₹ 2 lakh crore in the next three years. The volume of bilateral trade in 2010-11 was ₹ 1.1 lakh crore". (Perry, 2012) Economically, the relative importance to each other has grown significantly. But what is significant is that Australia is eager to complement the trade relations with a serious strategic partnership. (Tellis, Ashley J., Tanner, Travis and Keough, Jessica, 2011)

Rise of China and Strategic and Security Overtures

Both India and Australia are apprehensive about the rapid rise of China and its maritime claims in the Asia-Pacific and especially in South-China Sea and in India-Pacific. China has been raising objections to Australian and Indian maritime movements in the region. Protection of sea-lanes passing through the Indian-Ocean is essential for both the countries as almost all their trade passes through the region. China's increasing assertiveness in the sea waters is seen as a challenge to free trade and larger security in the region. To meet these challenges there is a visible shift away from the old policy of 'Defence of Australia' to more offensive-minded 'Australia Defense Force'. (Snyder, 2009) The goal is to be adaptable and versatile in meeting and sustaining the demands of diverse operations and the potential threat of great power confrontation in the Asia Pacific between China and the US. (Snyder, 2009)

A white paper released in May 2009 by the government of Australia, "Defending Australia in the Asia Pacific Century: Force 2030," emphasizes that "over the period to 2030, the Indian Ocean will join the Pacific Ocean in terms of its centrality to Australia's maritime strategy and defence planning", (Australian Department of Defence, 2009: 41-45). The paper is based on the assumption that China will increasingly dominate the region, alongside India and a re-emerging Russia. [1] Australia is unsure about the effectiveness of the traditional security cover provided by the US. As a result, Australia is compelled to seek new allies and become more self-reliant in defence preparedness. (Hunt, 2009)

The upgradation of the Indo-Australian relationship to the level of 'Strategic Partnership' through the Joint Declaration on Security co-operation in November 2009,   Australia-South Korea Security Declaration (2009), Trilateral Security Dialogue among Australia the United States and Japan, Australia-Japan Security Declaration (2007), the India-Australia specific MoUs on Air Services and Intellectual Property (2008), Science and Technology (2008), Defence Cooperation (2006), Customs, Information and Communications Technology, Combating International Terrorism (2003), Water Resource Management, bi-annual second-track security dialogue meeting since 2001 are indicative of the growing convergence. (The Yomiuri Shimbun, 2010)

In this emerging scenario, it is argued that the defence and security relationship between the two countries has the most intriguing potential of any area, with the capacity to significantly enhance both Indian and Australian geo-political, strategic and security interests working to build a rule-based maritime order in the Indian Ocean, and supporting one in the South China Sea, (Varghese, 2012) Australia is developing a hedging strategy based on its assessments of present and future capability of China and other major players in the region. (Varghese, 2012) It involves increasing Australia's own military weight, intensifying the US alliance, and building security links with large democratic Asian partners, including India. (Varghese, 2012)

The growing strategic and security relationship between India and Australia has to be seen in this background. Australian ambassador to the US Kim Beazely said in February 2012 referring to the Australian decision to sell uranium to India "...We sell enough uranium...so that's not important to us. What is important to us is the character of the relationship we have with India that is why we made changes". (The Hindu, 2012b) In supporting her proposal to reverse the Australian ban on uranium exports to India, Prime Minister Julia Gillard argued at the Australian Labour Party's conference in early December 2011, "We should take a decision that is in our nation's interest, a decision about strengthening our strategic partnership with India in this, the Asian century". (Jha, 2012) This larger threat scenario and the shared values and interests between India and Australia constitute the context and rationale of the emerging strategic and security partnership in the Asia-Pacific. [2]

India's response to these strategic overtures has been reserved and cautious. In 2012 Defence Minister A.K. Antony remarked that, "We are definitely looking to further expand our defence cooperation with Australia, especially in counter-terrorism and maritime security, but on a one-to-one basis. There is no security grouping in the offing". (Pandit, 2011) India wants to be 'a neutral player' in the ongoing geo-political rivalry between the US and China in the Asia-Pacific region. India has made it clear that while India has expansive defence ties with the US, there is no grander design of collaborating with Washington, Tokyo and Canberra to forge a trilateral or quadrilateral strategic axis to target China. (Pandit, 2011) India has earlier rebuffed overtures by NATO for formal cooperation in fields like missile defence or even anti-piracy patrols in Gulf of Aden. After China lodged a strong protest against the Indo-US 'Malabar' naval exercise in Bay of Bengal in 2007, which was expanded to include Australian, Japanese and Singaporean navies, India has largely restricted the exercise to a bilateral one with the US. Again India decided not to attend Australia's 2008 Kakadu 1X naval exercise, to which Japan sent a destroyer and where even Pakistan showed up. (Medcalf, 2012) It is reflective of a fundamental lack of trust between the two countries that are based on certain cultural and political discords.

Cultural and Political Differences

The fundamental discord in Indo-Australian relationship is the cultural and political alienation between two of the yester years extending and impacting on the present day relations. Australia practiced racialism openly and its indigenous people were subjected to systematic discrimination. The White Australia Policy (WAP) gave credence to the purity of race, had sustained discrimination against Indians in Australia. Restrictions on Indian immigration based on X'ian identity and British values all through 19th century and the glorified WAP of the 20th century were to keep Australia as an outpost of British race. Officially, the WAP came to an end in 1973 and Australia has been evolving into a multicultural society. But the legacy of racism could be found in the negligible presence of ethnic minorities and immigrants in national decision making process and membership in political community. Racism once again became a factor in the relations following attacks on Indian students and revelation of racist emails circulated by Victorian police.

The cultural gap between India and Australia has a geo-political dimension. Australia falls into two geo-strategic landscapes–the Asia-Pacific. Politically it is an active member of the global Anglo-American alliance, while   geographically a part of the Asia-Pacific region. It was isolated from its neighbours for most of the time–a feeling of isolation as a Western power in Asia-Pacific and sought security from Asia and not security with Asia. Historically, Australia was 'protected' by the British Empire. In strategic and security realms, during the Cold War days, Australia followed a policy of 'Forward Defense', where Australia sought to protect itself from hostile regional forces by closely aligning itself with the US. (Snyder, 2009)

As such it was preoccupied with the US led Cold War pacts and alliances and Australia's military involvements in the conflicts in Korea, Vietnam and Malaysia. Australia was considered West's early warning system in Asia. (Barber, 2011) On the other hand, colonial subjugation of the racial genre influenced the conduct of India's foreign policy and its international behaviour. Two important bases of free India's foreign policy were anti- racialism and pro-Asianism. Indian position was that "Asia affairs were to be solved by Asians by Asian methods in accordance with Asian interests". (Reddy, 2008:162) Robert Menzies dismissed Asia as, "irrelevant and as being too difficult for any occidental to understand". (Meg, 1992-93:510-27) The Australian support to apartheid regime in South Africa and the policy of WAP kept the countries at a distance for quite some time.

India viewed Australia's participation in military alliance, particularly the SEATO as antithetical to the tenants of NAM. (Gordon, 1974:342) India was particularly unhappy over Australian initiatives in Kashmir. The political differences were further explicit in the issues of Suez crisis, Soviet invasion of Hungary, West Irian in Indonesia, India Ocean as Zone of Peace and supply of 50 Mirage 111 aircraft to Pakistan. These divergent positions brought in a political gap between the two. (Meg, 1992-93: 514) The pro-India attitude in Indo-China conflict in 1962, the prompt recognition of

Bangladesh and the warmth generated by Rajiv Gandhi's visit to Australia in 1986 and even the opening up of the India economy could not wipe out the remnants of these basic discords completely.

The fact is that India and Australia are politically and culturally unsure of each other. [3] The political and cultural distrust account for the vacillations in Indo-Australian relations. This was the reason that personalities and personal temperament of the heads of government and the vagaries of domestic politics came to decide the nature of relationship. Personalities become a critical factor when there is a lack of strong political and cultural foundation for the relationship. During Nehru-Menzies period, their egos and differing perceptions were cited as the reasons for the cold relationship. Menzies successors such as John Gordon, Gough Whitlam of the labour party, Malcom Fraser of Liberal, Robert Hawk of the Labour and, John Howard in spite of their good personal equations with Indian leaders could not improve the relations beyond a point.

Similarly, the leading parties in Australia, the Labour and Liberal have different views regarding the sale of uranium to India. The differing perceptions among various political parties are also partially the result of a lack of strong political and cultural foundation for the relationship. Given this basic handicap, to what extent can we improve the relationship is a moot question.

The lack of political and cultural understanding between India and Australia could be explained by looking at the special relationship between the US and Australia. The relationship between and among Australia, US and with most of the other Western countries have a different degree of alliance and understanding. The relationship between Australia and the US is bounded by their common European origin and identity. It is similar to the special relationship and racialised peace between the US and Britain in which the American and British foreign policy elites framed themselves as members of a single supreme and messianic Anglo Saxon race. (Vucetic, 2011: 416)

The relation between the US and Australia is time tested and have better and deeper understanding. The US plays a central role in Australia's security. In a testimony before the House Committee on Foreign Affairs Sub-committee on Asia and the Pacific in March 2011, Kurt M. Campbell, Assistant Secretary, Bureau of East Asian and Pacific Affairs, stated that Australia remains a strategic anchor for regional stability and plays an incredibly important role in maintaining global security, the US and Australian forces fight side-by-side, extending a legacy of co-operation that goes back a century, and Australia is the largest non-NATO contributor to the coalition effort in Afghanistan. (Campbell, 2011) The 25th Australia-US Ministerial Consultations (AUSMIN) in November 2010, announced the launch of the Australia-US Force Posture Review Working Group, which envisages expanded US-Australia military co-operation to optimize US force posture in the Asia-Pacific region. (Campbell, 2011)

In other words, there is a fundamental cultural and political understanding between Australia and the US, which is absent between Australia and India. Commonality of positions on various security and political issues is built up on this special relationship. Australia's interest in Asia-Pacific is dominated by China clashes with none of their cultural and political goals. Whereas all the big talk about a strategic partnership between India and Australia is the result of changing realities in world politics, particularly in Asia. The relationship between India and Australia depends on the nature of the relationship between India and the US.

Attack on Indian Students

Education is the third largest export earner for Australia. Arrival of over 100,000 (constitute 19 percent of the total number of international students) Indian students in Australia by 2009 over a period of five years was the biggest thing to happen to Australia-India relations since the 1990s. Ironically, the biggest damage to India-Australia relationship was also caused by a series of attack on Indian students in 2009 and the reactions and responses to it.

The media in India sensationalized the issue in racial overtones. The Federation of Indian Students of Australia concluded racism as one of the bases of the attack. (Sploc and Murray, 2009) It created an impression that Australia is an unsafe racial country for Indians. Most of the studies showed that the attack was not essentially racial as has been depicted by many a media. (Sploc and Murray, 2009) At the same time, it was also recognized that racialism is factor in Australia's social milieu. The Race Discrimination Commissioner, Tom Calma, commented, "We need to recognise that racism does exist in Australia. It doesn't mean the whole society is racist but it does exist with individual's actions and small group actions". (Sydney Morning Herald, 2009) It widened the cultural gap and raised questions about cultural understandings and imageries of the two.

Nuclear and Uranium Issues

Nuclear policy and the question of uranium supply has been a major issue in India-Australia relations. Australia consistently refused to supply uranium to India on the ground that it has not signed the NPT. India's excellent record of non-proliferation and commitment to global nuclear disarmament has not found deserved appreciation in Australia. India considers the treaty discriminatory as it legitimizes the right of five Nuclear Weapon States to test and possess nuclear weapons to the exclusion of other countries. The security threats from its 'nuclear neighbourhood' and huge energy requirements give India no option but possess nuclear weapons. Australia severely criticized the May 1998 nuclear test by India as an 'an ill-judged step' that would have 'damaging consequences for security in South Asia and globally' and imposed sanctions and withdrew the High commissioner in India. What surprised India was the severity of its condemnation. (Bonnor, 2001)

Even after New Delhi's NSG waiver, under the Indo-US civilian nuclear deal in 2008, which Australia actually supported, Canberra's no uranium policy seemed incongruous with India's support to the global disarmament measures and its restrained nuclear postures such as no first use of nuclear weapons in conflict, moratorium on nuclear testing and the decision to join the Fissile Material Cut Off Treaty (FMCT) negotiations. (Government of India, 2008)

Also there is uncertainty over Australia's stand on India's membership of the world's four non proliferation-export control regimes, namely, the Wassenaar Arrangement, the Nuclear Suppliers Group (NSG), the Australian Group, and the Missile Technology Control Regime (MTCR).Things reached such a state that Indian Prime Minister Manmohan Singh actually skipped the Commonwealth Heads of Government Meeting in Australia in 2011to express New Delhi's displeasure on the issue. Thus, Australia's current position on uranium sales is a "huge road block to a real strategic partnership. (Sheridan, 2011)

In fact, Australia has been following a double standard in nuclear policy towards India. On the one hand, it stridently opposed nuclear policy of countries such as India and in the beginning of China. On the other hand, it has a special nuclear relationship with the US and Britain and was always under the extended protection of their nuclear weapons of these countries. (Defence White Paper, 1994:96) [4] Similarly, the not so perfect proliferation behaviour of both Soviet Union and China had not stopped Australia's uranium supply to these countries. (Medcalf, 2011:7-8) Of these particularly offensive was the supply to China despite the latter's proliferation record vis-à-vis Pakistan. All these were construed as a sign of inconsistency and ambiguity in Australia's stated desire to strengthen ties with India. Australia changed its nuclear policy towards India under American persuasion as is evident from that fact that such a decision came when the US president visited Australia in 2012. (Kumar, 2011)

Prospects of Strategic Relationship

The prospects of a strategic partnership between India and Australia depend on the complex interplay of the discords and concords that are characteristic of the bilateral relationship. The concept of strategic relations goes beyond the normal strengthening of co-operation between parts or even the reconfiguration of the dynamics that guides the parts in their relationship, having a more systemic role. It refers more to deeper understanding and strengthening of political, military and security aspect of the relationship. Emerson understands strategic partnerships as a kind of relationship, which "involves two actors that are powerful and capable of taking strategic action together". (Emerson, 2001:45) Strategic partnership should be between equal partners and it is more a political instrument. More importantly, a strategic partnership could be evolved if only there is a basic understanding and agreement on a whole lot of things which includes primarily security, political and cultural factors. Strong political and cultural bonds are required for a strategic relationship to take off and flourish. Factually, such cultural and political bonds are missing in Indo-Australian relationship.

The resurgence in the relationship between India and Australia is a marriage of convenience and not of convictions. Other than the scope for a strong economic relationship, 'Australia and India have limited bilateral security interests in common', and that 'neither country is central to the other's strategic planning'. (Bonnor, 2001) Gordon commented that 'Australia has mostly been the suitor and Indian the reluctant bride'. (Gordon, 2007:46) It points to the incoherence of the strategic relationship. In spite of the shared values and perceived common threats, Australia does not hold much strategic significance for India. The time may come when Canberra must choose not only between Beijing and

Washington but also between Beijing and New Delhi (Medcalf 2011). India wants to maintain its strategic autonomy and does not want risk being a party to the US led counter-China Strategy. (Latif, 2012)

The rise of China and the loosening of grip of the US in Asia-Indo-Pacific region is the basis of the security threat perceived by Australia. Australia and the US have a number of security concerns based on their political and cultural bonds. These commonalties are based on their shared past, common ethnic origin and visions of a future world order. Their relationship is historically inherited and time tested. The level and degree of political understanding between these countries are of a different genre. Culturally, they belong to the same caste and colour. Race has always been a factor in international relations as in the beginning it was the study of inter-racial relations. The excessive media hype that the issue of attack on Indian students in Australia received shows the underlying significance of race as a factor in the relationship, though it lies dormant. Even now race continues be a factor in international relations as could be derived from US president Obama's 2011 address to the British parliament which expressed intention to dominate the world by the Anglo-Saxons.

The US is expanding its alliance with Australia from a Pacific partnership to an Indo-Pacific one, and indeed a global partnership and considers Australia's counsel and commitment indispensable to strengthening regional architecture in the Asia-Pacific. (Clinton, 2011) Both Australia and the US wants to ensure that India is a key link in the 'hub and spokes' security alliances that the US is trying to revive in the Asia-Pacific against China. That is why India continues to perceive Australia as 'something of a pale shadow of the US'. The idea of strategic partnership, security architecture and military alliances contradict India's basic foreign policy precepts. Even after the end of Cold War and the post-Cold War shift in India's foreign policy priorities, the traditional impulses of an independent course in foreign policy and aversion to military and security alliances are still very strong. India had not been a party to and is not used to any military and strategic alliances.

Therefore, entering into a strategic partnership with Australia contradicts India's concept of strategic autonomy in foreign policy. One area where relationship is likely to flourish is trade and economics. That alone cannot generate and sustain a strategic relationship. The chequered nature of the relationship beset with occasional hiccups such as attack on students and controversy over nuclear policy is the result of cultural dissimilarities and lack of political trust between the two. The new found commonalities and values are insufficient to elevate the relationship to strategic realm.

Conclusion

The warmth of the new relationship between India and Australia is the result of the growing significance of India and China in particular and Asia in general. Most of the factors that have been identified and highlighted as shared values and principles were present ever since India became independent in 1947. But these factors could not strengthen the bilateral relationship because of the underlying cultural and political discords in the context of the interplay of Cold War equations. It was the prevalence of these incongruences that have blown out of proportion issues like attack on Indian students and created a longstanding ambiguity and confusion on the supply of uranium to India. India and Australia do not have any common security threats. During the Cold War, Australia was under the security coverage provided by the US. India became a factor in Australia's security in the context of the challenge that the US is facing at the hands of China in the Asia-Pacific.

The strategic partnership and common security threats that Australia is talking about is deceptive and a part of the US led Western hegemonic machinations in the Asia-Pacific. Australia envisages a politico-strategic relationship of the multilateral alliance pattern with India. Entering into any sort of strategic and security alliances with Australia, beyond the economic realm, is detrimental to India's interest. It would not only derail Sino-India relations but also keep Asia a divided house. The way forward for India is to engage Australia in normal diplomatic relations with an extra emphasis on economic matters and in fighting issues of global commons.

End Notes

1. By the end of Second World War, the US forward-deployed military forces, alliances, and extended nuclear deterrence was the bedrock of geo-political stability in the Western Pacific and the Indian Ocean. But this region, though has US presence since the 19th century, was not the primary focus of its foreign policy endeavours till recently.
2. The decision of the US in 2012 to open a naval training centre at Darvin in Australia, close to South-China Sea, is seen as an effort to contain China in its neighbourhood.
3. Australia always extended its defence facilities such as ports for US nuclear ships. It even permitted the UK to detonate twelve nuclear weapons on Australian soil. See Michael Hillman, (2000), The Grand Old Duke of York: Indo-Australian Relations Post Test, *South Asia,* Vol. 23, pp. 153-54. K. Subramanyan (1995), Australian N-Stand, *The Economic Times*, New Delhi, 27 June, 1995. Richard Broinoswki (2000), India, China and Australia: The Fractured Triangle, *South Asia*, Vol. 23, p. 125.
4. The Asian security architecture, that the US and Australia has devised, is an attempt to meet the Chinese challenge in the context of a rising Asia.

References

Australian Department of Defence (2009), Defending Australia in the Asia Pacific Century, Force 2030.

Canberra,http://www.defence.gov.au/whitepaper/docs/defence_white_paper_2009.pdf.) accessed 15-3-2012.

Barber, Lionel (2011), Asia's Rise, the West's Fall?, *Financial Times,* Sydney, 17 November.

http://aboutus.ft.com/2011/11/17/the-2011-lowy-lecture-lionel-barber-asia percentE2 percent 80 percent99s-rise-the-west percentE2 percent80 percent99s-fall/ accessed on 12-03-2012.

Bonnor, Janelle (2001), Australia-India Security Relations: Common Interests or Common Disinterests?, in Working Paper, Australian Defence Studies Centre, Canberra.

Campbell, Kurt M. (2011), Asia Overview: Protecting American Interests in China and Asia, Testimony, *Bureau of East Asian and Pacific Affairs, Government of US,* Testimony Before the House Committee on Foreign Affairs Subcommittee on Asia and the Pacific Washington, DC, March 31.

Clinton, Hillary Rodham (2011), America's Pacific Century, *The US Department of State,*
http://www.state.gov/secretary/rm/2011/10/175216.htm,
accessed on 30-4-2012.

Defence White Paper (1994), Defending Australia,
https://catalyst.library.jhu.edu/ catalog/bib_203590   accessed on 25-5-2012.

Devahuti, D. (1976), Pre-historic Links Among Australia, South-east Asia and India, *The South Asia Review*, Vol. 1, No. 1, August. Also see Kirk, R.L and Thorne, A.G. (eds.) (1976): *The Origin of Australians*, Australian Institute of Aboriginal Studies, Canberra.

Emerson, Michael, Tocci, Nathalie, Vahl, Marius and Whyte Nicholas (2001), The Elephant and the Bear: the European Union, Russia and their Near Abroads, *Centre for European Policy Studies,* Brussels.
http://library.northsouth.edu/Upload/Thepercent20Elephant percent20and percent20 the percent20Bear.pdf accessed on 12-4-2012.

Gordon, Greenwood (1974), *Approaches to Asia: Australian Post-war Policies and Attitudes,* Sydney, McGraw-Hill Book Co.

Gordon, Sandy (2007), *Widening horizons: Australia's New Relationship with India,* The Australian Strategic Policy Institute Limited, Canberra,
http://www.aspi.org.au/publications/
publication_details.aspx?ContentID=127&pubtype=5   accessed on 12-9-2011.

Government of India (2008), "Statement by External Affairs Minister of India Pranab Mukherjee on the Civilian Nuclear Initiative', September 5,
http:www.nti.org/e_research/source_docs/india/ministry_externa l-affairs/6.pdf accessed on 12-01-2012.

Hunt, Luke (2009), Against the Ropes: Australian Defense Policy, *World Politics Review,* 3 August, www.worldpoliticsreview.com accessed on 15-4-2012.

Jha, Saurav (2012), India-Australia Relations and the Obama Pivot to Asia, *World Politics Review*, 10 January, www.worldpoliticsreview.com   accessed on 13-4-2012.

Kumar, A. Vinod (2011), *Uranium from Down Under: Can Madam Gillard Pull it off? IDSA Comment,* November 21. http://www.idsa.in/idsacomment/UraniumfromDownUnderCan MadamGillardPullitoff_avkumar_211111 accessed 19-01-2012.

Kuruppu, Nihal Randolph and Henry (2000), An Indian Perspective on the Relationship between India and Australia, 1947 to 1975: Personalities and Policies, Ph.D. thesis, Victoria University of Technology, Melbourne.

Latif, S. Amer (2012), US-India Defense Trade: Opportunities for Deepening the Partnership, Centre for Strategic & International Studieshttp://csis.org/publication/india-and-new-us-defense-strategy accessed on 30-6-2012.

Medcalf, Rory (2011) "Australia's Uranium Puzzle; Why China and Russia and not India", *Australia India Institute,* The Frearless Nadia Occasional papers on India-Australia Relations, Vol. 1.

Medcalf, Rory (2012), Australia Grand Stakes: Australia's Future between China and India in Ashley J. Tellis, Travis Tanner, and Jessica Keough (ed.) *Strategic Asia 2011-12: Asia Responds to its Rising Powers China and India Restrictions on Use:* (Executive Summary) The National Bureau of Asian Research, Washington.http://www.nbr.org/ publications/strategic_asia/pdf/Preview/SA11/SA11p_Australia. pdf accessed on 15-03-2012.

Medcalf, Rory (2009), Problems to Partnership: A Plan for Australia-India Strategic Ties, Policy brief, November *www.lowyinstitute.org,* accessed on 18-02-2012.

Mediansky, Frederick Alexander (1971), *Australia's Relations with India 1947-64, with Special Reference to Diplomatic Exchanges.* Ph.D. thesis, University of Sydney, Sydney.

Meg, Gurry (1992-93), Leadership and Bilateral relations: Menzies and Nehru, Australia and India, 1949-1964, *Pacific Affairs,* V.65, N.4.

Nabeel, A. Mancheri (2011), India-Australia: Scepticism beyond the economics, February 16th, *http://www.eastasiaforum.org/tag/skepticism/*accessed on 12-02-2012.

Pandit, Rajat (2011), India snubs Australia, US move to check China, TNN, December 2, http://timesofindia.indiatimes.com/indiaIndia-snubs-Australia-US-move, accessed on 15-02-2012.

Perry, Grayson (2012), India-Australia trade to touch Rs. 2 lakh crore in three years, *http://articles.economictimes.indiatimes.com/*2012-02-06/news/31030640_1_india-australia-trade-bilateral-trade-indo-australia.

Reddy, Y. Yagma (2008), India-Australia Relations: Pattern of Alternation between Convergences and Divergences in D. Gopal (ed.), *India Australia Relations: Convergences and Divergences*, Shipra Publications, New Delhi.

Sheridan, Greg (2011), "Domestic Instability Obscures Big Strategic Changes", *The Australian*, June 23, http://www.theaustralian.com.au/news/opinion/domestic-instability-obscur accessed on 11-01-2012.

Snyder, Craig A. (2009), 'Strategic Posture Review: Australia', *World Politics Review*, 1 May, www.worldpoliticsreview.com accessed on 15-3-2012.

Sploc, Peter and Murray, Lee (2009), Indian Students in Australia Victims of Crime or Racism or the media. http://proceedings.com.au/isana2009/PDF/paper_Spolc.pdf.

Sydney Morning Herald (2009), 'Racism exists in Australia, says chief', 14 June, http://news.smh.com.au/breaking-news-national/racism-exists-in-australia-says-chief-20090614-c73b.html> accessed on 12-04-2012.

Tellis, Ashley J., Tanner, Travis, and Keough, Jessica (eds.) (2011), *Strategic Asia 2011-12:Asia Responds to its Rising Powers China and India Restrictions on Use:* (Executive Summary) The National Bureau of Asian Research, Washington http://www.nbr.org/publications/strategic_asia/pdf/Preview/SA11/SA11p_Australia.pdf accessed on 15-03-2012.

7

China's Growing Influence in South Asia and India's Response

S.Y. Surendra Kumar

China would like to have a foothold in South Asia and we have to reflect on this reality [1]
—PM Manmohan Singh (*September 2010*)

The international security environment is witnessing a power shift from the West to Asia, led by the rapid rise of China and India. More than India, it is rise of China a major concern for major powers like US, EU and Japan. Generally, the rise of China in the last few decades is attributed to rapid economic growth rate of more than 10 percent per annum in last two decade. Subsequently, China today is third largest economy in the world and also emerged as largest trading partner to US, EU, India and Japan. It is also estimated that China's economic size will match America's by 2035 and double it by mid-century. [2]

China's economic growth has also enhanced its military power for further modernization. In addition to high defence budget, worth more than 100 billion (2012); it is transforming from a mass army designed for a protracted conflict on its territory to one capable of fighting and winning short-duration, low or high-intensity conflicts beyond its region. At the same time, China has also won diplomatic recognition from other countries, broadened its diplomatic activities, playing a key role at international institutions, and wielded more geopolitical influence in Asia and around the world. As a result, China is undoubtedly the second most influential country in the world after the US. For instance, its role in stimulating world economy and even resolving nuclear issues in the Korean Peninsula (North Korea) and the Persian Gulf (Iran), is certainly crucial. [3]

In this new order, China is becoming a more responsible player on the global stage and addressing transnational issues, such as terrorism, environmental degradation and global warming, energy security, international crime, international peacekeeping and nation building, nuclear proliferation, public health, and the stability of the global financial system and so on. [4] Thus, China to sustain its peaceful rise, it is increasing its influence around the world and South Asia is no different.

Guiding Factors of China's South Asia Policy

Initially, China's Asia policy focussed more on Northeast and Southeast Asia region, however, in the recent times South Asia has also gained its importance in China's foreign policy since India began to look eastward, the former began to look southward to counter India's rise.

There are many factors that have shaped China's South Asia policy–some of them are as follows.

The geographical proximity continues to be vital factor in shaping China's policy, as it shares common borders with four South Asian countries Bhutan, India, Nepal and Pakistan. Although, the border dispute has been peacefully resolved with Nepal and Pakistan, but, the border disputes with India and Bhutan continues to be unresolved. Subsequently, South Asia is strategically well located, as it is in midway between the oil rich Middle East and the South East Asian regions and South Asia countries borders with China's southern boundary, gives the latter an alternative option of opening direct access through South Asia to the international sea lanes of Indian Ocean, which would enhance safe trade.

South Asian region also holds a number of attractions for China in terms of availability of natural resources like coal, iron ore, hydro carbon, natural gas and oil, some of them are yet to be fully exploited. The region has growing economies and billion populations provide enormous potential for trade and huge market for Chinese goods.

At the same time, the region also poses serious security threats to China like South Asia has become a source of inspiration for Jihadi terrorism and separatism in China's Xinjiang province. Similarly, the presence of large number of Tibetan refugees in India and Nepal with strong anti-Chinese sentiments continues to be a source of potential trouble for China. Apart from this, China is also concerned over security threats in Indian Ocean region, like piracy, terrorism, drug and material trafficking, weapons of mass destruction and so on, which will hurt its trade and energy security.

Above all, China's policy towards South Asia has been mainly, 'India Centric' as over the years India has emerged as an economic power, combined with regional military power; nuclear weapon and missile capability, which threatens China's rise in the region and beyond. Subsequently, growing India's strategic partnership with the US and Japan continues to be China's security concerns. Thus, as the Chinese saying goes, 'one mountain cannot accommodate two tigers", China's is determined to prevent the rise of India, which is emerging as a competitor in Asia and beyond. As a result, China has always supported political leaders, insurgency movements in India and its neighbours; it has being even supplying arms to dilute India's growth and influence in the region. Thus, Beijing policy towards South Asia is aimed to increase its own influence in the region and to lessen influence of India and also to reduce the ability of potentially hostile powers like US and Japan in harming its interest in the region.

Political Realities

Over the years the political relations between China and South Asian countries have drastically enhanced through the frequent high-level exchanges, such as in 2010 and 2011 the head of states from Bangladesh, Sri Lanka, Pakistan, and Nepal visited China–Prime Minister Sheikh Hasina (March

2010), Sri Lankan President Mahinda Rajapaksa and Nepal President Ram Baran Yadav (October 2010), and Pakistan Prime Minister Gilani (May 2011).

The year 2011, also marked the 36th, 54th, and 60th anniversary of the establishment of diplomatic ties with China vis-à-vis Bangladesh, Sri Lanka, and Pakistan respectively. Subsequently, the Chinese counterpart have also undertook high-level visit to these countries to boost the bilateral relations.

Apparently, increasing exchanges have also being undertaken through number of political, economic, military and academic delegations. Even the engagements at the institutional level has being intensified leading to greater interaction with the army, bureaucracy and police. For instances, according to *Xinhua,* in 2010, the number of China's bilateral personnel exchanges with Nepal reached 74,000. [5] As a result of frequent exchanges at all level has strengthened the political relations between China and South Asia countries.

The strong political relation has been strengthened through cooperation on many bilateral, regional and global issues. For instance, before the Mumbai attacks (26/11), China blocked United Nations (UN) sanctions, despite a global consensus favouring ban on Lashkar-e-Taiba (LeT) and Jamaat-ud-Dawa (JuD), who later on were responsible for planning and executing 26/11. Moreover, after the killing of Osama Bin Laden by the US raid (mid-2011), Beijing was the only major power defended Islamabad and supported the ignorance of Pakistani government about bin Laden's presence on its territory. Moreover, the Chinese Premier Wen Jiabao during Prime Minister Gilani's visit in May 2011 affirmed that "Pakistan has made huge sacrifices and contribution in combating international terrorism, that its independence, sovereignty, and territorial integrity must be respected, and that the international community should understand and support Pakistan's efforts to maintain domestic stability and to realize economic and social development". [6]

At the 17th UN Human Rights Council (UNHRC) Session in May 2011, China opposed any international intervention on Sri Lanka and put down any attempt to reopen the debate on Sri Lanka's conduct at the end of the war. [7] Subsequently, in March 2012, China has opposed similar resolution initiated by the US for the protection of human rights in Sri Lanka. In the case of Bangladesh, the Chinese have assured to help in ensuring food security and in combating militancy and terrorism. Thus, China's support has come at a crucial juncture to Pakistan, Bangladesh and Sri Lanka, which in a way has deepened bilateral relationship.

Apart from China's support to these countries on critical issues, the South Asian countries have also reciprocated like the Sri Lankan government's support on China's position on the Nobel Peace Prize given to Liu Xiaobo, and did not even send any representatives to attend the Nobel Peace Prize Award Ceremony in Norway. Sri Lanka, Bangladesh, Pakistan and Nepal continued to give China staunch support on Taiwan and Tibet-related matters and prevented any forces to use their territory for any anti-China activities.

On the SAARC front, Pakistan, Sri Lanka and Nepal, persuaded India to grant China's observer status, if not, they threatened to veto Afghanistan's entry into SAARC. Thus, all these developments indicate a stronger political relation between China and South Asia countries.

Economic Situation

China's economic relations with South Asian countries have improved in the recent times. Here, the economic aspects include extending loans on low interest and commercial terms, aid, project financing, infrastructure financing etc. Over the years the bilateral trade has increased, such that Sri Lanka, Bangladesh, Pakistan and Nepal's export to China has grown over the last five years, but at the same time, import from China has also grown at faster rate than exports leading to trade deficit. Nevertheless, China in order to boost South Asia countries export, in May 2010, signed exchanged notes with Nepal, where the former would offer zero-tariff treatment to 60 percent of Nepal's products covering 4,721 categories with no strings attached. [8] Similar agreement has been signed with Bangladesh, which came in effect from July 2010. In addition, China has signed the *Agreement on Economic and Technical Cooperation with Bangladesh* (June 2010) *and Nepal* (December 2010) which has boosted bilateral trade, such that Nepal's trade with China has increase by 80 percent, worth US$ 744 million in a single year from 2009-2010. [9]

In the case of Sri Lanka, the Sri Lankan Board of Investment (BoI) had also taken important steps to facilitate the needs of investors from China, like the demarcating a separate zone for Chinese investors at Mirigama; established an investment promotion office in Shanghai and also earmarked a special five-year visa for investors. [10] Subsequently, it allocated an exploration block in Mannar Basin and in 2010, Sri Lanka agreed to buy plant and machinery equipment for road construction from China at a cost of US$ 115.8 million, to boost the infrastructure. [11] Pakistan has a free trade agreement with China, and the former imports from China now constituting around 11 percent of Pakistan's total imports. At the same time, the two sides are committed for achieving a trade target of US$ 15 billion by 2015. [12] Even, during Chinese Premier Wen visit to Pakistan (December 2010), the two sides signed 35 new pacts, expected to bring US$ 30 billion of investment into Pakistan over the next five years. [13] Thus, the bilateral trade has been enhanced through mutual beneficial agreements.

More than the bilateral trade, it is the Chinese growing investment in the infrastructure that has enhanced its influence in the region like in Sri Lanka, they have invested in construction of Puttalam Coal Power Plant, Hambantota Port, the National Performing Arts Theatre; [14] Expressway from Colombo to the Katunayake Airport. In 2010, China signed a total of US$ 5.6 billion of project contracting and labour cooperation contracts in Sri Lanka. In Pakistan the development of Gwadar port and the railroad from Gwadar through the Karakoram Mountains leading into Xinjiang province of China, provides latter with an alternative energy supply route. Subsequently, China is building the strategic transport corridor in Pakistan Occupied Kashmir (PoK), despite Indian objections.

In Nepal, the Syafrubensi-Rasuwagadhi Road Project and 770 km. railway connecting the Tibetan capital of Lhasa with the Nepalese border town of Khasa also exists. Subsequently, it has built highways and financed a tourist resort; small airport at Pokhara into an international airport; Melamchi water project, hydel and other telecommunication projects, including the development of Lumbini and Pokhara. [15] In case of Bangladesh, development of Chittagong Port and construction of six vital bridges across major rivers. Subsequently, during the visit of Chinese Vice-President Xi Jinping to Dhaka on June 2010, he proposed to give assistance to Bangladesh for building a deep seaport in Chittagong and installing the country's first space satellite. [16] At the same time, these countries are also concerned over the catch in Chinese investment for development, as most of the labourers being employed for these projects are Chinese and not necessarily creating employment opportunities for local citizens. Nevertheless, the South Asia countries hungry for investment will drive its relations with China.

China's aid to South Asia countries have also increased over the years and has emerged as leading aid donor in the region. For instance, China's aid to Sri Lanka was just few million in 2005, but now it is more than US$ 1 billion. Interestingly, in 2009 alone, China emerged as Sri Lanka's biggest donors lending about US$ 1.2 billion of the total foreign aid received was US$ 2.2 billion, even surpassing Britain, which provided only £1.25 million in humanitarian aid in 2008. [17] Similarly, China's aid to Nepal has also being on rise, like in January 2011, during the Chinese Premier Wen

Jiabao visit to Nepal, announced an aid of US$ 119 million, and the amount to be spent on mutually identified projects. [18] In addition, China has also announced a one-time grant of US$ 20 million, to be spent on the rehabilitation of former Maoist combatants and increased its annual assistance to Nepal from RMB 150 million to RMB 200 million. [19] Similar has been with Pakistan and Bangladesh, who continue to benefit China's aid. Although, China's aid compared to US and EU's aid to South Asia countries is less, but greater acceptability for China's aid due to ''no-strings attached'' to the aid, unlike US, EU and other nations.

Furthermore, China to address its energy security needs, has established a substantial naval presence along vital maritime chokepoints, which is popularly known as China's 'String of Pearls', a plan to acquire several strategically placed ports, naval bases and listening posts in friendly countries like Gwadar (Pakistan), Hambantota (Sri Lanka), Sittwe (Myanmar) and Chittagong (Bangaldesh) to protect the billions of dollars worth trade that pass through strategically sea lanes such as the strait of Hormuz or the Malacca straits to Middle East, Africa and Latin America. [20] This string of pearls also allows China to access several preferential resources and a market access at highly subsidized terms. This strategy does not have any parallel strategies either by the US, Japan or any power in the world. Thus, this strategy has also enhanced the rise of China and influence in the region.

Military Status
China's military initiatives in the region are in forms of weapons sale, military training, and providing access to weapon technology. In the case of Sri Lanka, the Eelam War IV, (began in July 2006), provided an opportunity for expanding its military ties with China. As a result, China provided billions in loans and military hardware to Colombo to defeat LTTE. Subsequently, it signed an arms deal worth US$ 37.6 million with Beijing-based Poly Technologies.

Apparently, the arms sales included Chinese Jian-7 fighters, JY 11-3D air surveillance radars, armoured personnel carriers, T-56 assault rifles, machine guns and anti-aircraft guns, rocket-propelled grenade launchers and missiles, which were beneficial for Colombo in defeating LTTE. Moreover, it is alleged that Beijing went to the extent that it provided six fighter aircrafts (F-7 jets) free of cost. [21] Thus, China's military support was crucial to the regime's ultimate victory, and came at time, when the international community, including the US and other powers had withdrawn their support over human rights violations during the course of the war.

China continues to have stronger military ties with Nepal irrespective of regime, like in 2005, it supplied more arms to King Gyanendra, and in 2008 it announced military aid package of worth 1.3 million and 2.6 million non-lethal military aid. [22] Apart from this, frequent high level military exchanges have taken place, which have intensified supply of military equipments/weapons like General Chen Bingde, Head of the PLA General Staff Department, visited Nepal in March 2011 and signed a number of contracts worth US$ 20 million to build a military base on the Tibetan border. Moreover, China has always reiterated its commitment for enhancement of defence cooperation with Nepal army.

The strongest China's military ties with South Asia countries are with Pakistan, as China continues to be Pakistan's largest defence supplier, and with few joint ventures that produce armaments like JF-17 fighter aircraft used for delivering nuclear weapons; an Airborne Warning and Control System, and the Babur cruise missile. In May 2011, China agreed to assist modernization of Pakistan's military and provide Pakistan with 50 new JF-17 Thunder multi-role jets under a co-production agreement. Moreover, China is also helping Pakistan to build and launch satellites for remote sensing and communication, even as Pakistan is reportedly already hosting a Chinese space communication facility at Karachi.

At the same time, China is behind the Pakistani nuclear weapons program. China has gone one step further by emphasising on signing a China-Pakistan civil nuclear agreement, similar to Indo-US civil nuclear agreement, knowing Pakistan as proliferator of nuclear weapons technology, and further in 2006 it supplied 2000 megawatt nuclear power plant, bypassing Nuclear Suppliers Group (NSG) regulations despite China being member. To woo China, even Pakistan is insisting the former to take over the operation of Gwadar port in the Arabian Sea west of Karachi, upgraded to a naval base for Chinese use, however, China has rejected the offer keeping in mind the US and India reactions.

Apparently, China has always justified its military ties with South Asia countries on the grounds that it is legitimate and normal state-to-state relations to bolster their security, and it is well within the purview of the five principles of peaceful co-existence. Subsequently, argued that India is also selling weapons to South Asia countries and even emerging as largest weapons importer in the region. Furthermore, it has emphasised that China does not have any aggressive or malevolent intention to counter India or attack. Nevertheless, China's influence in the region continues to be major concern for India.

Why is this Happening?

Generally, there are many vital reasons for growing China's influence in South Asia, such as:

1. China's quest for accessing resources to sustain its rise has led to expansion of its influence in most of the region and in the process it continuous to extend support to undemocratic regimes, which has been shunned by the western powers like Cuba, Venezuela, Iran, North Korea, Zimbabwe, Myanmar and so on. In this regard South Asia is no different, as China from time to time has supported successive military regimes in Pakistan and Bangladesh. It had stronger ties with King Gyanendra, when he was fighting the Maoists and when the Maoists overthrew him, China changed sides overnight, such that it even increased

its aid to the Maoist regime by 50 percent from 80 million Yuan to 120 million Yuan. Thus, unlike India, the China relations with South Asia countries is not grounded on democracy, human rights and rule of law, as China itself is lacking in these fronts. As a result, India's sympathy for democratic forces has often been seen as a major threat to the undemocratic regimes in South Asia. Moreover, China does not have any serious emotional or cultural bonds with South Asia countries like India, so it can easily relate itself with any political force in control of the country. Nevertheless, in the recent times, India is also balancing both democratic values and strategic interest vis-à-vis the undemocratic regimes like Iran and Myanmar.

2. China follows the policy of 'non-interference' in internal affairs of state, be it in Africa, Latin America or South Asia. As a result, China has been successful in avoiding the weakness of Indian diplomacy which is dubbed 'arrogant' and unnecessary interfering in neighbours internal affairs. Although India is largest foreign investor in the countries like Nepal, Bangladesh and Sri Lanka, but its neighbourhood policies are seen with scepticism and China's increased assistance is seen as a positive balance to India. It is rightly pointed out by Kanti Bajpai, states "China has managed to project itself as disinterested neighbour and a remarkable attractive alternative to big brother India". [23]

3. The dominant discourse on India in the South Asia countries has been hegemonic power or 'big brother', always attempting to dominate over the region for its own strategic interest. This perception has been to certain extent strengthened by incidents of India's hegemonic behaviour in the past like the closure of some transit points between Nepal and India in 1988; the food 'bombing' in Jaffna in 1986; sending of the IPKF to Sri Lanka under Indo-Lanka Accord; India's intervention in the Maldives in 1988; India insisting political solution to Tamil ethnic

problem in post-war Sri Lanka etc. Moreover, India's growing strategic partnership with US is also perceived by neighbours as former seeking US help to continue its dominance in the region. Thus, these prevailing perceptions has hindered India's influence and allowed China's growth in the region. As a result, many infrastructure projects which are in the interest of India and its neighbours, are awarded to China like the development of Chittagong port. Thus, the key to China's success in South Asia is the fear and suspicion of latter countries over India' domination. As a result, India's efforts to have a normal relation with its neighbours continuous to be major challenge.

4. To certain extent, India itself has given space for China, by not meeting the requirements or needs of the neighbouring countries at critical juncture. For example, due to political reasons, India was reluctant in selling necessary weapons to Sri Lanka, which China readily made available. Moreover, initially, the Sri Lankan government had offered the development of Hambantota port to India, however, due to latter's lukewarm response it went to China. Moreover, in the recent time, India is very much obsessed with strengthening its strategic partnership with US, Russia, EU, Japan, Australia, Israel and so on to sustain its rise and meet its energy requirements and increase its global presence, as a result, South Asia is not in top priority list of Indian policy makers, which has allowed China to fill that space.

5. Domestic compulsions have also hindered India's pro-active policy towards South Asia, which is not the case for China. For example, West Bengal shares border with Bangladesh and Tamil Nadu is closer to Sri Lanka, are not always in same wave length as Indian government like Mamata Banerjee declined to sign the Teesta Treaty, which indented to sharing of river waters between India and Bangladesh and she also pulled out of PM Manmohan Singh's trip to Dhaka in September 2011. As a result, it

was huge embarrassment to the United Progressive Alliance (UPA) government and the treaty was put on hold, however recently the consultations have begun. Similarly, India's policy towards finding a lasting political solution in Sri Lanka is shaped by Tamil Nadu politics, like the political parties and the present government have insisted Manmohan Singh to persuade the Sri Lankan government for early political solution to Tamil problem and to take necessary steps against the Sri Lanka Navy for attacking India fishermen in the Palk strait, which the Sri Lanka government see it as India's unnecessary interference in its internal affairs. Moreover, Manmohan Singh has not made a very significant bilateral visit to Sri Lanka, precisely due to pressure from the Tamil political parties in Tamil Nadu. Even in the case of Nepal, the UPA government was initially reluctant in establishing relations with the Maoist led government, due to the prevailing Maoist insurgency problem in country. Thus, these domestic compulsions have prevented Indian government in adopting a pro-active neighbourhood policy.

6. At the same time, the South Asia countries have also deepened their ties with China through supporting on issues concerning China's sovereignty and national interests, inducing issues of Tibet, Taiwan and human rights in China. Most of the countries have worked towards preventing any anti-China activities in its land like Nepal the PM Prachanda ruled out the possibility of granting the Dalai Lama representative permission to function from Kathmandu and stated categorically that his party would not condone any action that could displease China. [24] Subsequently, Prachanda in 2008, stated there is need to review the Indo-Nepal friendship Treaty of 1950, however, accepted the draft of a 'Peace and Friendship' treaty submitted by China. Moreover, all the South Asia countries ensured the successful entry of China as 'Observer Member' of SAARC and now pushing for

China's full membership. Thus, the South Asia countries have successfully crafted their relationship with China, in way to neutralise India dominance in the region.

In addition, unlike India, China does not have any serious contentious issues affecting its bilateral relations with these countries. Subsequently, the political, economic and social problems within and between South Asian nations and India's limitation in interfering in the affairs, has offered a fertile ground for increasing China's influence through political, military and economic means.

India's Response

Generally, the shared history, common heritage, linguistic and cultural ties, ethnic linkages, music, art and literature have shaped India's policy towards South Asia countries. Subsequently, India's geographical proximity, huge population, economic and military potentials wields a strong holistic influence not matched by any other country in this region. As a result, India's neighbourhood, policy for many years, has been focussed on pluralistic society, democratic cultures, political instability, stable economy, terrorism and violence. However, in the recent times, India is concerned about the influence and presence of extra-regional powers, particularly the Chinese influence, which poses a great threat to India's regional hegemony and threats to national security. [25]

Apparently, many strategic analyst and policy-makers perceive Chinese presence in South Asia countries as a design to circumvent what was once considered its 'sphere of influence'. Thus, to counter China's assertiveness and growing influence in South Asia, India has to respond with a combination of rhetorical, diplomatic, infrastructural and defence-led initiatives with South Asia countries and at the same time without effecting the its bilateral ties with China. In this context, India's already initiated measure to counter China's influence in the region.

Strategic Partnership with the US

Since 2004, India-US relation has been transforming into a strong strategic partnership, which has laid the foundation for a mutual cooperation in key sectors. Under the Strategic partnership the Bush administration proclaimed that the US would facilitate India's quest for global status and make India a strategic partner of the US. As a result, in January 2004 an agreement was signed in the form of 'Next Steps in the Strategic Partnership' (NSSP) in which India's concerns related to space, nuclear power and high technology were adequately addressed. In June 2005, India signed the 10-year framework agreement with US on expanding defence cooperation. Indian Prime Minister Manmohan Singh visited Washington in July 2005 signed the Indo-US nuclear deal. This agreement was significant for India, as it recognized India as a de facto nuclear power; decades of technological sanctions on India were removed and the energy option for India was addressed through the nuclear deal.

Finally, in strategic terms, India got global leverage as a partner of the US, especially in ensuring India's security in Asia and also in South Asia. Hence, these developments laid foundation for a comprehensive strategic partnership between both the countries.

In addition, to certain extent China factor has also shaped the strategic partnership, as both the countries have concern about the long term implications of China's rise and its growing influence in the region and beyond. On the other hand, China has also expressed its concern about growing Indo-US relations, mainly to counter its growth. For instance, Chinese President Hu Jintao in September 2010 stated that "the forging of Indian security links with the US continuous to be a source of concern". [26] Thus, India in order to counter China's influence in the region is building strategic partnership not only with the US, but also with Japan and other South East Asian countries.

Engaging China

The six decades of India-China relations can be summarised as one that of conflict and cooperation. The India-China relations began to take new dimension since the year 2000, that of cooperation on resolving transnational issues and shaping a shared vision for peaceful rise of both the nations. The year 2006 was marked as India-China friendship year coinciding with President Hu Jintao's visit that led to the formulation of 10 point agenda on multifarious cooperation, regional and global level cooperation, which was accepted by India. [27] This was reciprocated by Prime Minister Manmohan Singh's visit to China in January 2009, during which he emphasized on further deepening of economic cooperation through agreement on a number of practical issues- aviation, agriculture, water resources, planning, education, environment, S&T Research, Confucius Institutes, Issue of Market Economy Status and Free Trade Agreement (FTA), joint military training and exercise to fight piracy.

The Chinese Premier Wen Jiabao's visit in December 2010 marked the sixty years of diplomatic ties between India and China and emphasized on an important milestone in their economic relations, with bilateral trade expected to breach US$ 60 billion with signing of Memorandum of Understanding (MoU) worth US$ 16 billion as against US$ 10 billion worth of agreements signed during the US President Barack Obama visit to India in November 2010. [28] Overall, India-China relations are becoming stronger and stronger, at the same the time there are many unresolved outstanding issues causing tension and misunderstanding between the countries.

Although India and China have cooperated on strengthening economic ties and on many translational issues like terrorism, global warming, economic crisis, piracy, drug trafficking, and other security issues, there are many irritant which has the potential of snowballing into a major conflict like territorial and border disputes, river water disputes, China's overwhelming economic, military, nuclear and political support to Pakistan, China's assertive influence in South Asian region, Tibet issue and so on.

Thus, conflict and cooperation has been core elements of India-China relations. Nevertheless, many analyst and policy makers have advocated that engaging China is also a way of managing. At the same time, there is wide opportunity for both the nations to work closely in addressing common issues in South Asia like growing instability in Pakistan, religious and radical fundamentalism in Pakistan and Bangladesh, terrorism and violence, climate change, piracy at Indian Ocean, economic and social issues and so on. Overall, India is engaging with China, which in a way can reduce China's influence in the region.

Strengthening of Bilateral Relations

Over the years, India has also strengthening its neighbourhood policy through the frequent high-level contacts among the foreign minister levels and below, including visits of head of state of South Asia countries to India and vice versa in the recent times. The contacts and meeting between the different sectors like defence, science and technology, commerce, education and so on, have also deepened the relationship. On the economic fronts, India is among the fourth largest investor in Sri Lanka, Bangladesh, Nepal and Maldives, like in 2010, India was the top investor in Sri Lanka, constituting more than 20 percent of its total investment. [29]

India's trade with the neighbours have increased drastically and vice-versa and India continues to be an important trading partner for South Asia countries and tourist arrivals. In addition to humanitarian assistance, India has also being giving economic assistance, like it has extended line of credit to Bangladesh, Nepal and Sri Lanka for range of projects including road and railway infrastructure, supply of locomotives, power, village development. Moreover, Indian armed forces and intelligence wings have also played leading role in helping Nepal, Sri Lanka and Bangladesh to defeat the insurgents groups; modernise their armed forces and also supplying equipment and training. In addition, parliamentary cooperation, institutional mechanisms related to trade, security, water transit and technical cooperation, cultural exchanges and so on, have strengthened the cooperation with the South Asia countries. Thus, the growing India's bilateral ties with South Asia countries certainly will neutralise China's assertiveness in the region.

Concluding Observations

China's influence in South Asia will continue to grow, as the region is strategically vital for China's peaceful rise and to counter India's rise. At the same time, the South Asia countries are pro-active in deepening their ties with China for their own growth and development and also to balance India's dominance. Although, China has emphasised that its growing influence in the region is not to encircle India, however, the former should be worried about the long-term implications, regardless of Chinese intentions and should work towards countering China's influence in South Asia and beyond, through strategic partnership with US, Japan and other major powers.

India is surrounded by weak states that pose serious challenges to its national security as well regional stability. At the same time, given India's stronger bondage with the South Asian countries, India has the responsibility to bring the region to the path of political stability and socio-economic development.

Although India is also helping South Asia countries in building and investing in infrastructure development, but not as aggressively as China, which has large cash reserve built from its huge trade surpluses and the reservoir of excellent construction engineers with experience in infrastructure building. Nevertheless, India should give due importance to South Asian region, rather than focusing entirely on sustaining its rise at the global level.

The region is confronted with vast challenges such as political stability, economic stagnation, and transnational issues such as terrorism, economic migration, environmental degradation, drug and human trafficking, organized crime, and so on. As a result it is in the interest of both India and China to work towards a stable and manageable South Asia through cooperation, rather than involving in confrontation. At the same time, the South Asia countries will continue to balance both the giants, i.e. benefiting from both India and China without antagonizing or aligning completely with one power against the other, for their own growth and development.

Hence, both India and China should co-exist for their respective rise and work towards bringing peace and prosperity in the region.

End Notes

1. "India and China Eye Each other Warily", (2010), *Strategic Comments*, 16 (10):1.
2. Tao Xie and Benjamin Page, (2010), "American's and the Rise of China as a World Power", *Journal of Contemporary China*, 19 (65) and Albert Keidel, (2008), *China's Economic Rise–Fact and Fiction* Washington, DC: Carnegie Endowment for International Peace, p. 1.
3. Chintamani Mahapatra, (2010), "Fairy Tale of America Decline and China's Rise", *Strategic Analysis*, 34(4): 520 and Chris Patten, (2010)."The Rise of China", *The RUSI Journal,* 13(3): 54-57.
4. David Shambaugh, (2005), "The New Strategic Triangle: US and European Reactions to China's Rise" *The Washington Quarterly*, 28 (3):7.
5. Nihar Nayak, (2012), "Chinese PM in Nepal: A Short Visit but a Long Trail?", 18 January. www.idsa.in/idsacomments/ChinesePMInNepalAshortvisitbutal ongtrail Nihar Nayak_180112.
6. Harsh V. Pant, (2012), The Pakistan Thorn in China-India-US Relations" *The Washington Quarterly*, Winter, 35 (1): 83.
7. "China, Cuba and Pakistan speak for Lanka at UNHRC Session", (2011), *The Daily Mirror*, 31 May Available at http://print.dailymirror.lk/news/front-page-news/ 45547.html.

8. "China-Nepal Relations", (2010), available at
    http://www.fmprc.gov.cn/eng/wjb/ zzjg/yzs/gjlb/2737/
9. Bhavna Singh, (2011), "China's Nepal Focus", 14 July,
    available at,
    http://www.ipcs.org/article/india/chinas-nepal-focus-3431.html.
10. Bharti Chhibber, (2009), "Indo-Sri Lankan Economic
    Cooperation: Contemporary Scenario", *Mainstream*, XLVII (32)
    25 July.
11. "China to undertake Mega Road Construction Job", (2011), *The
    Daily Mirror*, 3 June. available at,
    http://print.dailymirror.lk/news/news/45872.html.
12. Harsh V. Pant (2012), p. 86.
13. Anwesha Ray Chaudhuri, (2011), "India and Pakistan-China
    Nexus in Gilgit-Baltistan", *IDSA Comment,* 16 March, p. 9.
14. "China-Sri Lanka Relations", (2010), available at,
    www.fmprc.gov.cn/eng/wjb/zzjg/ yzs/gjlb/2737/
15. Bhavna Singh (2011).
16. B. Raman, (2011), "China's Strategic Eggs in South Asia", 12th
    July, available at,
    http://www.southasiaanalysis.org/percent5Cpapers46
    percent5Cpaper4595.html.
17. Sithara N. Fernando, (2010), "China's Relations with Sri Lanka
    and the Maldives: Models of Good Relations among Big and
    Small Countries", *China Report*, 46 (3): 289.
18. Nihar Nayak (2012).
19. Ibid.
20. Iskander Rehman, (2009), "Keeping the Dragon at Bay: India's
    Counter-Containment of China in Asia", *Asian Security*, 5
    (2):122 and Lawrence S. Prabhakar, (2009), "China's String of
    Pearls in Southern Asia-Indian Ocean: Implication for India and
    Taiwan" in M.J. Vinod, Yeong-Kuang Ger and S.Y. Surendra
    Kumar, *Security challenges in the Asia-Pacific Region,* New
    Delhi, Viva Books, p. 44.
21. B. Raman, (2008), "China Doing a Myanmar in Sri Lanka?", 27
    June, available at,
    www.southasiaanalysis.org/percent5Cpapers28
    percent5Cpaper2748.html.
22. Satish Kumar, (2011), "China's Expanding Footprint in Nepal:
    Threat to India", *Journal of Defence Studies*, 5 (2): 82.
23. Ibid, p. 83.

24. Nihar Nayak, (2009), "Involvement of Major Powers in Nepal Since the 1990s: Implications for India", *Strategic Analysis,* 33 (1): 43.
25. Smruti Pattanaik, (2011), 'India's Neighbourhood Policy: Perceptions from Bangladesh', *Strategic Analysis*, 35(1): 72.
26. "India, US need to partner to balance China in Indian Ocean", *The Indian Express*, 2 September 2010, available at, www.indianexpress.com/news/india-us-need-to-partner-to-balance-china-in-indian- ocean/676275/2.
27. David M. Malone and Rohan Mukherjee, (2010), "India and China: Conflict and Cooperation", *Survival*, 52(1): 144.
28. Sujit Dutta, (2011), "Managing and Engaging Rising China: India's Evolving Posture", *The Washington Quarterly*, 34 (2): 127 and Joe Thomas Karackattu, (2010), 'India-China Relations: It's the economy, and no one's stupid", *IDSA Issue Brief*, 28 December, pp. 1-12.
29. Government of India, Ministry of External Affairs, "India-Sri Lanka Relations", January 2012, available at www.mea.gov.in.

8

Emerging Indo-US Equations

Venkat Lokanathan

In the late 1940s, the Cold War between the United States and the Soviet Union was threatening to consume and divide the world into two blocs. The economies of the seemingly impregnable erstwhile imperial European powers like Britain and France was in tatters. In West Asia, the controversial creation of the state of Israel and the ensuing conflict with its Arab neighbours was threatening to unleash a new World War. In the Far East, Japan was reeling in the aftermath of the devastating effects of the nuclear bomb. It was in this intensely complex environment, which was threatening to uproot the foundations of global security and peace, that democratic India became independent. Not only was its external environment volatile, India was also the theatre of a violent partition internally that resulted in a bloodbath of its people and a break up of its pre-independent territory. Soon after, in 1949, its big neighbour, China went the communist way. Such external and internal challenges meant that India required strong and decisive leadership. India's first Prime Minister, Jawaharlal Nehru gave, at that crucial juncture in time, precisely what it required.

In this context, this paper will make a modest attempt at analysing and evolving responses to some pertinent questions in an effort to fuel a larger debate. First, how did India, under Nehru's leadership evolve its foreign policy and more specifically its relations with the United States? Second, did Nehru's visionary framework create a strong foundation that ultimately led to strengthening of bilateral relations post-Cold War? Third, does the Nehruvian framework continue to be relevant in the emerging Indo-US equation of the 21st century?

Intertwining Democracy and Secularism

Jawaharlal Nehru defined the meaning and content of nationalism thereby saving it from introversion. He gave direction and purpose to the struggle for freedom with a vision of India after it. He was also engaged in the difficult task of creating, out of a religious-cultural entity called India, a modern nation-state. From the moment of its birth, the Indian political system ensured the widest democratic rights and liberties. Whereas in Europe, population as well as democratic rights and liberties grew with the growth of wealth, in India the situation was the other way round with the economy presenting the picture of a wasteland. The Indian state was established and its constitution was evolved with great care providing a realistic framework.

Nehru had the vision, the wisdom and the perception to see that a country like India, with its linguistic, cultural and ethnic diversities could not survive unless its policy rested on the principle of secularism. Without secularism as a binding force and a common denominator for unity, it was impossible for Nehru to construct the policy of India. He was also able to forge unity in the midst of extreme diversity. This was, all the more a marvel at the time, because neighbouring Pakistan, which became independent at the same time, chose to be an Islamic state. Nehru's constant reiteration and insistence upon the values of secularism were responsible for the infant nation's continued survival as an entity and possibly a reason why it is even now observed that there is a method to the madness in India. If, despite Indian poverty, democratic institutions and democratic processes continued to flourish and show strength even in the midst of extraordinary difficulties, it was because of Nehru's insistence on secularism as a guiding principle not merely of state policy but of the thought processes and behaviour patterns. [1]

Importantly, Nehru also grasped that democracy in India

had to be universal. It could not be restricted and qualified by some elitist concept on the assumption that only those who are educated are capable of exercising the franchise. In fact, the experience of our elections has shown that there is no obvious correlation between political wisdom and formal education. From time to time, the Indian electorate has shown that despite poverty and deprivation, despite lack of formal education, it can act with remarkable wisdom in times of distress, in times of crises. When contemplating the entire panorama of history after the Second World War, one cannot fail to be struck by the durability of democracy in India as against its destruction in many parts of Asia, Africa and Latin America. Most importantly, by nurturing the true spirit of democracy enshrined in his historic objective resolution which subsequently became the philosophy behind the Indian Constitution, Nehru laid a stable foundation for India's political future. It is to his credit that India, has witnessed only 15 general elections in the last 65 years.

Science and Technology for a Stable Economy

In a way, the battle for secularism and parliamentary democracy was relatively easy to win. However, the most difficult problem was to transform the barren wasteland of India living at the level of subsistence, with more than eighty percent of the people pressing on very limited land, to convert the wasteland into green fields and to strike a balance between the town and the village. Nehru was aware that without changing the economy, it would be impossible to make a dent on India's social structure, ideas and value systems which sustained it. This, in turn, meant bringing about an industrial revolution in a short space of time and carrying it through without causing excessive human suffering. To stimulate economic growth and development in spite of the extreme paucity of resources was the most difficult problem. Nehru saw clearly that to span the centuries of backwardness the remedy lay in proper application and development of science and technology and in making the correct choice of a mix of technologies appropriate to India.

To develop science was not easy and to apply it in the socio-cultural environment of a traditional India was even more difficult. Some of these difficulties were overcome by Nehru's personal attention and passionate attention to science and technology. He was never tired of speaking in his own simple way about the need for a scientific temper, or of fighting irrationality. As is well known, given his scientific temper, he wanted to channelise science for developmental purposes. However, the nuclear energy was dual technology; it could be used for constructive and destructive purposes. A careful reading of Nehru's speeches and policy declarations clearly reveal that he did not foreclose the nuclear option for ever. It goes to the credit of Jawaharlal Nehru that he laid the strong foundations of atomic research, so that when the country decided to exercise the nuclear option, it could do so without much difficulty. On June 26, 1946, Nehru declared, "As long as the world is constituted as it is, every country will have to devise and use the latest scientific devices for its protection. I have no doubt that India will develop its scientific researches and I hope the Indian scientists will use the atomic force for constructive purposes. But if India is threatened she will inevitably try to defend herself by all means at her disposal. I hope India in common with other countries will prevent the use of atomic bombs."

In January 1956, Nehru announced in Parliament that if adequate resources were delivered, an Indian bomb could be made in three or four years. In December 1959, speaking before the Parliamentary Committee on Atomic Affairs, Dr. Homi Bhabha, who was chosen by Nehru to implement his vision, declared that India has progressed to such a stage where, if a political directive was received, a bomb could be made without external assistance. In 1961, when the Zerlina reactor went critical, Nehru stated that although India could make the bomb in two years, it chose not to do so. Dr. Bhabha created the structures and norms that have endured to this day, despite his passing away soon after Nehru's death.

Thus secularism, rationality and a concern for the growth of science and technology imparted to an ancient India a new style of living and thinking. Nehru added to it the concept of planning in the form of five year plans. Talking in simple language to millions of people across the country, Nehru made the concept of planning understandable, as he made secularism and democracy look part of India's heritage. Hence, whatever may have been the pitfalls, Indian planning has continued to endure even today. [2]

External Challenges

The Congress' foreign policy since the mid-1920s was formulated to a very large extent by Jawaharlal Nehru. His visit to Europe in 1926-27 as the representative of Congress to the International Congress of Oppressed Nationalities held in Brussels in February 1927, which assembled on one platform the representatives of the colonial peoples of Asia, Africa and Latin America, brought him in touch with Left-wing political workers, organisations and thinkers from all parts of the world, and constituted a landmark in formulation of his ideas and attitudes. Jawaharlal Nehru's visit to the Soviet Union in November 1927 made a deep impact on him. His admiration for the Soviet Union as the greatest opponent of imperialism deepened with time. The Congress also decided to set up a Foreign Department to develop contacts with its counterparts in other parts of the world. Jawaharlal Nehru emerged as the chief Congress spokesperson on world affairs, and the Congress used his services to formulate all resolutions on foreign policy. [3]

Relations with the United States

India and the United States, being separated from each other by thousands of miles, had few opportunities to come close to each other. The British also did not want the two countries to establish direct contact, for it feared that India might get inspiration from the United States for intensifying its political struggle. The Second World War marked the beginning of official Indo-US relations. After the Japanese attack on Pearl Harbour in December 1941, the United States realized the need for India's cooperation in the war effort. The strategic importance of India as a base of operations against Japan was one of the chief factors that influenced the Roosevelt Administration to take interest in the Indian political problem. President Roosevelt wanted a solution for the Indian problem but hesitated to involve himself directly in the efforts. He suggested to the British Prime Minster, Winston Churchill in March 1942, for the formation of a Government in India representing the various religious, geographical, occupational groups, the British Provinces and native princes which could be treated as a "temporary Indian Dominion Government".

Roosevelt also sent Colonel Louis Johnson to India as his personal representative with the rank of Ambassador in April 1942. During the stay of the Cripps Mission in India, Colonel Johnson held unofficial talks with many important Indian political leaders. Johnson's participation in the Cripps negotiations impressed Jawaharlal Nehru because the United States was, for the first time, showing an active interest in the solution of the Indian problem.

Though the Cripps Mission failed to achieve any result, it heralded the beginning of Indo-American political relations. The two countries, though quite different from each other in their geographical setting, race, culture and habits, cherished common ideals. They had both lived under subjection to a common power for a long time and had fought vigorously for their independence, though with different methods. While the American people got freedom through violence and bloodshed, India preferred the path of non-violence.

Soon after independence, India tried to develop friendly relations with the United States. It acknowledged with gratitude the positive role played by the United States during its struggle for independence. The democratic ideals of the United States also greatly fascinated Nehru and he tried to develop intimate relations initially. However, due to divergence of security and strategic interests, both India and the United States manifested serious differences on several international issues. Essentially, India and the United States took fundamentally different approaches while dealing with similar issues.

First, the United States, the World's oldest democracy was expecting India, the World's largest democracy to be a natural ally during the Cold War. However, Nehru was convinced that it was best for India to keep out of the Cold War and stay non-aligned. He chose to create the non-aligned group with Indonesia, Egypt and Yugoslavia. Although the term "Non-Alignment" was coined by V.K. Menon in his speech at the United Nations in 1953, Nehru referred to it for the first time during his speech in 1954 in Colombo, Sri Lanka where he described the five pillars called Panchsheel which would serve as a guide for Indo-Sino relations. Nehru went so far as to say, "If these principles were recognized in the mutual relations of all countries, then indeed there would hardly be any conflict and certainly no war". [4]

The five principles were subsequently incorporated in modified form in a statement of ten principles issued in April 1955 at the historic Asian-African Conference in Bandung, Indonesia, which did more than any other meeting to form the idea that post-colonial states had something special to offer the world. The Five Principles as they had been adopted in Colombo and elsewhere formed the basis of the Non-Aligned Movement, established in Belgrade in 1961.

For Jawaharlal Nehru the policy of non-alignment was an indigenous product, emanating from India's long struggle for freedom. His concept of nonalignment brought India considerable international prestige among newly independent states especially in the Third World that shared India's concerns about the military confrontation between the superpowers and the influence of the former colonial powers. India used nonalignment to establish a significant role for itself as a leader of the newly independent world in such multilateral organizations as the United Nations (UN) and the Non-aligned Movement. However, India's policy of non-alignment became a major source of irritation for the United States, which was obsessed with containing communism. [5]

Second, when the United States, in an effort to increase its power, launched an arms race by creating the nuclear bomb, India called for universal disarmament and a nuclear free world. An essential feature of the policy of non-alignment was the emphasis on peace, universal disarmament, and elimination of the element of fear. To Nehru, peace was indivisible. He stated on January 12, 1951, "What we need is a passion for peace and for civilised behaviour in international affairs. It is the temper of peace and not the temper of war that we want, even though peace is sometimes casually mentioned...If we desire peace, we must develop the temper of peace and try to win even those who may be suspicious of us or who think they were against us. We have to try to understand others, just as we expect them to understand us. We cannot seek peace in the language of war or threats".

The commitment to peace also involved tackling the root cause of the social, economic and political conflicts, reducing international tensions and resolving conflicts without recourse to violence. He was aware that a peaceful approach would not necessarily guarantee peace, but he wanted to give it a fair trial. The resolution of conflict through discussion, negotiation and accommodation was his way. Brought up in Gandhian traditions of non-violence, and given his abhorrence of violent conflicts and commitment to peaceful resolution of international disputes, it was but natural for Jawaharlal Nehru to openly oppose the manufacture of nuclear weapons. In November 13, 1945, he declared, "The revolution, caused by discoveries, having to do with atomic energy can either destroy human civilization, or take it up to unheard of levels". The peaceful use of nuclear energy was the official policy of the Government of India. This point was highlighted in bilateral agreements with Canada, UK, USA and USSR.

Third, when the United States emerged, in the early 20th century, from its Isolationist policy to fight two World Wars and begin a Cold War, India strongly urged for a peaceful resolution to all conflicts without the use of force by stressing the importance of protecting individual human rights. Nehru interpreted India's interests in a manner which did not conflict with the interest of maintaining world peace. Following his lead, the Indian National Congress at its Calcutta session declared that the Indian struggle was part of the worldwide struggle against imperialism. He saw that War had ceased to be an instrument of policy post Second World War and that modern technology had significantly reduced the importance of this concept. Even the structuring of a system of a balance of power was impossible as the sanction behind it was War. Hence, Nehru observed that the problem of foreign policy for every country, including India, was to interpret its national interest in a manner that did not conflict with overall international interests. Subsequently, India's refusal to join the military alliances sponsored by the United States and its opposing stands taken on the Korean Crisis of 1950 further annoyed the United States.

Fourth, when the United States invested in the Monroe Doctrine, in the early 19th Century, largely to pre-empt and stop the emergence of a geographically proximate competitor, Jawaharlal Nehru was against creating positions of strength or playing the game of power politics. The doctrine of balance of power did not find favour with him. To Nehru, national self-interest was not a narrow self-centred concept, but one in which there was no incompatibility with the interests of other nations. He was for the reconciliation of the national interests of one nation with that of the other. He repeatedly laid emphasis on pursuing a deliberate policy "of friendship with other countries" which he believed would go a long way in strengthening the security of the environment.

Speaking in the Constituent Assembly of India in 1948, he observed, "Whether a country is imperialist or socialistic or communist, its Foreign Minister thinks primarily of the interests of that country. But there is a difference, of course. Some people may think of the interests of their country regardless of other consequences, or take a short-distance view. Others may think that in the long-term policy, the interest of another country is as important to them as that of their own country. The interest of peace is more important because, if war comes, every one suffers, so that in the long-distance view, self-interest may itself demand a policy of co-operation with other nations, goodwill for other nations, as indeed it does demand. Every intelligent person can see that if we have a narrow national policy it may excite the multitude for the moment, just as the communal cry has done, but it is bad for the nation and it is bad internationally, because we lose sight of the ultimate good and thereby endanger our own good. Therefore, we propose to look after India's interests in the context of world co-operation and world peace, insofar as world peace can be preserved".

As such Jawaharlal Nehru saw India's national self-interest both in the context of better world co-operation and India's long-term interests. In his view the interest of one nation was not necessarily in conflict with that of other nations. Nehru devoted his attention to cement close and friendly relations with neighbours. Treaties of friendship were concluded with Bhutan in 1949 and with Nepal in 1950, two northern neighbours with whom India was closely bound by historical, cultural and social ties. India signed treaties of friendship with both Indonesia and Bhutan in 1951 and with the Philippines in July 1952.

The same pattern of friendship was adopted with regard to her relations with Afghanistan, Egypt, Iran, Iraq, Muscat, Syria and Turkey. The agreement of February 1954 with Sri Lanka on the presence in that country of people of Indian origin demonstrated the intentions of both India and Sri Lanka to work on this matter for a mutually acceptable arrangement. He also looked with pragmatism at the problem of Indians overseas, particularly in Burma, Fiji as well as East African countries. He advised Indian settlers to acquire local citizenship and associate themselves more with the interests of the people of that country. India was, however, against any discrimination towards them on the basis of colour and religion, and opposed the ill-treatment of the people of Indian origin in South Africa, a country with whom she served diplomatic relations as early as 1946.

Jawaharlal Nehru considered friendly relations with China essential for peace in Asia and worked for developing co-operative relations with that country. The Communist Revolution of 1949 in China was seen as a threat to the U.S. policy of containing Communism. However, India promptly recognized the new Communist regime of China on December 30, 1949–one of the first Asian countries to do so. India always supported the move to admit Communist China as a member of the United Nations. It offered the olive branch by stressing on the spirit of the Panchsheel principles in the 1950s. Under an agreement with China, in April 1954, India accepted Tibet as an autonomous region of China. India and China also worked out the modalities of trade between India and the Tibet region of China. This difference over China embittered the Indo-US Relations.

Fifth, the United States went to war with its immediate neighbour, Mexico, when confronted with problems over delineation of border lines in the mid-19th century. Meanwhile, Nehru hoped that geography, common history and language would help in furthering friendly relations with Pakistan but unresolved problems—the legacy of partition—proved a hindrance. Pakistan's invasion of Kashmir which had legally acceded to India complicated matters. Nehru referred the Jammu and Kashmir dispute, with its neighbour Pakistan, to the United Nations in the hope that a neutral third party might be able to find a long lasting solution. The United States maintained a cryptic silence about India's complaint of declaring Pakistan as the aggressor. Instead it laid emphasis on the need to settle the issue by means of a plebiscite in Kashmir. The role of the United States in the Security Council all through the discussion of the Kashmir question was that of supporting the case of Pakistan and was naturally not appreciated in India. The resolution was ultimately not passed and adopted due to the veto used by the Soviet Union.

The United States, through direct negotiations, began taking a very keen interest in the affairs of Kashmir. It realized the strategic importance of Pakistan to its plans for establishing military bases all around the Communist world. When Nehru and Mohammad Ali, Prime Minister of Pakistan, met in Karachi in July 1953 and later in New Delhi in August 1953, the US proposal for military aid to Pakistan came up and queered the pitch. Moreover, Pakistan's joining Western-sponsored alliances, namely, SEATO in 1954 and the Baghdad Pact in 1955, put her at complete variance with the policy of non-alignment being pursued by India.

In the wake of the Chinese invasion of its northern territories in October 1962, Nehru, considering that the threat was communist in nature, shrewdly asked the United Kingdom and the United States for direct and substantial military help to meet the Chinese onslaught. This was the first time, out of sheer compulsion, that Nehru had changed his earlier stand on non-alignment. Remarkably, here the United States despite initial reluctance helped India in accordance with her policy of containment of Communist China. Even as the war ended, the fundamentals of the Indo-US relations had altered. Although India continued to talk of non-alignment, there was a rapprochement in relations with the US in their efforts to confront China. There was a military understanding between the two countries for the supply of US arms and equipment for this purpose. There was also a political quid pro quo—India's defence plans would have to be approved by the US before it would agree to provide necessary supplies, and India would have to initiate a dialogue with Pakistan on Kashmir.

After early 1962, Nehru's vigour and along with it, his political influence began to wane. Added to that, the death of some dear colleagues, the unexpected Chinese aggression in 1962, and a prostate illness sapped his energy. Although Nehru remained the strongest figure in Indian politics, his pronouncements and policies were no longer accepted without challenge. The executive committee of the Congress parliamentary group operated with a new independence of spirit and was less intimidated by Nehru.

As Nehru reminded himself on the eve of his death he had 'many promises to keep and miles to go' before he slept: it was not as if he was unaware that in order to carry out the transformation of the society one needed a new instrumentality. Yet, he was brought up prior to independence to regard maintenance of that unity in the midst of extreme diversity as so important that he felt that the Congress Party needed to be changed only with the greatest care. Hence, the Indian National Congress (INC), the party in power that Nehru led, was a typical embodiment of an amalgamation of different opinions and voices that worked under one large umbrella.

When Nehru died on 27 May 1964, Ambassador Bowles observed, "However frustrating Nehru may have been on occasion, he was a great man whose impact on India will continue for generations. His control over the Congress Party organization and the minds of the Indian people had almost no precedent among modern democratic societies. With some notable exceptions, he was extraordinarily skilled in his grasp of basic principles. He had a clear concept of what he wanted India to be, with a proud commitment to democratic concepts. His sense of political timing was often brilliant". [6]

Contemporary Relevance of the Nehruvian Philosophy

It was the demise of the Soviet Union thereby ending the Cold War and India's policy of market liberalisation that created a favourable environment to kick-start political relations in the 1990s. It was again to Nehru's credit that the socialist pattern of development had laid a strong economic foundation in the formative years thereby making the domestic industry competitive when India opened up its markets. Subsequently, India's economic growth, its democratic stability, the increasing challenge from China and the unreliability of Pakistan meant that the United States could no longer afford to keep India out of its strategic global vision. Hence, despite US technological and economic sanctions post India's nuclear tests in 1998; a monumental shift in bilateral relations began in President Clinton's second term itself. The Clinton administration termed this monumental shift in bilateral relations as the "bonding of two democracies" in an effort to appreciate India's ability to remain democratic despite being surrounded by political instability and authoritarian regimes–again for which credit must go to Nehru for emphasising on building strong democratic institutions in the formative years.

Through the first decade of the 21st Century, India and the United States gradually expanded cooperation in the areas where they mutually benefited. The Next Steps in Strategic Partnership (NSSP) for cooperation in strategic areas such as nuclear, space, defence technology and export control was initiated in January 2004. Subsequently, both countries decided to move beyond the NSSP to a Strategic Dialogue in March 2005. This Strategic Dialogue, for collaboration in a number of areas including energy, climate change, trade, education, and counterterrorism, was launched in July 2009. The first and second session of the Strategic Dialogue, held in June 2010 and July 2011 respectively, led to extensive discussions on areas such as education, science and technology, defence, security and counter-terrorism, trade, and women empowerment.

In addition, there has been a tremendous growth in people to people contacts between both countries over the last decade.

Indians have received almost half of all H1B visas issues worldwide and more than 44 percent of all L1 intra-company transfer visas in the past four years. About 650,000 Indians travelled to the United States in 2010, an increase of 18 percent from 2009. Over 100,000 Indian students have travelled to study in colleges and universities across the United States in 2010. Simultaneously, about 2,700 American students travelled to study in India in 2010. The United States has created the Passport to India initiative to encourage an increase in the number of American students studying and interning in India. It is remarkable that many of the areas that were identified as critical by Jawaharlal Nehru are now influential factors in strengthening Indo-US relations.

Benefits of Investment in Science and Technology

Scientific and technological cooperation between India and the US has taken place for more than five decades now. In the 21st century, this relationship has already reached three important new milestones: the launch of Indo-US Science and Technology Forum (IUSSTF) in March 2000 and the signing of the Indo-US Science and Technology Agreement in October 2005. The IUSSTF was launched to catalyse bilateral collaborations in science, technology, engineering and biomedical research when President Clinton visited India in March 2000. A High Technology Cooperation Group (HTCG) to focus on building knowledge economy in the areas of biotechnology, nanotechnology, defence and information technology was formed in November 2002.

An umbrella Science and Technology (S&T) agreement, signed in October 2005, established intellectual property rights protocol and other provisions necessary to conduct active collaborative research in areas such as basic sciences, space, energy, nanotechnology, health, and information technology. [7] The National Oceanic and Atmospheric Administration in cooperation with Indian Space and Research Organisation have helped in bringing monsoon forecasting data to India's farmers recently. Additionally, a Science and Technology Endowment Fund has been established which will award US$ 2-2.5 million per year to promising technology projects that produce material benefits for both countries.

Achieving Energy Security through Nuclear Cooperation

In late September 2001, President Bush, keeping in mind the increasing bonhomie in relations, lifted sanctions imposed under the terms of the 1994 Nuclear Proliferation Prevention Act following India's nuclear tests in May 1998. An Energy Dialogue, which was part of the July 2005 summit, sought to expand cooperation by creating working groups on oil and gas, coal, power and energy efficiency, new technologies and renewable energy, and civil nuclear power. [8] The process for finalising the landmark Indo-US civilian nuclear agreement was initiated when President Bush visited India in March 2006. Subsequently, the historic Henry J. Hyde United States-India Peaceful Atomic Cooperation Act, allowing direct civilian nuclear commerce with India for the first time in 30 years, was passed in December 2006.

In July 2007, both countries reached a historic milestone in their strategic partnership by completing negotiations on the 123 agreement which was later signed in October 2008. Crucially, the Nuclear Suppliers Group then in an unprecedented move granted an "India specific" clean waiver opening the door for American and Indian firms to participate in each other's civil nuclear energy sector. [9] Again, Nehru's emphasis on using nuclear technology constructively for peaceful purposes meant that India had a strong record on non-proliferation and was considered as a mature nuclear nation-an argument that was used by the United States to get the clean waiver for India from the NSG.

Recently, both countries have established a Joint Clean Energy Research and Development Centre to mobilise up to US$ 100 million for advancing clean energy. The United States Geological Survey is helping explore options for shale gas development and determine if India's shale, will allow fracking technology with which it has had success in the US. Simultaneously, the Overseas Private Investment Corporation is exploring initiatives in renewable energy especially in the field of Solar. The United States' Department of Energy and India's Department of Atomic Energy has signed an Implementing Agreement on Discovery Science that provides the framework for cooperation in accelerator and particle detector research and development at Fermi National Accelerator Laboratory, Thomas Jefferson National Accelerator Facility, and Brookhaven National Laboratory. [10]

Growing Economic Potential

Economically, India has grown at an average of 7.6 percent in real terms over the last decade, according to International Monetary Fund statistics, with only a modest decline due to the global economic crisis in 2008 and 2009. After charting 10.4 percent growth in 2010, the Indian government believes that it can sustain rates of 8 to 9 percent economic expansion for the foreseeable future. It is apparent that over the next two decades India is on a path to become a global economic powerhouse.

In this context, India and the United States have been working together in a wide range of areas resulting in enhanced trade and investment and mutual job creation. Both countries have rightly focused on building strong institutional mechanisms to promote bilateral trade. An interagency collaboration, the Indo-US Trade Policy Forum, created in 2005, is the principal trade dialogue between both countries. It has five Focus Groups: Agriculture, Investment, Innovation & Creativity (intellectual property rights), Services, and Tariff and Non-Tariff Barriers. Indian and US Focus Group chairs are meeting periodically to work towards resolution of issues that impede trade and investment flows.

The Economic Dialogue, initiated during the July 2005 summit, includes a forum of chief executive officers from leading corporations to advise both governments on how to accelerate economic cooperation. The Private Sector Advisory Group, created in 2007, comprises of leading trade experts from both countries to provide strategic recommendations to the Trade Policy Forum. Both countries are also holding exploratory talks on a bilateral investment treaty since 2008 that would provide binding legal rules regarding one country's treatment and investments from another country. [11]

There has been tremendous progress in the recent past which has opened up numerous opportunities for economic cooperation. The United States has also remained one of the top sources of foreign direct investment in India, bringing important managerial expertise, capital, and technology with it to the dynamic Indian market. Bilateral trade has grown from a US$ 5.6 billion, twenty years back in 1990, to US$ 48.7 billion in 2010; a phenomenal growth of around 760 percent. [12]

Additionally, as part of the "Framework for Cooperation on Trade and Investment" signed in March 2010, both countries have launched an initiative called "Integrating US and Indian Small Businesses into the Global Supply Chain", which will expand trade and job-creating opportunities for U.S. and Indian companies. [13] Industry chamber Assocham has signed an agreement with the Denver-based National US India Chamber of Commerce (NUICC) on the side lines of the July 2011 strategic dialogue with an aim to strengthen economic ties further. Additionally, both countries have also identified a short term goal of doubling bilateral trade to US$ 100 billion in another five years. [14]

Common Concerns over Democracy

India has demonstrated an enduring commitment to democratic values. Indian democracy has prospered despite endemic poverty; extraordinary ethnic, religious, and linguistic diversity; and foreign and internal conflicts. It has provided Indian society the resilience and adaptability necessary to overcome and respond to the myriad challenges the nation has faced since independence. India and the United States share the objective to strengthen pluralist and secular democracies worldwide, and India's rise as a democratic great power promotes that profound global objective. [15] Indian culture and diplomacy has generated goodwill in its extended neighbourhood. India has positive relations with critical states in the Middle East, in Central Asia, in Southeast Asia, and with important middle powers such as Brazil, South Africa, and Japan—all of strategic value to the United States. India's soft power is manifest in wide swaths of the world where its civil society has made a growing and positive impression. This includes the global spread of its private corporate sector, the market for its popular culture, its historical religious footprint, and the example of its democracy and nongovernmental institutions.

The power game over the last two decades has shifted away from the West to the East and more specifically to Asia represented by its huge population, cheap labour and growing markets. India and China are rapidly emerging as global players of this century. From an American perspective, China with its history of communism and penchant for maintaining secrecy is an antithesis. The unreliability of its political structure, its rapid economic growth, its ability to engage in cyber warfare, its ambitious military, naval, space and air modernisation programmes and its aggressive forays into South, Central Asia, Africa makes China a threat to US global ambitions. Alternatively, India, with its thriving democracy, open society, huge market, cheap labour and a strong service sector led by a large English speaking workforce has many commonalities with the United States. The US Secretary of State Hillary Clinton, on the side-lines of the July 2011 strategic dialogue, reiterated American support for the rise of India both as a regional and global power and specifically appreciated its Look East policy:

"India and Indonesia in particular are two of the most dynamic and significant democratic powers in the world...the United States is committed to broader, deeper, more purposeful relations with each. And we want to actively support India's Look East policy as it grows into an Act East policy.

Soon after President Obama seconded this—we want India to not only "look East", we want India to "engage East"—because it will increase the security and prosperity of all our nations." [16]

After 9/11, the United States has revoked sanctions and pumped about US$ 22 billion in assistance and military reimbursements to Pakistan and designated it as a major non-NATO ally in June 2004. It has also spent nearly US$ 100 million since 2001 on a classified program to help secure Pakistan's strategic weapons. [17] However, there have been increasing differences between both countries on the counter terror strategies in the post-2003.

Despite increasing tensions post Osama's killing, the United States will attempt to actively engage with Pakistan. India has become critical in the existing scheme of things as Washington will continue to push for resumption of peace talks between India and Pakistan as continuous flare-ups will only divert Islamabad's attention from the Afghan front and push it closer strategically to China. [18] The United States and India are making efforts to discuss whether their respective policies toward Pakistan can be improved. They are intensifying their efforts to reach out to civil society and the business community to strengthen and sustain a democratic government in Pakistan. They are making efforts to strengthen the existing law enforcement and intelligence cooperation on Pakistan-based terrorist groups. Crucially, India is continuing to push the United States to condition all military and economic aid on sustained concrete antiterrorist measures by the Pakistan military against groups targeting India and the United States, including in Afghanistan. [19]

Controlling the porous border between Pakistan and Afghanistan is the central issue for the United States. The American and NATO forces have continuously focused on pre-empting and stopping brazen attacks by the Taliban and in training the Afghan National Security forces. The United States is increasingly concerned that Pakistan's obsession over India's efforts to encircle it, by gaining influence in Afghanistan, has in part led to continued Pakistani ambivalence toward the Taliban. The US military and intelligence officials have repeatedly warned that Pakistan's tribal areas along the Afghan border continue to serve as safe havens for the Taliban and Al-Qaeda to stage attacks against Afghanistan. [20]

This situation has been further complicated by President Obama's initial announcement to drawdown troops from Afghanistan by July 2011 and then postponed subsequently to December 2014. It is becoming increasingly evident that the United States cannot realise its goals for India, Pakistan and Afghanistan simultaneously without taking all these players on board collectively. [21] India is also increasingly concerned over its future in Afghanistan post the US exit in 2014. It has attempted to convince the United States to avoid making a hurried exit from Afghanistan. Simultaneously, the United States has been highly appreciative of India's active involvement in supporting international efforts to rebuild Afghanistan. [22]

End Notes

1. P.N. Haksar (1974), "The Relevance of Jawaharlal Nehru", 6th Jawaharlal Nehru Memorial Lecture, University of Cambridge, 16 May, available at,
   http://www.cambridgetrusts.org/assets/documents/Lecture_6.pdf
2. Ibid.
3. P.V. Narasimha Rao (2009), "Nehru and Non Alignment", Mainstream, Vol. XLVII, No. 24, May 30, available at,
   http://www.mainstreamweekly.net/ article1399.html.
4. Nehru (1958), "The Colombo Powers' Peace Efforts", broadcast from Colombo 2 May, 1954, Jawaharlal Nehru's Speeches, Vol. 3, March 1953-August 1957 New Delhi: Government of India, Ministry of Information and Broadcasting, p. 253.
5. The full text of this agreement (which entered into force on 3

June 1954) is in United Nations Treaty Series, Vol. 299, United Nations, pp. 57-81, available at, http://treaties.un.org/doc/publication/unts/volume percent20299/v299.pdf.

6. Kalyani Shankar (2007), "India and the United States: Politics of the Sixties", Macmillan Publishers India, New Delhi, pp. 1-10.

7. Indo-US Science and Technology Forum, available at, http://www.indousstf.org/fullstory. aspx?storyheadline=History&prevmytitle=About percent20IUSSTF§ionid=S150 Accessed on 2 December 2011.

8. Richard Fontaine (2011), "The strategic relationship between the U.S. and India: Coming along nicely", Foreign Policy, 20 July, http://www.cnas.org/node/6709; accessed on: 21 November 2011.

9. Editorial (2011), "US-India Strategic Dialogue: Science, Technology and Education Ties Forged", Asian Scientist, July 20, available at, http://www.asianscientist.com/topnews/2011-us-india-strategic-dialogue-science-technology-education-ties-forged/Accessed on: 15 October 2011.

10. Remarks by Robert D. Hormats, Under Secretary for Economic, Energy and Agricultural Affairs and Robert Blake, Assistant Secretary of State for South and Central Asian Affairs, US Department of State (2011), "US-India Strategic Dialogue", at East West Centre, Washington DC, 15 July, available at, http://iipdigital.usembassy.gov/st/ english/texttrans/2011/07/20110715104141su0.1004864.html?CP.rss=true#axzz1TTJIs6ml Accessed on 10 November 2011.

11. Office of the United States Trade Representative, available at, http://www.ustr.gov/countries-regions/south-central-asia/india accessed on: 3 December 2011.

12. Rohit Sharma (2011), "Trade Watch: India-US biz boom in 2011", India BIZNEWS, July 21, available at, http://www.indiabiznews.com/?q=node/1723 Accessed on: 5 December 2011.

13. US India Trade Policy Forum (2010), "Framework for Cooperation on Trade and Investment", 17 March, available at, http://geneva.usmission.gov/2010/03/17/u-s-indiacooperation/

14. Sandeep Dikshit (2011), "Hillary seeks greater investment,

Krishna wants better environment for IT sector", The Hindu, 19th July.

15. Office of the Press Secretary, The White House (2010), "Remarks by the President to the Joint Session of the Indian Parliament in New Delhi, India", November 08, http://www.whitehouse.gov/the-press-office/2010/11/08/remarks-president-joint-session-indian-parliament-new-delhi-india, accessed on 15 December 2011.

16. Office of the Press Secretary, The White House (2010), "Remarks by the President to the Joint Session of the Indian Parliament in New Delhi, India", November 08, http://www.whitehouse.gov/the-press-office/2010/11/08/remarks-president-joint-session-indian-parliament-new-delhi-india, accessed on 15 December 2011.

17. Alan Kronstadt (2005), "Pakistan-US Relations", Congressional Research Services Issue Brief, The Library of Congress, January 28, pp. 8-13.

18. Alan Kronstadt (2011), "Pakistan-US Relations: A Summary", Congressional Research Services Issue Brief, The Library of Congress, October 21, pp. 4-10.

19. n. 7.

20. Walter K. Andersen (2011), South Asia, India and Afghanistan: An Evolving Triangle", Foreign Policy Research Centre, Journal No. 7, October.

21. Stanley Wolpert, Professor Emeritus, University of California, Foreign Policy Research Centre, No. 7, October 2011.

22. Council for Foreign Relations and Aspen Institute India (2011), "The United States and India: A Shared Strategic Future", Joint Study Report, September.

9

China's Involvement in South Asia and India's Concerns

Anil Kumar P

South Asia is a most complex, volatile and one of the most socially and politically divided and region of the world. The region of South Asia mainly consists of eight states: Bangladesh, Bhutan, India, Maldives, Nepal, Pakistan, Sri Lanka and Afghanistan. It is home to 1.4 billion people, more than 20 percent of the world population. Thus, about one-fifth of humanity lives between the western reaches of Afghanistan and Pakistan on one side and the eastern reaches of Bangladesh and India on the other. It is a region that lies between the sea routes of the Indian Ocean (Persian Gulf and the Asia-Pacific) and the land routes of Central Asia connecting Europe to the East. It is a large reservoir of natural and human resources, making it a prime destination for finance capital, a lucrative market for trade and a source of cheap raw material. It also sits at the confluence of the richest sources of oil, gas, rubber, manganese, copper, gold, tea, cotton, rice and jute and is the transit point for most of the resources and manufactures that criss-cross the world. Moreover, it is the most heavily militarized and bureaucratized zone in the world and it has a variety of complex and violent primordial ethnic groups.

Historically, South Asia had been the finest passage of invaders from Central Asia, Persia, the Arab world and even Greece for thousands of years. Later, the region was colonized first by the Muslims and then by the European powers and ultimately it comes under the suzerainty of British Empire. Thus, British India was the base from which England projected its power towards China and Russia as part of the infamous *Great Game* in the 19th century.

The region has been recognized as a geographical area of major strategic significance through, which the routes connecting Europe, Africa and Asia. The region of South Asia is important because of its connection with the vital sea-lines of communication in the Indian Ocean and is sandwiched between two politically volatile and economically critical regions, i.e. the Persian Gulf and Southeast Asia. (Beazley, 1979:6-23) Thus, South Asia forms an integral part of Mackinder's "World Island," that is, the Euro-African-Asiatic land mass, the most important single geographical unit in the world. (Parker, 1982:32-56) Moreover, the major actors of the region, India and Pakistan, were divided in terms of polarisation between the United States, the Soviet Union and China. During Cold War India has functioned as an important ally of the Soviet Union and Pakistan has functioned as a broker for the West in relation to moderate Muslim countries in the Middle East and the Gulf areas and in relation to China.

China and South Asia

South Asia remained as a very unique segment of China's foreign policy just as China remains integral to South Asian reality and ethos. Since ancient times South Asia was the only periphery of China which was never described as one inhabited by barbarians yet-to-be civilised. Instead thanks to the influence of linkages of Buddhism, this subcontinent was always revered as *Tian Zhu* (Western heaven) in Chinese commentaries and epics. (Singh, 2003:11) Until their liberation towards the 1940s, mutual interactions between the Chinese and South Asians were guided largely by the external visions of colonial powers. But in 1990s, it was gradually moved away from its critical politico-strategic concerns towards-pragmatic approach of economic engagement making mutual benefit as basis of their policy initiatives.

For China's first foreign policy crisis lay in the need for

countering possibilities of South Asia being used as a foot hold by anti-China forces as Western powers. While Pakistan had already been clearly recruited into Western military alliances from early 1950s, India's steering clear of any military alliances by adhering to its non-aligned movement was also interpreted as a clear reflection of India's ambitions for Asian leadership. Therefore, while Beijing may have been preoccupied with its regular shelling on Quomoy and Mitsu Island between Taiwan and Fijian province yet, China was all the time very alive to various developments in South Asia that was so critical to its most fragile regions where western powers could have most easily started nibbling into its body politics. This sense of insecurity about these regions, that made China's South Asia policy so security and strategic centric. (Singh, 2003:311)

In operative terms, it was China's 'liberation' of Tibet since early 1950 that was to bring South Asia face to face with the nature of new communist regime. It has now proved that India had made concessions on Tibet with an understanding to achieve larger regional peace and agreement on their complex boundary question. (Singh, 2003:311) However, the events inside Tibet, especially arrival of the Dalai lama in India March-April 1959 followed by China-India war of 1962, were to gradually push China at the centre stage of South Asian psyche.

In response to China's liberation of Tibet, South Asian states like Bhutan, Sikkim and Nepal ended their policy of accommodation of China and revived various older treaties of the British times. Assuming India to be the successor state of the British, the Himalayan states of Nepal, Bhutan and Sikkim were to strengthen ties with New Delhi almost on the lines of their earlier treaties with the British. [1] Even India's arch rival, Pakistan was to seriously pursue the idea of building a South Asian 'joint defence' against the Chinese and this had been one favourite proposal of President Ayub Khan till the very late 1950s. (Singh, 2003:312)

All these further strengthened India's stature amongst South Asian states and bring India to the centre-stage of Beijing's South Asia policy. But China applied their pragmatic strategy to get a good friend in South Asia. Beginning from the Border Settlement Agreement of 1963 between China and Pakistan and their 'special relationship' was to make China all the more integral to South Asian affairs and thereby make Pakistan for more rigid and aggressive in dealing with India. (Singh, 2003:313) As result, the problematic bipolar equations between India and Pakistan were to also encourage other smaller states to either play one against the other or use Pakistani example to invite external powers to deal with their anti-India grievances. These trends were to facilitate and encourage a more intrusive approach to South Asia by China's leaders. (Hussain, 1977:32) This fluidity of smaller South Asian states to swing between New Delhi and Beijing was to only further re-enforce the fact that both China and South Asia were still integral to each other's policies and profile.

Boundary disputes have been the root cause of inter-states suspicions and threat perceptions between China and South Asia. What makes these boundaries especially so critical is that all of these have been disputed and often have populations that overlap into each other's claimed areas. Though China has resolved most of its land boundary disputes with other smaller countries, its unresolved boundary with India make these smaller states very critical buffers between China and India and thus increasing their significance for both China and India. Even countries like Bangladesh, that was not in the picture until 1971, and does not directly share boundaries with China remain important for China as, at one stage, Chinese had toyed with idea of using this state for finding an outlet into the Indian ocean. The same is also true of Myanmar which, despite not being part of the conventional British definition of South Asia, provides China tremendous leverage in making China integral to South Asian security scenario.

Amongst China's special relationships' with South Asian

military regimes, the China-Pakistan axis perhaps presents the most critical element of South Asian security environment. It is a unique example of inter-state relations which has no comparison whatsoever. This is a unique case where one nuclear weapon state has been primarily responsible for propping another nuclear weapon state. Similar attempt was later made by China with Burma's military rulers yet, China's indulgence has had only a limited success with other South Asian countries during Cold War period.

Given the proximity and historical interdependence of these smaller South Asian countries with India, Chinese indulgence has not resulted in any formal military alliance with any of India's neighbours. (Singh, 2003:316) At the same time, however, this indulgence did have a major impact on South Asian threat perceptions which has been mainly responsible for vitiating the South Asian vision about China. This has also provided an opportunity for other outside powers to seek influence in this region. Despite absence of ideological linkage or military alliance, China has tried to tie down India to South Asia by seeking influence by building economic engagement with smaller South Asian states. Table 9.1 and Table 9.2 will tell us about the import and export data of China and the major South Asian countries including India's arch rival Pakistan during the Cold War.

China keeps a high amount of trade volume with other major South Asian counties, especially with Pakistan compared to India. Between 1956 and 1973, when China-India ties were at their lowest ebb, nearly 20 percent of China's total world aid was targeted to these South Asian countries, with Pakistan receiving 13.1 percent, Sri Lanka 3.5 percent and Nepal 2.9 percent. The main focus was generally on supplying these countries with military equipment resulting in China emerging as the single largest supplier of military equipment to Pakistan, Sri Lanka, Bangladesh and Burma. (Singh, 2003:316) To quite an extent this equation has since continued to be decisive in determining the nature of military capabilities of these states. This extreme indulgence has also to be understood in terms of Beijing's strategic vision of emerging as the Asian leader which has a direct bearing on the South Asian security environment.

Table 9.1: China's Exports to South Asia during the Cold War Period (in million dollars)

Year	1977	1979	1982	1985	1989	1991
China's Total Export (US$ bn)	7.6	13.7	22.0	27.4	52.6	72.0
Pakistan	49	122	22.0	185	368	597
India	1	-	203	84	169	144
Bangladesh	17	-	101	76	192	204
Sri Lanka	28	95	90	61	69	118
Nepal	-	-	37	17	27	32

Source: Atul Kumar (2006), *China-Pakistan Economic Relations*, IPCS Special Report published on September 2006, p. 3.

Table 9.2: China's Import from South Asia during the Cold War Period (in million dollars)

Year	1977	1979	1982	1985	1989	1991
China's Total Import (US$ bn)	7.2	15.7	18.9	42.3	59.1	63.8
Pakistan	19	30	143	58	224	89
India	1	-	81	39	102	120
Bangladesh	17	-	22	12	35	9
Sri Lanka	52	62	7	13	4	5
Nepal	-	-	4	2	5	1

Source: Atul Kumar (2006), *China-Pakistan Economic Relations*, IPCS Special Report published on September 2006, p. 3.

Before 1980s China tried to offered counterweight to small states in South Asia against Indian hegemonism. But following improvements in Sino-Indian ties since early 1980s, Beijing has gradually lost its motivating force to prop smaller states against India. But India-Pakistan war of 1971 was introduced a new player–Bangladesh in the region. It transformed South Asia's security system from being a largely bilateral balance of power in to a multilateral one, that too in favour of New Delhi. This was the first major watershed event in the evolution of China's South Asia policy which was to strengthen 'special relationship' between China and Pakistan and make China integral to South Asian affairs during much of 1980s and 1990s.

The most critical determinant of China-South Asia mutual policies remains the nuclearisation of South Asia since 1974. Beijing's policy of supplying sensitive military technologies to Pakistan in bargain to promote a China-Pakistan relationship of dependency and thereby to use Islamabad as its bulwark in its South Asia policy was bound to have its implications for India's threat perceptions. (Singh, 2003:321) China-Pakistan nuclear axis had become the single most disturbing element in New Delhi's foreign and nuclear policy making.

Regarding most visible part of China-South Asian ties, China has been the most reliable, most affordable and also the most appropriate supplier of weapons to most of the smaller South Asian countries. During Mao's regime, during its first 25 years, the Chinese arms exports were focused more towards China's ideological allies and these were distributed virtually free amongst various communist states and communist inspired insurgent groups. But from late 1980s, Deng China took its arms exports in his new spirit of entrepreneurship and by mid-1990s, China's share in world market had moved from being under 1 percent during late 1970 to being the 5th largest arms exporter. (Chakrabarti, 1984:810) Of course this was partly the result of collapse of Soviet Union which had led to a drastic decline in weapons transfers from early 1990s. But at the same time, China's supplies to South Asia were not entirely guided by collapse of Soviet Union though they did show substantial expansion during 1990s.

At the end of 1980s, China emphasized state-to-state relations while at the same time building engagement with all the segments of each of South Asian nations.

Post-Cold War Strategy

China's broad objective in South Asia in the post-Cold War period is to expand multi-dimensional cooperative relations with all the countries of that region. "Multi-dimensional" signifies military ties as well as more innocuous political and economic cooperation. "All" means both India and India's smaller neighbours: Pakistan, Myanmar, Nepal, Sri Lanka, Bangladesh, Bhutan, and the Maldives. India has sometimes objected to China's relations–especially military-security ties–with these countries. Beijing views South Asian countries as "neighbours" with whom it is especially important to have friendly, cooperative ties both to increase China's own economic and political influence and to lessen the ability of potentially hostile powers (currently the US) to injure China's interests.

Except India and Pakistan, all other smaller powers of the South Asian region are searching for their allies for economic development and strategic interests. In the post-Cold War period, China is investing in the economies of South Asian countries with multiple targets. South Asia's increasing defence ties with the United States and unprecedented Chinese influence in the region created a platform for smaller countries to come forward with their demands and play bargaining diplomacy. The post-Cold War world offers new avenues of challenges and opportunities to the powers that be in the global scenario. The world witnesses intense struggles for strategic resources, strategic locations and strategic dominance.

This makes every part of the world significant for the global actors. With the emergence of China and India as the new economic power houses of the world, Asia has entered into the limelight of international community. Nuclearisation of India and Pakistan, presence of Taliban-Al Qaeda elements in Afghanistan, and the strategically vital Indian Ocean has made South Asia a high profile area in international relations.

This has prompted countries like the US and China to concentrate their attention on South Asia. Moreover, the military presence of the United States in Afghanistan and the cementing of Indo-US relationship have forced China to make some strategic moves in South Asia.

South Asia borders most of China's sensitive southern boundary. This gives China the strategic option of opening direct access through South Asia to the international sea lanes of Indian Ocean. The Indian Ocean region has always been the scene of power play between Russia, the US and the West, and the theocratic Islamic states because 75 percent of global merchant shipping passes through it.

In recent times, South Asia has also become a source of inspiration for Jihadi terrorism and separatism in China. Western parts of South Asia bordering China had been the fountainhead of Jihadi terrorism inspiring fellow Muslims across the borders in Xinjiang province. Similarly, the presence of large number of Tibetan refugees in India and Nepal with strong anti-Chinese sentiments had always been sources of potential trouble for China. (Hariharan, 2008) These factors have importance in the formulation of China's South Asian policy.

Core of China's South Asian strategy in the post-Cold War period is to contain and encircle India (concircle) through the creation of different pro-China 'micorpoles'. So China concentrates in the strategy of building alliances and partnerships. China's entry in South Asia gained momentum only after its conversion to the market economy in the 1980s, which filled its coffers with trade and investment dollars. Its resultant economic strength opened the path into South Asia, beyond Pakistan. China skilfully deployed economic incentives to draw Bangladesh, Nepal, Pakistan, and Sri Lanka into its strategic orbit. China's recent strategic manoeuvres in and around the Indian Ocean threaten both India's economic as well as security interests. China's naval capabilities have significantly expanded over the past few years with induction of new warships and submarines.

It has nearly surrounded India by forming strategic alliances with countries of the Indian Ocean. As part of China's naval strategy to encircle India, Beijing is in the process of building a number of bases around India in Pakistan, Sri Lanka, Maldives, Myanmar and Bangladesh. China's Sanya naval base in South China Sea, an underground nuclear submarine base, is about 1,200 nautical miles from the strategic Malacca Strait and the nearest naval base to India. With the construction of Gwadar naval base in Pakistan (400 km. east of the Strait of Hormuz), China plans to restrict the movement of Indian Navy in the Arabian Sea. The strategically important Gwadar will also reinforce Pakistan's Karachi naval base against India. Very interesting thing related to Gwadar port is that 80 percent of this US$ 250 million project is funded by China.

From strategic point of view China always attempted to minimise India's hegemonic role in South Asia. It is clear from their role in the emergence of Pakistan as a nuclear weapon state and nuclear missile state. China's clandestine contributions stand well documented by CIA and US Congress documents. China, not only supplied 'off-the-shelf' nuclear capable missiles with IRBM ranges, but also set up missile productions facilities in Pakistan. Objective behind the Chinese designs here were not to contribute to Pakistan's defence capabilities or deterrence but to strategically defend India. In addition to this China made every effort to all weather and all dimensional friendship with Pakistan. Pakistan is the first country which recognised China's full market economy status (December 15th, 2004) and the only one till now that signed the Free Trade Area (FTA) with China (November 24th, 2006) in South Asia. On April 17th, 2007, during the visit of Pakistani Prime Minister Shaukat Aziz to China, the two side inked 27 agreements and Memorandums of Understanding aimed at further expanding ties between the two countries. The annual trade volume between these two has reached 5 billion in 2006 making 23.1 percent increasing than previous year.

Besides the fast growing economic cooperation between these two old friends, their traditional politics and security links are also getting closer. During the visit of Chinese Premier to Islamabad in 2005, the two governments signed *Treaty of Friendship, Cooperation and Good-neighbourly Relations between the People's Republic of China and the Islamic Republic of Pakistan* as an important legal foundation for the strategic partnership between China and Pakistan. From March 6th to 13th, 2007, the Chinese navy task group participated in the naval exercises held in the Arabian Sea with Pakistan, which is the first time for Chinese navy force to participate the multinational naval exercises. And before this, the "Friendship-2006" China-Pakistan joint anti-terrorism exercise was initiated on December 11th concluded on December 19th in the hilly area of northern Pakistan's Abbottabad. These exercises renewed and enriched the long-term defence cooperation between China and Pakistan. Now there are reports from Pakistan that it started to strengthen their nuclear weaponisation programme. Definitely China's position is important in this regard in the following days.

After 9/11, the new strategic development (beginning of the US offensive in Afghanistan) changed the security environment in Asia. US military presence in Uzbekistan and Afghanistan and the new military relationship of the US with Pakistan and India completed the US military involvement in the whole of the Asian continent. This also compelled China to make possible alliances in this region to counter US influence. One of the cardinal principles of Chinese foreign policy in the post-Cold War era is the peaceful rise. So China also believed that an economic, diplomatic, and military partnership with the South Asian region would maximize its influence in the region, and ensure that threats to China did not emanate from that region.

China's relationship with Bangladesh is strengthening day

by day. Total trade between China and Bangladesh was around US$ 3.5 billion in 2007, up about 8.5 percent from the previous year. China is an important source of military hardware for Bangladesh and increasingly is investing in Bangladesh's garment sector. With natural gas deposits in Bangladesh estimated at between 32 trillion and 80 trillion cubic feet, Bangladesh has gained strategic importance for both China and India as a potential source of energy. But Bangladesh recently turned down India's proposal for a tri-nation gas pipeline with Burma. For China, Bangladesh is a doorway into India's turbulent north-eastern region, including the Indian state of Arunachal Pradesh, to which China lays territorial claims.

Taking advantage of a sharp downturn in India's relations with Bangladesh over issues ranging from illegal immigration to Islamist terrorism, transit and trade, Beijing has upgraded its ties with Dhaka to gain naval access to the Chittagong port, to establish a road link with Bangladesh via Myanmar and to acquire Dhaka's immense natural gas reserves. China is already the largest supplier of weaponry to Bangladesh. Chinese Premier Wen Jiabao's recent offer to provide Dhaka with nuclear reactor technology has led to speculation as to whether Beijing would replicate in Bangladesh the sort of military, nuclear and missile collaboration it has with Pakistan. Bangladesh and Nepal are also expected to join Pakistan in concluding peace and friendship treaties with China in the near future.

A *Defence Co-operation Agreement* was signed between Bangladesh and China during the visit of Bangladesh Prime Minister, Begum Khaleda Zia's visit to China from December 23 to 27, 2002. The Bangladesh-China Defence Cooperation Agreement, presently being termed as only a consolidation of different defence agreements between the two countries, carries in it an inbuilt potential of serious strategic implications, not only for India but also for the United States and for the South Asia region as a whole.

China is also apparently planning to develop a submarine base at Marao in Maldives to counter the Indian navy's Southern Command. After Burma and Bangladesh, to complete the "arc of influence" in South Asia, China is determined to enhance military and economic co-operation with Maldives and Sri Lanka. Given China's known interest in developing bases around the Indian Ocean littoral, a Chinese base in Maldives would not be surprising. Although China claims that its bases are only for securing energy supplies to feed its growing economy, Indian experts perceive the Chinese base in Maldives as motivated by Beijing's determination to contain and encircle India, and thereby limit the growing influence of the Indian Navy in the region.

Regarding Nepal there has been a major shift in China's foreign policy towards it since the Maoist ascendance to power. China had earlier adopted a policy of 'non-intervention' in the internal matters of Nepal and largely stayed out of Nepalese internal politics. However, the demise of the monarchy and the ascendance of political parties have forced China to reshape its Nepal policy. Moreover, frequent protests by Tibetans in recent months alerted the Chinese to the possibility of the China-Tibet border being misused. Consequently, China has sought to engage Nepalese political actors at all levels, primarily to secure the border with Nepal. With the Maoists in power, China also hopes to use its ideological commonalities to suppress the Tibetan movement in Nepal. (Nayak, 2009)

When the Maoists emerged victorious in the April 2008 elections, China adopted a wait and watch policy because it was unsure of their intentions. After all, the Maoists were backed by India and were catapulted to the political centre stage only after a comprehensive peace agreement in which India had played a substantial behind the scenes role. However, media reports reveal that after several interactions with Maoists leaders, China has begun to feel quite comfortable with the Maoist-led government. The Maoists' ideological linkages with China and their keenness to neutralize India's influence in the region have also made them an obvious choice for engagement.

In fact, twelve high-level Chinese delegations, including two military teams, visited Nepal in the course of 2008-2009. During these visits, China has repeatedly assured economic, technological and military aid to Nepal. The Maoist-led government was also asked to adopt a 'One-China' policy, not to allow Nepalese land for anti-China activities, take strong action against Tibetan refugees and grant special facilities for Chinese investments in strategic sectors. Beijing has also initiated Track-II diplomacy with Nepal and invited Nepalese scholars to undertake visits to Chinese think tanks.

The increasing level of bilateral engagement also indicates that China is wooing Nepal as a new strategic partner. This has been confirmed by the statements made by various Chinese officials. For example, on 16th February 2009, Chinese Foreign Minister Yang Jiechi said in Beijing that China would prefer to work with Nepal on the basis of a strategic partnership. In fact, Vice Minister of International Department of the Central Committee of Communist Party of China, Liu Hongcai said in Kathmandu in February 2009 that "we oppose any move to interfere in the internal affairs of Nepal by any force". (Nayak, 2009) Similarly, on November 04, 2008, Liu Hong Chai, International Bureau Chief of the Chinese Communist Party, stated that "China will not tolerate any meddling from any other country in the internal affairs of Nepal- our traditional and ancient neighbour". (Nayak, 2009) During Chinese Premier Wen Jiabao's visit to Nepal in the first half of 2012 the two state leaders declared 2012 as "Nepal-China Friendly Exchange Year". In short, the increasing relationship between Nepal and China is no doubt a major concern for India from strategic angle.

Sri Lanka has generally enjoyed cordial ties with China since relations were first established with the recognition of the People's Republic of China in 1950 and the signing of the

Rubber-Rice Pact in 1952. Since then, and especially in the last decade, trade between the two countries has steadily expanded, culminating in the signing of a China-Sri Lanka Joint Communiqué in September 2005. This served as a benchmark for future expansion of the bilateral relationship. Gotabaya Rajapakse, Sri Lanka's Defence Secretary stated that "the President went to China three times, I went five times. Sometimes, the President speaks to the Chinese premier by phone. We have set up good relations. We have understood who is important to us." (Ranasinghe, 2010:3)

The growing ties have benefited Sri Lanka in a number of ways. For example, China was willing to supply arms to Sri Lanka at concessionary prices when India was restricted in the type of military assistance it could provide due to opposition from its state of Tamil Nadu. Also, China demonstrated an interest in investing in the development of Sri Lanka's infrastructure by providing interest-free loans and preferential loans at subsidised rates.

As a result, Chinese aid and commercial investments have increased markedly throughout President Rajapakse's term, most notably the Hambantota Port Development Project (US$ 1 billion); Norochcholai Coal Power Plant Project (US$ 855 million); the Colombo-Katunayake Expressway (US$ 248.2 million) and the National Performing Arts Theatre (US$ 21.2 million). Indeed, from 2006 to 2008, Chinese aid to Sri Lanka grew fivefold, replacing Japan as Sri Lanka's largest donor." (Ranasinghe, 2010:3) China views Sri Lanka as a strategically vital gateway for securing access to shipping arterials in the Indian Ocean.

Hambantota will be more than three times the size of Colombo harbour and is designed to function as a service and industrial port when fully completed, 14 years from now. It also has the potential to be developed into a major transhipment port. In addition, the port will be able to accommodate a new generation of mega-ships and is to include four terminals (12 berths), bunkering and refuelling facilities, liquefied natural gas refinery, aviation fuel storage facilities, bonded export processing zone and dry docks. The project is expected to generate more than 6000 jobs directly for the impoverished south of Sri Lanka, and another 50,000 indirectly in what is also President Rajapakse's home constituency.

As the main symbol of growing Sino-Lankan relations, the new Hambantota port (construction of which began in January 2008) will serve as a key transit point for oil and gas tankers accessing the Red Sea, Persian Gulf, Malacca Straits and the ports of Gwadar in Pakistan and Sitwe in Burma. Hambantota will also serve as a key maritime transit point to China's expanding investments among Indian Ocean island nations. However, the strategic value of Hambantota and its commercial/naval potential has raised Indian suspicions of China's intentions in what it sees as its sphere of influence, and in the process has contributed to an escalating India-China rivalry.

The four-day visit of Sri Lankan President Mahinda Rajpaksa to New Delhi from 9 June 2010 was followed by the visit of the Chinese Vice-Premier Zhang Dejiang to Colombo from 12 June. Strategic analysts and observers argued that it was not a coincidence and it was the part of Sri Lanka's fine balancing act to keep both these mighty neighbours in good humour, while at the same time benefiting from both.

The relationship between the two countries received a major boost during the recent three-day visit of 30 member delegation led by Chinese Vice-Premier Zhang Dejiang to Colombo, during which as many as six agreements were signed. The agreements cover highways development, enhanced cooperation in information technology and communication, development of maritime ports and the second phase of the Hambontota Port Development Project and maintenance of the Bandernaike Memorial International Conference Hall. Beijing offered US$ 200 million to Sri Lanka for the second phase of the Hambontota port. Zhang, who met

President Rajpaksa, reiterated China's commitment to the economic development of Sri Lanka (Das, 2010).

A statement issued by the Sri Lankan President's office described the meeting as cordial and constructive. It further stated that the Sri Lankan President thanked China for its continued assistance in the efforts to defeat terrorism and economic and social development both during and after the conflict. As a gesture of goodwill, Beijing recently donated 30 Chinese motorcycles to President Rajpaksa's younger brother Basil Rajpaksa, a minister in his brothers' cabinet, for use by officials in his constituency. In the past few years, particularly during the regime of President Rajpaksa, China and Sri Lanka have forged a comprehensive strategic relationship. This growing relationship is a concern for India from its strategic angle.

Regarding Afghanistan, China's interest remained marginal until Karzai's government opened up its energy, mineral and raw materials to foreign investment. In 2007, China emerged as Afghanistan's fifth-largest trading partner, behind Pakistan, European Union (EU), the US and India. China has been involved prominently in Afghanistan's infrastructure development, including telephone networks, irrigation projects, public hospitals, and several other reconstruction projects. Chinese companies like Zhong Xing Telecommunication Equipment Company Limited (ZTE) and Huawei have sought collaboration with the Afghan Ministry of Communications to implement digital telephone switches. Moreover, Chinese companies and workers have been hired by the EU for various reconstruction projects, including road restoration and infrastructure development

Though the bilateral relations during 2001-2006 remained at best cordial, it was in 2007, having won the contract for the copper mines in Aynak that Afghanistan emerged prominently in China's economic calculus. Since then China's growing economic clout has been most telling in its relations with Afghanistan. It is already a major source of consumer goods for Afghanistan. Since 2006, China has applied zero tariffs on 278 items of export products from Afghanistan. Although the Afghan economy accounts for less than one-tenth of one percent of China's overall trade, the availability of cheap natural resources on its western border is of tremendous interest to China.

Aynak Copper Mine deal which represents the world's largest untapped copper deposit estimated to be worth up to US$ 88 billion which is more than double Afghanistan's gross domestic product (GDP). The Chinese consortium Metallurgical Group purchased a 30-year lease for approximately US$ 3.5 billion, which makes this the largest direct foreign investment in Afghan history. To put this in perspective, this amount is equal to 20 percent of all foreign aid to the country since 2001, and the annual royalties alone from mining operations will represent 45 percent of the Afghan national budget just in this one project. (Kleponis, 2009:2) In terms of local development, the Chinese have committed to building a 400 megawatt plant to support the mine, as well as Kabul, and water development and purification, all of which will be available to the local population.

The Company, also known as M.C.C., will dig a new coal mine to feed the plant's generators. It will build a smelter to refine copper ore, and a railroad to carry coal to the power plant and copper back to China. If the terms of its contract are to be believed, M.C.C. will also build schools, roads, even mosques for the Afghans. Indeed, the cost of building numerous infrastructures in a volatile security environment like Afghanistan is prohibitive for many private firms. But the price tag is tolerable for the Chinese state firm because the project contributes to Beijing's plans for the development of western China and its regional trade links, which is part of a broader strategic outlook.

There are numerous indications suggesting that China is set to increase its investments and presence in Afghanistan in the near future. Afghanistan has substantial reserves of oil and natural gas in the northern parts of the country. The rising demand for natural gas has compelled China to explore alternate overland energy supply diversification in the neighbouring states in Central Asia, and also potentially in Afghanistan.

President Karzai's three-day state visit to China, beginning 23 March 2010, culminated with the establishment of the China-Afghanistan comprehensive cooperative partnership. President Karzai has publicly reiterated his ambition to emulate 'America's democracy and China's economic success' in Afghanistan. (D'Souza, 2010:7) This first visit after the Afghan President's re-election evoked immense international attention as an attempt by a beleaguered leader to indulge other big powers in the region at a time when he faces increasing criticism on corruption, cronyism and electoral reforms at home and abroad. Considering the fact that China's role in Afghanistan thus far has remained limited, this visit has sparked speculations regarding increased Chinese engagement in that country. In a joint declaration, Chinese President Hu Jintao emphasised on five aspects of the cooperative partnership: (1) political and diplomatic; (2) economic and trade; (3) humanitarian; (4) security and police affairs; and (5) multilateral efforts to build the comprehensive cooperative partnership of good-neighbourliness, mutual trust and friendship for generations.

Both Afghanistan and China pledged to step up greater economic engagement and cooperation in the security sector. The three agreements signed by the two countries span wide-ranging economic and technological cooperation that include providing favourable tariffs for some Afghan exports and technical training programmes. The reported bilateral trade which reached US$ 155 million in 2008 is set to further enlarge following the signing of these agreements. President Hu Jintao has called for deepening political ties, while urging greater cooperation in mining, agriculture, hydro-electric and irrigation and infrastructure projects.'

China has further expressed its willingness to 'support and

aid Afghanistan in its peaceful reconstruction and support Afghanistan's efforts to establish sovereignty, independence and territorial integrity'. Chinese Prime Minister Wen Jiabao pledged to extend aid and economic support for Afghanistan's reconstruction, while calling for both nations to jointly fight terrorism and drug trafficking. Beijing has pledged to provide a grant worth 160 million Yuan (US$ 23.4 million) to Afghanistan. In a separate meeting, Chinese Defence Minister Liang Guanglie pledged military assistance to Afghanistan in talks with his Afghan counterpart Abdul Rahim Wardak.

In short, economic interests remain central to China's involvement in Afghanistan. However, it remains to be seen for how long it can choose to pursue 'only economic activity' in Afghanistan. Given the dangers of Islamic extremism engulfing the region and spilling over into its restive Xinjiang province coupled with increasing cross-border drug trade, China will have to do a policy rethink. It may not tantamount to joining the US-led war, but would certainly involve steps that would have direct implications on the peace and stability of Afghanistan. China will have to prepare for a scenario of the US withdrawal from, or downsizing in Afghanistan, and the challenges posed by such an eventuality. In the prescription of a regional solution for Afghanistan's woes, China will have a critical role to play.

The present Sino-Afghan cooperative partnership might not mean as much as the comprehensive strategic partnership agreements with its all-weather ally, Pakistan, but has significant pointers of a change in China's thinking in anticipation of the US draw down from Afghanistan. Given China's political and military relationship with Pakistan, it has considerable leverages to influence the latter's Afghan policy, which will be critical to any long-term stabilisation efforts in Afghanistan. In short, it is clear that China is strategically moving and investing in the economies of South Asia to prevent the threat and the rise of any kind of dominant force in the region in the future.

Conclusion

China's interest in South Asian region has three major aspects. First is to minimising South Asia's alignment with United States, especially with India; second is to contain the hegemony of India and to prevent the possibility of any kind of threat in future and third is to create good neighbourly relations with all the countries of South Asia through investing in their economies, which is necessary to protect their strategic interest and peaceful rise. India's growth as a major power and paradigm shift in its foreign policy towards United States compelled China's involvement in South Asian region in an unprecedented manner. Today, for several strategic reasons, a relation with each nation in South Asia is important for their national interest, especially for to contain India and to checkmate the western influence in the region.

With this purpose China strategically weaving its web to 'concircle' India through the creation of pro-China micro poles. For this they investing in the smaller economies of Bangladesh, Nepal, Pakistan and Sri Lanka to gain a strategic foothold and build a diplomatic profile in the region. Their involvement in major ports around India is a best example of this purpose (Gwadar in Pakistan, Marao in Maldives, Hambantota in Sri Lanka etc.).

All their efforts have now transformed the South Asian region from India's purported 'near abroad' into China's own 'backyard'. Even though in September 2012 Chinese Defence Minister Liang Guanglie says that Beijing's increasingly close ties with South Asia are aimed at ensuring regional "security and stability" and are not intended to harm any "third party", all their movements in the region is raising India's strategic and security concerns day by day.

End Note

1. These include: 'India-Bhutan Treaty of Friendship' signed on 8th August 1949; 'Treaty of Peace and Friendship' between Government of India and Government of Nepal signed on 3rd July 1950, and 'India-Sikkim Treaty of Peace' was signed on 5th

December 1950. For more details, see A. Appadorai (1982) Select Documents on India's Foreign Policy, 1949-1972, Vol. 2, Delhi: South Asia Books.

References

Appadorai A. (1982), *Select Documents on India's Foreign Policy 1949-1972*, Vol. 2, Delhi: South Asia Books.

Beazley, Kim and Ian Clark (1979), *The Politics of Intrusion: The Superpowers and the Indian Ocean*, Sydney: Alternative Publishing Cooperative.

Bhattacharjea, Mira Sinha (2001), *China and the World and India*, New Delhi: Samskrithi.

Bhatttacharya, Abanti (2008), China and Nepal: Challenges for India, May 23 accessed from IDSA, available at, http://www.idsa.in.

Bruce Vaughn (2010), "Bangladesh: Political and Strategic Developments and US Interests", *CRS Report for Congress*, Congressional Research Service, R41194.

Chakrabarti, R. (1984), "China and Bangladesh", *China Report*, New Delhi, Vol. 30, No. 7, October.

Colonel Greg Kleponis (2009), "China's Role in the Stabilization of Afghanistan", *Of Interest,* Strategic Studies Institute, July 8.

Garver, John W. (1992), "China and South Asia", *The Annals of American Academy of Political Science*, No. 519, January.

Garver, John W. (1993), *Foreign Relations of the Peoples Republic of China*, Englewood Cliffs, NJ: Prentice Hall.

Gopal Pradhan, Radhe (1983), *America and China: A Study in Co-operation and Conflict,1962-1983,* Delhi: UDH Publishers.

Hariharan (2008), *China's Influence in India's Neighbourhood,* C3S Paper, No. 200, August 12 accessed from http:/www.c3sindia.org/strategicissues/305> on 20August 2008.

Hussain, T. Karki (1977), *China-India Conflict and International Politics in the Indian Sub-continent, 1962-1966,* Faridabad: Allied Publishers.

Khairul Islam, A.K.M. (2006), "The Post-Cold War US-China Relations: Win Win or Zero-Sum Game", *Asian Affairs*, Vol. 28, No. 24-25, April-June.

Kumar, Atul (2006), *China-Pakistan Economic Relations,* IPCS Special Report, September IPCS, New Delhi.

Mavara Inayat (2007), "The South Asian Association for Regional

Cooperation in Regionalism in South Asian Diplomacy", SIPRI Policy Paper No. 15, February.

Nayak, Nihar (2009), Nepal: New Strategic Partner for China, March 30 accessed from IDSA, available at, http://www.idsa.in.

Next Steps for the US in Afghanistan (2010), Task Force Report, Henry M. Jackson School of International Studies, University of Washington.

Parker, W. H. (1982), *Mackinder: Geography as an Aid to Statecraft*, Oxford: Clarendon Press.

Poorna Rodrigo (2010), *President Nasheed's China 'phobia'*, *Asian Tribune*, Accessed on 28 September 2010, available at, http://www.asiantribune.com/news/2010/05/04/news-analysis-president-nasheeds-china-phobia.

R.N. Das (2010), "China's Foray into Sri Lanka and India's Response", IDSA Comment, August 5, accessed on 6 August 2010, at http://www.idsa.in/idsacomments/ChinasForayintoSriLankaandIndiasResponse_rndas_050810.

Sergei, DeSilva-Ranasinghe (2010), "Sri Lanka: The New Great Game", *Strategic Analysis Paper*, Future Directions International-Independent Strategic Analysis of Australia's Global Interest, March 24.

Shambaugh, David (1991), *Beautiful Imperialist: China Perceives America, 1972-1990*, New York: Princeton University Press.

Shanthie Mariet D'Souza (2010), "Karzai's Balancing Act: Bringing 'China' In?", *ISAS Insights*, National University of Singapore, No. 98, May 7.

Sigh, Swaran (1994),"China's Arms Trade: Taking Off Again", *Strategic Analysis*, New Delhi: IDSA, Vol. 12, No. 7,October.

Singh, Swaran (2003), *China-South Asia: Issues, Equations and Policies*, New Delhi: Lancers Books, p. 11.

Sinha, Radha (2003), *Sino-American Relations: Mutual Panorama*, New York: Palgrave.

10

India and Pakistan in Afghanistan

Khursheed Ahmad Wani

"I dream of a day, while retaining our national identities, one can have breakfast in Amritsar, lunch in Lahore and dinner in Kabul. That is how my forefathers lived. That is how I want our grand children to live" [1]

—Prime Minister Manmohan Singh

Indo-Pakistani competition in Afghanistan long precedes the advent of the Hamid Karzai regime. Both states, since their emergence from the break-up of the British colonial empire in South Asia in 1947, have had ties with a range of Afghan governments. Afghanistan is not just the frontline state in US fight against the Taliban, but also a battleground for proxy war between India and Pakistan from last three decades. Pakistan is a security state defined by its ideational opposition to India. The Pakistani military remains obsessed with the idea of gaining 'Strategic Depth' against India in Afghanistan. Its worst nightmare remains an Afghanistan friendly to and dominated by its arch-enemies. So, Delhi's growing influence in Kabul after 9/11 has been causing panic in Pakistan. Pakistan claims India is using Afghan territory and India established their consulates in Afghanistan to foment trouble in Pakistan, especially in the province of Baluchistan.

India rejects these allegations and insists that its assistance to Afghanistan is purely developmental in nature and claims that the attacks against Indian assets in Afghanistan were the handiwork of Pakistani supported militant groups. But on the other side, Indian presence in Afghanistan has increased substantially, primarily in the sphere of institution building, capacity creation, and infrastructure and development assistance, with involvement in a large number of social, education and government sector projects. The message for India was that it could only operate successfully in Afghanistan with Pakistan's tacit approval.

Bilateral reapproachment between the nuclear neighbours is necessary for the development of Afghanistan. Another large scale war would have deep effects on the well-being of Afghanistan because the games both countries play in their countries will directly affect the stability in the coming years. India and Pakistan must both reflect on their own past actions in Afghanistan as well as their own limitations and strengthens, in framing their future Afghan policy.

Peace and stability in Afghanistan will not only help Afghanistan but will also help in the regional Integration in South Asia. In such conditions the paper will try to analyse both Pakistan and Indian interests in Afghanistan particularly after 9/11 and how the two countries are trying to override the other. Finally, the paper gives some recommendations for building a close friendly, cooperative and trustworthy relationship between these countries for the welfare of South Asia in general and Afghanistan in particular.

I

The Islamic Republic of Afghanistan as a linchpin to Persian Gulf, Central Asia, East Asia and shortest overland links to Europe need not be overstressed. Afghanistan is a landlocked country covering an area of about 6,53,000 square kilometres with no independent access to sea, nearest accessible port has to be either through Iran and Pakistan. The very fact that the Afghanistan shares 76 km. of border with China, 936 km. with Iran, 2,430 km. with Pakistan, 1,206 km. with Tajikistan, 744 km. with Turkmenistan and 137 km. with Uzbekistan testify to the strategic salience. [2]

The history of Afghanistan over the last two centuries reflects continuous interplay between domestic political forces and external actors, whose intervention has ranged from intellectual and politico-economic influences to physical occupation. Afghanistan has been in limelight since the Soviet invasion in December 1979 when it became a geopolitical issue in the Cold War between Soviet Union and the US. Both the superpowers fought costly proxy wars at the cost of Afghanistan. During the Cold War, the US helped Afghanistan militarily and economically in tooth and nail but after the disintegration of Soviet Union in 1991 the US abandoned Afghanistan. [3] Neighbouring countries like Iran and Pakistan, who had their own axes to grind, stepped into fill the vacuum by supporting their favourite warlords.

The ten-year War and national uprising against the Soviet and local communist forces thus turned into an on-going twelve-year civil War fought on ethnic, linguistic and religious grounds. After the rise of Taliban, other regional powers, such as Russian Federation and the newly independent countries of Uzbekistan and Tajikistan, also joined in. India, Saudi Arabia, Turkey and western intelligence followed them, aiding the opposition warlords against with arms, international publicity, food and medicine.

Pakistan and Afghanistan despite sharing hundreds of miles of unguarded border–historically speaking–and a bulk of population of the same Pashtun ethnicity which comprises the major ethnic group here in Afghanistan and second in Pakistan have witnessed souring diplomatic relations, thanks to the Durand Line, throughout the history since the inception of the later one. The Pukhtunistan issue had been an apple of discord between these two countries. Afghanistan government never accepted the Durand Line. The first confrontation was taken place in early 1950s when Pakistan applied for the membership of the UN.

Afghanistan opposed their membership on the plea that Pakistan is not willing to implement basic tenets of UN values and it has violated it through negating the right of plebiscite of the Pathans of the frontier. [4] The Af-Pak bilateral ties, last time, was badly hurt following the assassination of Professor Burhanuddin Rabbani on September 20, 2011 for which Kabul blamed Pakistani-based militants. The relations was further driven to the lowest ebb when the US military targeted the Pakistani border check post on November 26, 2012 killing at least 24 border security guards which consequently resulted in halting the NATO supply route and more strained relations between the trilateral partners in the war on terror. [5]

President Hamid Karzai in a speech during the annual opening of the parliament on 21st January 2012 said that Afghanistan is not a place for foreigners to do their political experiments or a laboratory that every few years they test a new political system. Too many of our civilians, soldiers and security forces lost their lives in order to defend this country. [6]

However during the recent trilateral summit (Afghanistan-Pakistan-Iran) in February 2012 on regional cooperation, Afghanistan President Karzai's meeting with Prime Minister Yousaf Raza Gillani saw the two sides reiterate their commitment to work together for restoring peace and stability in Afghanistan. According to a statement put forward out by the Prime Minister's Secretariat, Mr. Karzai termed Pakistan's support as critical to the success of Afghan owned and Afghan-led peace process and reconciliation in the country. He also quoted that Pakistan and Afghanistan were twin brothers and therefore should cooperate in the same spirit for the cause of peace and stability in both countries. [7]

With the resurgence of Taliban on both sides of the Durand line, Pakistan is eroding its sovereignty in Tribal Areas. Pakistan created Taliban in 1990's to achieve the notion of "Strategic depth", but now she is falling into what N.K. Jha said "Strategic ditch". [8] In fact, now in return Taliban is achieving "Strategic depth" in Pakistan, which seriously threatens Pakistan's own existence. Pakistan has strong and deep interests in Afghanistan. Most of the scholars accepted that Pakistan's security establishment viewing Afghanistan almost entirely through the prism of the Indian threat. Islamabad's principal objective in Afghanistan is to limit Indian influence. Pakistanis want American forces to withdraw in an orderly fashion from Afghanistan; cease all unilateral intelligence gathering, special operations, and drone strikes in the border areas, and provide no-strings-attached financial and military aid to Pakistan. In short, they want a free hand on both sides of the Durand Line. [9]

However, some of the scholars are of another view that Pakistan now regards Afghanistan increasingly through the prism of the existential threat to the Pakistani state posed by the Pakistani Taliban rather than through the prism of an Indian threat. They recognize that Pakistan itself is now the prime locus of a militant extremist insurgency that poses an existential threat to the Pakistani state. Hence, Pakistan seeks urgently to close off the Afghanistan war in order to focus at home. [10]

In addition to strategic interests, Pakistan is providing critical transit access to the sea and bilateral trade to Afghanistan. Pakistan has pledged an estimated US$ 330 million for the reconstruction of Afghanistan, including infrastructure, education and health projects. These include the new Torkham-Jalalabad road, the Nishtar Kidney Centre in Jalalabad, a 200-bed Jinnah Hospital complex in Kabul and educational facilities in various universities across Afghanistan. Another half a dozen large projects, including two eye hospitals, a limb centre at Badakhshan and two nuclear medical centres in Kabul and Jalalabad, are in the pipeline.

The two states have also made a provisional commitment to the TAPI gas pipeline project. Pakistan has offered 1,000 scholarships, subsequently doubled in March 2010, to Afghan students; 60 percent of all Afghan students who study abroad attend educational institutions in Pakistan. More than 1.7 million Afghan refugees continue to live in Pakistan. [11] But in spite of economic support, Pakistan is not popular in

Afghanistan. In one of the survey conducted by GALLUP regarding the role of NATO and regional players in Afghanistan in 2009, 33 percent Afghans said that Pakistan is supporting the Taliban leadership and only 30 percent people said that Pakistan's role is constructive. For India, 56 percent people supported India's role in reconstruction. [12]

II

India was keen on Pakistan's perception of Afghanistan and its policies there. From independence until 1992, India supported what government was in power in Kabul. Things changed after 1992, when the Pakistan backed Mujahideen entered Kabul. During the civil war period, India supported the group which was against the Pakistan. After the Taliban came into power, India for the first time supports the opposition group and not the government. India became a solid supporter of Northern Alliance. [13] Presently, India is a significant player in Afghanistan. It has the world's 5th largest aid programme there, having committed US$ 2 billion in developmental assistance. It has played a key role in reconstruction and has developed training programme for Afghan civil servants and police. [14] A wide spectrum of programs includes highway repair, communications, energy, health care, and capacity building in contributions to secondary education and the training of diplomats and bureaucrats. Indian-donated Tata buses are a key part of Kabul's public transportation. Assistance to Afghanistan's reconstruction advertises India's claims to be a regional economic power, ready to assume regional responsibilities. [15]

India has positive attitude towards the development of the Afghanistan. Indian Prime Minister Dr. Manmohan Singh at the Council on Foreign Relations on November 23, 2009 said, "...The road to peace in Afghanistan will be long and hard. But, given the high stakes involved, the commitment of the international community must be sustained by the firm resolve and unity of purpose. Democracy in an ancient land like Afghanistan will take root and come to terms with country's history and tribal tradition". [16]

On 23-24 January, 2007 then Indian External Affairs Minister, Pranab Mukherjee remarked, "India-Afghan bilateral relations are fast developing into a partnership which is very special to us...we are glad to be able to contribute to the reconstruction and rebuilding of Afghanistan". [17]

Afghan president Hamid Karzai's visit to India and the signing of wide ranging Strategic Agreement on October 4, 2011 set the stage for cooperation between two countries. Mr. Karzai's visit also underscored the growing economic and security ties between India and Afghanistan. [18] This agreement for the Afghans is a reaffirmation of the positive role India has played in the reconstruction of their country and future commitment at a time when other countries are talking of downsizing or even complete withdrawal. The partnership agreement, being first of its kind in post-Taliban Afghanistan, is designed to address the challenges of transition as much as to prepare ground for preventing the reversal of gains beyond 2014. [19]

The agreement on Strategic partnership comprises: (i) general principles, (ii) political and security cooperation, (iii) trade and economic cooperation, (iv) capacity development and education, and (v) social, cultural, civil society and people to people relations. This partnership agreement would be implemented under the framework of a Partnership Council, which will be headed by the Foreign Ministers of both the countries. The council will convene annual meeting. The Council will consist of separate Joint Working Groups on Political and Security Consultations, Trade and Economic Cooperation, Capacity Development and Education, Social, Cultural, Civil Society and people to people Relations involving high level representatives from concerned ministries/authorities. [20]

The agreement, among other matters envisaged that India

might give training, equipping and arrange capacity building programmes to units of the Afghan security forces as the US seeks to withdraw its forces from the country in 2014. After the agreement Dr. Manmohan Singh said, "The greatest need today is for the Afghan people to have peace and stability. India will stand by the people of Afghanistan as they prepare to assume the responsibility for their governance and security after the withdrawal of international forces in 2014". India stands by the people of Afghanistan in their journey towards capacity building, reconstruction, development and peace. We will do all that is within our means to help Afghanistan. [21]

Apart for the strategic pact, the two countries also signed two MoUs for development of hydrocarbons and mineral resources.

The representatives of 27 countries met in Turkey in November 2011. The Foreign ministers of India and Pakistan attended the conference. In this conference three core issues were examined: Preventing Afghanistan's emergence in the future as a battleground for regional rivalry; National security of Afghanistan which is under threat of destabilisation from the Taliban; and ensuring that sufficient number of jobs were created in the country so that young people of Afghanistan were kept away from taking up arms or indulging in terrorism and drug-trafficking. [22]

The Bonn Conference (December 2011) on Afghanistan was attended by nearly 100 nations and international organisations including India to chart out Afghanistan political future. The Bonn Declaration promises an inclusive order, "representing the legitimate interests of all the people of Afghanistan, regardless of gender or social status". It insists that a future power sharing agreement must include "the reaffirmation of a sovereign, stable, and united Afghanistan", "The renunciation of violence", "the breaking of ties to international terrorism", "respect for the Afghan constitution, including its human rights provisions, notably the rights of women". [23] But in real terms no significant development takes place. Continuously for the 5th year the number of civilian causalities has been increased from 1527 in 2007 to 3021 in 2011. [24]

While there is no denying that India's strategic interests lie in the long-term stability of the country, most of these projects are directed at capacity building and triggering economic growth. India has been providing educational and vocational scholarship, health services; it has dug tube wells across Afghanistan and India has built Afghanistan's new parliament building and trained its legislators. It has also helped to build a power transmission line to Kabul and developed a hydroelectric project at the Salma Dam in Herat at a cost of US$ 180 million.

Furthermore, India has also been active in providing various forms of humanitarian assistance to Afghanistan. One of the most visible and strategic projects is the 218 km. Zaranj Delaram road connecting landlocked Afghanistan to the Iranian port of Chabahar was already completed. The road reduces Afghanistan's dependence on Pakistan, providing a potential alternative route connecting Central Asia. However, optimal utilisation of this road would require greater security mechanisms. [25] In addition to these developmental activities, India had also quietly sought to bolster Afghanistan's security capabilities.

According to one analysis, India has provided US$ 8 million worth of high-altitude warfare equipment to Afghanistan, shared high-ranking military advisors and helicopter technicians from its clandestine foreign intelligence and counter-espionage organization, the Research and Analysis Wing (RAW). [26] So India's interests in Afghanistan are predominately strategic (to prevent the return of Taliban rule and the establishment of terror camps) and developmental (to build Afghan capacities in infrastructure and human resource development to strengthen governance), while ensuring the security and safety of its projects and people in Afghanistan. [27]

III

The opposing objectives of India and Pakistan make the case for a proxy war all the more likely, threatening not only the security situation within Afghanistan, but further exasperating the already tense relationship between Delhi and Islamabad. Since the beginning of 2010, both India and Pakistan have sought to prepare for what might be called the 'end game', the scenario when US-led NATO troops begin–even in small measure–their exit from Afghanistan. The London Conference in January 2010 made clear that transition from International Security Assistance Force (ISAF) to the Afghan National Security Forces (ANSF) was a key objective for almost all NATO countries.

The expected security vacuum in a post-NATO Afghanistan, or at least in most of rural Afghanistan, is likely to be filled by proxies belonging to one regional actor or the other. As the Pakistani army's strategic interests are driven primarily by two concerns: First, "to ensure that a balance of terror and power is maintained with respect to India", hence, maintaining at least a tenuous link with jihadi groups who can be deployed when the time comes. Second, the rationale underlying direct or indirect support to groups like the Afghan Taliban or the Quetta Shura (QST) is to 'hedge' against a US withdrawal from Afghanistan and against "Indian influence in Kabul".

While India has two main concerns with regard to the future of Afghanistan, each of which counters Pakistani objectives. First, to make sure that the Afghan Taliban do not occupy a dominant political position in the future make-up of the Afghan body-politic. Second, Indian security elites are afraid that the South and East of Afghanistan may serve to host training camps of the LeT in its war against the Indian state. [28] What makes the issue of Indian and Pakistanis actions in Afghanistan so thorny is that, all three parties have overriding national interest in the situation.

For India, there are the issues of interest to a rising

regional and global power, including access to valuable resources. New Delhi sees its efforts going hand-in-hand with the needs in Kabul. Regardless of whether Pakistan's desires for its own strategic involvement in Afghanistan are outdated, Islamabad nonetheless sees itself as surrounded by inimical forces, with China viewed as its only friendly neighbour. India's growing presence and influence in Afghanistan undercuts the Pakistani military establishment's long-term obsession with the quest for "strategic depth" against India. Consequently, it will relentlessly work, and go to considerable lengths, to undermine a cordial Indo-Afghan relationship and threaten Indian officials and personnel within Afghanistan. [29]

The policy of accusing each other has been in existence for a long period. Pakistan has accused India since 2003 of using its consulates in Jalalabad, Kandhar, Herat and Mazir-i-Sharif to launch and promote "terrorist activities' in Pakistan, particularly in strife torn province of Baluchistan and FATA. Pakistan has seen India's rapid insertion of material support into Afghanistan as a strategic loss and as rolling back decades of efforts to establish an Islamic alliance between Islamabad and Kabul. [30] The whole support of India to Afghanistan is seen in Islamabad and even in the Pakistani military headquarters in Rawalpindi–as part of a deliberate strategy to encircle Pakistan. [31] India is now geared up to impart extensive training to the fledgling Afghan National Army at training institutions across the country. Three areas have been identified under the 'Strategic Agreement' so far. One, increase in number of Afghan trainee officers, two, specialized training to already serving mid and higher-level officers in Afghan National Army (ANA) and three, training Afghan soldiers in counter insurgency and counter terrorist operations. [32] Pakistan accusing India of creating a force of Indian character in Afghanistan and tries to strengthens its position.

On the other hand India is accusing Pakistan of playing a double role in Afghanistan. India claims that Pakistan supported the on-going war on terror effort to secure Afghanistan. Pakistan joined the campaign against the Taliban, its erstwhile client, in part due to international pressure but also in part because Afghan extremists were swiftly becoming a threat to Pakistan's own security. But Pakistan on the other hand also supported Pakistan based Taliban and other terrorist groups. [33] Pakistan has used some of the groups associated with the Pakistani Taliban as proxy fighters against India in the on-going Kashmir conflict.

These accusations are logically difficult to prove or refute. But one thing is clear that the intensions of both the countries are not as clear as they want to show to the world. Pakistan's double game of supporting war on terror as well the terrorist groups and the opening of consulates in southern region and sending a large sum of money to Afghanistan in spite of helping any other country by India raises a question mark. In these conditions peace for Afghanistan is a dream, what British Secretary Davil Miliband argued, "...Given the scale of the geo-political challenges in this region–including the long running tensions between India and Pakistan and the presence of Iran- it can seem that Afghanistan is fated to remain the victim of a zero-sum scramble for power among hostile neighbours. The logic of this position is that Afghanistan will never achieve peace until the region's most intractable problems are solved". [34]

IV

This essentially shows that Cold War politics is going on between India and Pakistan for the influence of Afghanistan. India is investing in Afghanistan to counter Pakistan's evil initiatives. As long as the two states contest, Afghanistan will not have peace and there will be always an opportunity for any foreign country to intervene. Any long term peace, stability in Afghanistan depends upon the peace in the region between India and Pakistan. If there is considerable improvement between their relations and Pakistan feels secure of India's territorial interests, Pakistan may not feel the need for "strategic depth". [35] India should also understand the role of Pakistan in Afghanistan, because Afghanistan's problems cannot be resolved without Pakistan support. Both India and Pakistan need to become more transparent in its activities about Afghanistan. The intelligence agencies RAW and Inter-Services Intelligence (ISI) could be persuaded to enter a dialogue to establish a permanent India-Pakistani body at the intelligence and military levels, where complaints can be lodged and discussed.

Both India and Pakistan should take some short term and long term steps to make some progress in real terms which will help the common people of Afghanistan. India and Pakistan should make engagement with the common people and local communities. The problem of drug trafficking is badly affecting the Afghanistan. Recently, in one of the international conference United Nations Secretary General Ban Ki Moon has said that Afghanistan cannot be a stable Country when its economy depends heavily on drug trade. He added that there cannot be sustainable development when opium production is the only viable economic activity in Afghanistan and 15 percent of GDP comes from drug trade worth US$ 2.4 billion. Because of the large scale opium production, it will not only affect Afghanistan but whole South Asian region. That is why, M.K. Bhadrakumar wrote, "the biggest threat to regional stability originates from Afghanistan in the activities of radical extremists and drug trafficker." [36]

Pakistan and India should try to encourage the farmers to produce other crops than opium by giving them new agricultural technology, financial loans and proper education. Both countries should adopt bottom-up approach in supporting the Afghanistan. Now Pakistan is giving more importance to make better trade relations with India than to Kashmir issue. Recently, Pakistan granted Most Favoured Nation (MFN) Status to India. In February 2012, a high level economic delegation visited Pakistan under the chairmanship of Commerce Minister Anand Sharma and it seems that mind-set is changing for the better. Praising the Indian Prime Minister on February 22, 2012, Pakistan Prime Minister Yousaf Raza Gillani said, he had a great regard for his counterpart, who is a sincere person desirous of Friendly and Cooperative bilateral ties. This shows the considerable change in Pakistan policy towards India. So trade should be enhanced with Afghanistan also and the Afghan government should be supported for the utilization of their own resources like iron, copper and cobalt. There are US$ 908 billion estimated total worth of mineral deposits in Afghanistan including some rare minerals like Lithium, Caesium, Beryllium, Niobium and tantalum etc. [37] Discussions should be made on important pipe line TAPI (Turkmenistan- Afghanistan-Pakistan-India pipeline).

The United States and International Community should help Pakistan, Afghanistan and India to encourage relationship and develop a link between energy needed South Asia and mineral rich Central Asia. The resurgence of Taliban's after 2006 shows that they have popular support in Afghanistan may be because of foreign interventions. The USA has failed to eradicate the Taliban groups from the Afghanistan and no country can ignore this fact. So India and Pakistan in this situation should try to engage Taliban in talks for the future benefit of Afghanistan and South Asia. India should now begin talks with Taliban and a policy should be made which will clear Pakistan's mind about India. Then only a better, prosperous and stable Afghanistan can be seen on the globe.

V

In conclusion, the situation demands that both India and Pakistan should make a Treaty of peace, security and friendship with each other. The peace deal is very much necessary for the welfare of Afghanistan as well as South Asia. India and Pakistan's aim should be to prevent Afghanistan from once again becoming a source of terrorism. Both countries should understand the importance and each other's strength and role in international arena for the maintenance of security of the region. The strained relations will always give an opportunity to other countries to intervene in South Asia, that happened in past and that will happen in future, if the situation continues like this. Now the time has come to make South Asia as Zone of Peace.

End Notes

1. Prime Minister Manmohan Singh address to FICCI on January 8, 2007.
2. Rajen Singh Laishram, (2011), "India's Afghanistan Policy: Beyond Bilateralism", World Focus, Vol. XXXII, No. 11-12, November-December, p. 775.
3. Rizwan Hussain (2005), Pakistan and the Emergence of Islamic Militancy in Afghanistan, Burlington: Ashgate, p. 1.
4. APS Chauhan and Sudhir Singh (2009), "Pakistan-Afghanistan Relations-Post 9/11 and its Implications", in Monidra Dutta, (ed.), Emerging Afghanistan in the Third Millennium, New Delhi: Pentagon Press, p. 137.
5. "Resuming Af-Pak bilateral Ties: Mutual Respect and Quality Core for success", (2012) Afghanistan Times (Kabul), Editorial, January 12, available at,
http://www.afghanistantimes.af/index. php?option=com.
6. Graham Bowley and Sharifullah Sahak (2012), "Karzai Underscores Afghanistan's Right to Decide its Future", The Hindu (Chennai), January 23.
7. "Pakistan Central to Afghan Peace Process, says Karzai" (2012), The Hindu (Chennai), February 17.
8. Nalini Kant Jha (2009), "Resurgence of Taliban in Afghanistan: Implications for India and Pakistan", in Monidra Dutta, (ed.), Emerging Afghanistan in the Third Millennium, New Delhi: Pentagon Press, p. 142.
9. James Shinn, James Dobbins (2011), Afghan Peace Talks: A Primer, (Pittsberg: RAND corporation), p. 39.
10. Ibid., p. 41.
11. Rahul Roy Chaudhury (2012), "Pakistan", in Toby Dodge and Nicholas Redman, (eds.), Afghanistan: To 2015 and Beyond, New York: Routledge Publishers, p. 171.
12. Julie Ray and Rajesh Srinivasan (2009), "Afghans Assess Roles for NATO, U.N., Regional Actors", November 20", available at, http://www.gallup.com/poll/124445/afghans-assess-roles-nato-

regional-actors.aspx.

13. Frederic Grare (2006), "Pakistan-Afghanistan Relations in the Post 9/11 Era", Carnegie Papers, No. 72, October, p. 11.

14. Satish Kumar (2012), "Indo-Pakistan Relations and Afghanistan", World Focus, Vol. XXXIII, No. 1, January, p. 47.

15. Marvin G. Weinbaum (2006), "Afghanistan and its Neighbours: An Ever Dangerous Neighbourhood", USIP Report, No. 162, June, p. 16. www.usip.org.

16. Rahul Bhonsle and N Manoharan (2011), "India: Afghanistan's Partner in Nation Building", in R K Sawhney, et al, Afghanistan: A Role for India", New Delhi: KW Publishers Ltd., p. 165.

17. Ibid., p. 165.

18. Jack Healy and Alissa J. Rubin (2011), "Afghanistan Favours India and Denigrates Pakistan", New York Times, October 4, http://www.nytimes.com/2011/10/05/world/ asia/afghanistan/Afghanistan-Favors-India-and-Denigrates-Pakistan.com.

19. Shanthie Mariet D'Souza (2011), "India-Afghanistan Strategic Partnership: Beyond 2014", ISAS Paper, No. 142, October 24.

20. "Text of Agreement on Strategic Partnership between the Republic of India and the Islamic Republic of Afghanistan", Minister of External Affairs, Government of India, October 4, 2011, available at, http://www.mea.gov.in/mystart.php?id=100018343&pid=2339.

21. "Pak in Mind, Karzai signs Pact with Manmohan Singh" (2011), The Times of India, October 5.

22. "Turkey meet looks beyond U.S withdrawal from Afghanistan" (2011), The Hindu (Chennai), November 3.

23. Parveen Swami (2011), "Sound and Fury Signifying Nothing", The Hindu (Chennai), December 10.

24. http://www.bbc.co.uk/news/world-south-asia-16883917 The Number of civilian's killings is continuously increasing, 2007-1528, 2008-2118, 2009-2412, 2010-2790 and 2011-3021.

25. Shanthie Mariet D'Souza (2011), "Securing India's Interests in Afghanistan", The Hindu, October 22.

26. Shashank Joshi (2010), "India's Af-Pak Strategy", RUSI Journal, February/March, Vol. 155, No. 1, p. 23.

27. Rahul Roy Chaudhury (2012), "India", in Afghanistan: To 2015 and Beyond, Nicholas Redman and Toby Dodge, (eds.), New York: Routledge Publishers, p. 234.

28. Rudra Chaudhuri (2011), "Balancing US Interests in India and Pakistan", The International Spectator: Italian Journal of International Affairs, Vol. 46, No. 2, pp. 85-86.

29. Sumit Ganguly and Nicholas Howenstein (2009), "India-Pakistan Rivalry in Afghanistan", Journal of International Affairs, Vol. 63, No. 1, Fall/Winter, pp. 126-127.

30. Ibid., p. 134.

31. Savita Pande (2009), "Pakistan-Afghanistan Relations", in Monidra Dutta (ed.), Emerging Afghanistan in the Third Millennium, New Delhi: Pentagon Press, p. 259.

32. "Indian role in Afghanistan spells Danger for Pakistan?"(2012), South Asia Monitor, 7 Feburary, available at, http://southasiamonitor.org/detail.php?type=n&nid=1498.

33. K. Shankar Bajpai (2003), "Untangling India and Pakistan", Foreign Affairs, Vol. 82, No. 3, May-June, p. 112.

34. Davil Miliband (2010), "How to End the War in Afghanistan", The New York Review of Books", April 1, http://www.nybooks.com/articles/archives/2010/apr/29/how-to-end-the-war-in-afghanistan/?pagination=false.

35. Lecture by Professor A. K. Pasha in Pondicherry University on December 22, 2011.

36. M.K. Bhadrakumar (2009), "Indian Interests in Regional Security", The Hindu, August 28.

37. "Strategic Geography", Adelphi Series, Vol. 51, No. 425-426, p. XVII.

11

Search for Public Sphere in the Radicalised Pakistan

Shibu M.P.

The public sphere represents the ideal of a democratic politics and the ground for moral and epistemic values that nourish and maintain democracy like equality, liberty and rationality. It is the informal sphere of sociality positioned somewhere between civil society and the state where subjects participate in the rational discussion in pursuit of truth and the common good. The public sphere in any society determines the social order which develops through shared culture that in turn helped the participants to ascertain and express their needs and interests for the conception of common good. (Gordon, 2005)

About the Islamic state like Pakistan, the common perception amongst the academic think-tanks and strategic experts is that social order is maintained by Islamic laws and authority, backed by the use of force and reasonable threat of punishment, which is argued as a reflection of the Hobbesian method of maintaining a social order. They spot recent developments in Pakistan as an outcome of this process. The main objective of this paper is to validate that argument by analysing the recent developments in Pakistan in the milieu of War on Terror.

The Islamic groups had a considerable role in helping the Pakistan from the desolation of partition and this in a way gave them additional organizational skills. This pattern was repeated forty years later when many Islamist group worked with millions of Afghan refugees. Immediately after Independence, the Islamic groups pressurised the Muslim League government to turn Pakistan into an Islamic state. Maulana Mawdudi, the founder of Jamaat-e-Islami, formulated the argument that Muslim League had shaped a state ruled by Muslims, a Muslim State, whereas an Islamic conducts its affairs in accordance with the uncovered guidance of Islam and accepts the sovereignty of Allah and the supremacy of Allah's laws. The Islamists wanted to replace the British derived civil and criminal laws with *Shariat* laws. These Islamic as well as sectarian provisions were also incorporated in the Pakistan's Constitution.

In Pakistan, the state regime was not threatened by radical Islamists especially before its engagement in War on Terror. The state especially the army allowed the Islamists to function on a wider stage, equipping and training them, and imparting them political and strategic guidance. Both democratic and military establishments cannot limits the affluent radical Islamists and banning these groups mean a name change or the temporary suspension of operations. The Pakistani civil society, which is characterised by disconcerted struggle between the practices and values of pre-capitalist society and new sorts of social life, between authoritarian legacies and democratic aspirations, have a mixed response in issues of radicalisation.

Radicalisation Tendency in Society

The blasphemy laws once again triggered a debate in Pakistan's civil society with the awarding of death sentence to Aasia Bibi under Section 295C of the Pakistan Penal Code (PPC) for allegedly making derogatory remarks against the Prophet. Since 1986, when 295C was added, hundreds of people have been charged with blasphemy. Another victim of the radicalisation process was the killing Salmaan Taseer, Governor of Pakistan's Punjab province by his own Elite Police Force guard for his stance against the country's blasphemy laws. Pakistan's only Christian Minister, Shahbaz Bhatti was another victim who was shot dead on 2 March 2011 for diluting the countries harsh blasphemy laws, in Islamabad.

There were similar attacks on those who backed minorities.

The brutal assassination of Salman Taseer, Governor of Pakistan, had sent a disturbing signal about the subtle spread of radical Islamist sentiment infiltrating even the elite security forces. [1] This could be seen as an instance of increasing radicalisation of armed forces. According to data collated by the Pakistan Institute for Peace Studies (PIPS) for its annual Pakistan Security Report, Pakistan was the most violent country in the region. The country witnessed over 10,000 killed in violent incidents across the country. [2] In 2010, there were 44 suicide attacks in Pakistan, which killed 1,033 and injured 1,992 people. As compared to 2009, there were 80 suicide attacks, out of which 20 took place in Peshawar. However, the intensity of suicide attacks in 2010 was more. One of the most deadly attacks last year occurred in Yakka Ghund of Mohmad Agency, which killed 108 people. Another major attack that jolted Pakistan took place in Lahore in which 95 worshippers were killed and 92 others were injured.

Increasing radicalisation in society is reflected in the public response in these issues. A rally organised by the Jamat-ud Dawa in Lahore turned out to be huge success as the militant group had taken over the role of uniting various religious parties in the country. Under the banner of Tehreek-e-Hurmat-e-Rasul (Movement for the Honour of the Prophet), the JuD's rally was attended both by Dobandi and Barelvi parties, all of whom called for the death sentence to anyone calling for a change in Pakistan's controversial Blasphemy laws. Almost all political parties including the ruling coalition partners in Pakistan backtracked from their previous stand of amending the blasphemy laws. Parties like Imran Khan's PTI, Nawaz Sharif's PML-N actively engaged in street protest in favour of blasphemy laws organised by the religious right. This was widely acknowledged as a concern for not only in Pakistan but for the entire South Asian region.

The terrorism in Pakistan involves a significant ideological basis, which is either political or religious. Ideology inspired violence carried out by militant extremist individuals and groups could be psychological also. The radicalisation process was often associated with youth, adversity, alienation, social exclusion, poverty or the perception of injustice to self and others. The term 'radicalisation' is being employed to refer the increasing tendency to use a peculiar brand of religion as the justification for conquest and control over territory, populations and resources, and the establishment of specific forms of judicial and social systems by the use of force. Some analysts like American author and counter-terrorism practitioner Marc Sageman rejects the notion that radicalisation can aptly be described in terms of a fixed sequence of stages while others view terrorism as the final destination along a path of radicalisation characterised by a quite orderly series of phases.

Radicalisation of Pakistani students in Universities, colleges and religious schools became a challenge to state security. The nature of educational system in Islamic countries is viewed by experts as prime reason for youth radicalisation. The education system and the socio-economic system in southern Punjab and FATA compelled poor parents to send their children to sectarian religious schools. There were linkages between biases in education and the incidences of extremism, hatred and violence in Pakistan.

According to Dr. Muhammad Memon, Hamidudin Alkirmani, Professor and Director of Programs at the Institute of Educational Development at Agha Khan University in Karachi, the lack of religious diversity acknowledged in the education system and more broadly has serious consequences on religious and inter-sectarian harmony. Fear and discrimination is one of the reasons for non-Muslims not pursing higher education and drop out of schools at early stages. (Hussain, 2011)

The extremist infrastructure, widespread terror networks of the militant groups, and poor governance in the country had created a climate of fear and harassment. This helped the extremist elements in Pakistan to take advantage and supersede the welfarism of Pakistani state and support in favour of more Islamisation. According to a Gallup survey, majority of Pakistanis wanted the government to take steps for the Islamisation of society and almost a third of them believes that the process should be completed in one go. The study was carried out by Gallup Pakistan, the affiliate of Gallup International.

According to Press Watchdog Reporters without Borders, Pakistan became one of the most dangerous countries for journalists. Since 2010 about 15 journalists had been killed. Killing of Saleem Syed Shahzad, Pakistani bureau chief of *Asia Times online* who had a reputation for courageous reporting, was the latest incidence. According to the United States based Committee to Protect the Journalists, in the nine years since the abduction and murder of the Wall Street ·Journal Reporter, Daniel Pearl, 32 media professional had been killed, 17 of them in targeted attacks for clear work-related motives. [3]

Even though some members of the political leadership tried to reform the blasphemy laws, later they changed their stands. Under pressure from the People's Party (PPP) leadership; former Minister Sherry Rehman dropped the idea of drafting a bill to reform the blasphemy laws in view of the threats to her life. Meanwhile, *Citizens for Democracy* (CFD) –an umbrella group of individuals and organizations opposed to the misuse of blasphemy law and religion in politics–urged the political class to take a clear stand against this practice. The Human Rights Watch asked the government to immediately drop blasphemy laws against 17 year old boy for allegedly including remarks about the prophet in his answer sheet in April 2010. [4]

The situation in Karachi was that more than 1,400 peoples were victims of targeted killings in 2010 as opposed to 11,000 killed all over the country in terrorism in 2010.

According to security officials, there were nexus between politics and crime in Karachi. Extortionists, kidnappers, drug-peddlers, gunrunners and even petty criminals have managed to find their niche in one political party or the other. All of them heavily armed and most of them have the connections needed to escape arrest and prosecution. [5] Over 70 target killing incident took place in January 2010 causing panic among citizens. Out of these 70 victims, around 20 were workers and supporters of different political parties, and one was a policeman while the rest were common citizens. [6]

The US State Department's report on human trafficking, released on 27 June 2011, underlined the issue of militants using children for terrorist attacks in Pakistan. According to the report, in Pakistan non-state militant groups kidnap children or coerce parents with fraudulent promises into giving away children as young as twelve to spy, fight, or die as suicide bombers in the Pakistan and Afghanistan. The militants often sexually and physically abuse the children and use psychological coercion to convince the children that the acts they commit were justified. Disabled children and adults are forced to beg in Iran. Girls and women are sold into forced marriages; in some cases moved them across Pakistani borders and forced them into Prostitution. [7]

According to Aurat Foundation, a women's rights organisation, incidents of honour killings increased in Pakistan and in the past year 36 women were killed. According to Ashfaq Mengal, programme coordinator of the Aurat foundation, the police and law enforcement agencies had stopped providing data to the foundation due to which it had to collect details through district coordinators. About 76 cases were registered during the last year. [8] All these cases reflect the level of radicalisation process taking place in Pakistani society. The public sphere is shrinking as there is wider support for Islamisation and radicalisation from the civil society as well.

Radicalisation and State-Civil Society Interface
The Islamic state of Pakistan finds it difficult to demarcate

the boundaries of Islamisation and radicalisation. After joining hands with the west in the War on Terror it gets even more difficult to convince the civil society, which is dominated radical elements. The 'war on Terror' frame of thinking hampered the Pakistani state's relationship with Islam. Its defective constitutional framework forced the Pakistanis to refer to their eccentric and personal views on life through the lens of Islam. Such state of affairs has the effect of concealing every political, material and economic demand behind theological verbiage and ultimately favours religious parties and militants who are willing to use violence. (Etenaz, 2009)

The democratic state cannot go against the wishes of the civil society as its views are reflected as the voice of the society at large. It is a state where political party, leaders and civil society support democracy at the normative and conceptual level. The civil society organizations are doing more pro poor activities in Pakistan with the huge amount of money they are getting for charity from foreign countries. This is one of the reasons for the shifting the tide of people's support towards civil society from the state. Another reason must be the Pakistan's involvement in War on Terror joining hands with the western alliances.

This happens in a country where state is considered as an agent for fulfilling the wishes of Allah propagated by Islamic thinkers like Maulana Maududi, who visualised the idea that "the sovereignty of the state of Pakistan vests in God Almighty and that the government of Pakistan shall be only an agent to execute the Sovereign's Will". Pakistan is recognised not as a secular state with an extremist problem but as an Islamic state overburdened with political ambitions couched in religious terms.

It is well understood that the dominant sections of the civil society in Pakistan encourages Islamisation and thereby radicalisation. But it support base from the public cannot be seen on religious bases. As civil society is considered different from the state, which is supposed to protect the citizens from the state abuse, therefore permits the realisation of sovereign rights for citizens. In the Pakistani society, these rights have to be seen in parallel with the Islamic principles. It has to be viewed different from the pluralist and self organizing civil society seen in a normal democratic country. Discourses on national security, developmentalism and identity politics had moved Pakistani civil society in different directions. (Mustafa, 2005)

Thus, the explanation of civil society by Micheal Walzer, the prominent political philosopher, is more suitable in the context of Pakistan. According to him, civil society is a space of uncoerced human associations with a system of relational networks formed for the sake of faith, interest and ideology. The quest of democracy in Pakistan and other Middle Eastern countries is contextualised with a formal structure of rigid Islamic state dominated by a strong religious hierarchy. The rich urban groups would prefer democracy and modernisation even though they would like Pakistan to become a truly Islamic state. (Karim, 2008)

Although social capital of civil society organisations in Pakistan is considered independent from the state functions, but the case of organisations like Jamaat-e-Islami upholds the role of democratic state in manipulating the ambit of social capital mobilisation. (Mustafa. 2005) As Coleman puts it, "Social capital is defined as norms of behaviour and the social and functional behaviour between individuals and groups, which may facilitate the action of the social actors. (Coleman, 1988) More than democratic state, military governments in Pakistan respected the social capital of civil society organisation, especially religious organisations. The overall support of military while criticising the democratic establishments from the religious groups strengthens this fact. Historically, the military government in Pakistan had taken initiatives towards Islamisation showing allegiance to Islamic groups: Revision of textbooks, switchover of the medium of instruction from English to Urdu in Schools, Changes in radio and TV programmes to spotlight national identity, establishment of Shariat benches for refraining laws according to the tenets of Islam and setting up of a post-graduate faculty of Shariat at Islamabad University to produce experts with thorough grounding in Islamic jurisprudence and Shariat. [9]

The issue to be addressed is that, how the Islamic state of Pakistan could respond to the issue of radicalisation which is intensifying day by day. The ideological puzzle, "reconciling the different permutations of state and religion in the country with widespread ethnic and linguistic conflict and a dysfunctional oligarchic political order (Philip, 2004:163)", put forward by Stephen Cohen got complicated with the issue of radicalisation in Pakistan. The state failed to play an effective role in issues of increasing militancy and terrorist incidents, sectarian violence due to the unequal distribution of resources in provinces, unemployment and the recruitment of youth in terrorist organisations and the deteriorating human development indexes.

The state could take the initiative in bridging the gap between the various civil society institutions and strive for an independent voice in the international arena like what Iranian establishment is doing now. This would encourage nationalism within the state of Pakistan and dilute the conflicting interest at the societal level and a state-civil society interface could be created where subjects participate in rational discussion in pursuit of common good for a social order, rather than exclusively identify with Islamic principles.

End Notes

1. The Times of India, 5th January 2011,
2. The Hindu, 21st January 2011.
3. The Indian Express, 2nd June 2011,
4. The Hindu, 4th February 2011.
5. Daily Times, 18th January, 2011.
6. Daily Times, 31st January, 2011.
7. Dawn, 28th June 2011.
8. Daily Times, 5th January, 2011.

9. Islamisation of an Islamic Republic' (1979), Reviewed works, *Economic and Political Weekly*, Vol. 14, No. 23, p. 966.

References

Coleman, J.S. (1988), 'Social Capital in the Creation of Human Capital', *American Journal of Sociology*, Vol. 94, pp. 95-120.

Etenaz, Ali (2009), *Pakistan is already an Islamic State*, accessed 5th March 2012 at,
http//www.dissentmagazine.org/online.php/id=235.

Karim, Afsir (2008), 'Radicalisation of Pakistan and its Impact on India', *ORF Issue Brief*, No. 11.

Gordon, James Finlayson (2005), *Habermas-A Very Short Introduction*, Oxford University Press, Oxford.

Hussain, Azhar and Ahmad Salim (2011), 'Connecting the Dots: Education and Religious discrimination in Pakistan: A Study of Public Achools and Madrassa', *United States Commission on International Religious Freedom*, Washington D.C.

Mustafa, Daanish (2005), 'Anti-Social Capital in the Production of an (UN) Civil Society in Pakistan', *Geographical Review*, Vol. 95, No. 3, pp. 328-347.

Philip, Stephen Cohen (2004), *The Idea of Pakistan*, The Brooking Institution, Washington DC.

12

India's Role in South Asia

Shyna V.V.

"The Indian elephant cannot transform itself into a mouse. If South Asia is to get itself out of the crippling binds of conflicts and cleavages, the seventh will have to accept the bigness of the eighth. And the eighth, that is India, will have to prove to the seventh that big can indeed be beautiful."

—Bhabani Sen Gupta [1]

The end of the Cold War brought about a fundamental change, a paradigm shift in international relations. The predominant strain was of the primacy of economies in a market-driven international politics. There have also been significant attempts by the world's rich to consolidate regionally in order to prepare for the global future. South Asian Association for Regional Cooperation (SAARC) established in 1985 is the largest of any regional organization in terms of sphere of influence; the combined population of its member-states being more than 1.5 billion.

Some of the primary objectives of SAARC are to promote the welfare of the peoples of South Asia and to improve their quality of life; to accelerate economic growth, social progress and cultural development in the region; to promote and strengthen collective self-reliance among the countries of South Asia; to promote active collaboration and mutual assistance in the economic, social, cultural, technical and scientific fields. The management of relations with neighbours is the first priority of every country's foreign policy.

A stable, friendly and peaceful neighbourhood helps to reduce political, economic and military burdens on a country.

India and its South Asian neighbours share strong civilisation, cultural, linguistic and ethnic ties. India tried to maintain good relations with its neighbours because an unfriendly neighbourhood means tensions and heightened danger of conflict that means more military expenditure and diversion of sources from development to security.

The Indo-centrality of South Asia has quite obviously sharpened focus on India's policy in the region. India's objective in SAARC is to promote economic co-operation despite the political differences among the member countries. India believed that such co-operation would promote peace, harmony and greater stability in South Asia. [2] India has been the single largest democracy in the world for the majority of its post-independence history, despite regional and cultural differences. India is a giant among South Asian countries.

Because of the various accessories of power, sizes of population, history, civilisational role etc., India is the major undisputed power in South Asia. South Asia has a total area of about 4488 million sq. km. Out of this India (3287 million sq. km.) occupies 73.2 percent of the total area of South Asia. It is four times larger than Pakistan, which is the second largest in South Asia and second thousand times larger than the tiniest Maldives. India also has correspondingly larger and ever-expanding responsibilities that flow from the expectations of other regional and global powers and from the demands of its citizens for health, education, security and overall welfare. It occupies a unique position in the South Asian region.

By the virtue of its size, location and economic potential, India assumes a natural leadership role in the region. So it remains the biggest power in South Asia, and its significance in terms of how India sees itself and how others see it, is a key consideration for regional politics. The present paper focuses on the regional interactions through the SAARC forum for ascertaining the degree of leadership or hegemony manifest in the policies of India and perceptions of other South Asian states.

Perceptions of India's Power in South Asia

In South Asia, India is the dominant regional power: its population, GDP and military expenditure are three times larger than those of all its neighbours combined. Military power in South Asia is also acutely concentrated. India's military and paramilitary forces vastly outnumber those of its neighbours, as do the weapon systems and platforms in its arsenal. India is arriving on the world stage as the first large, economically powerful, culturally vibrant, multi-ethnic, multi-religious democracy. India became a leading member of the "South Asia" and to play a key role in the great political struggles of the next decades. [3]

The primary objective and overriding concern of Indian foreign policy since the dawn of Independence in 1947 has been the establishment of India's predominance in South Asia- a predominance whose legitimacy would be accepted by other nations in the region. That quest for predominance derives not only from all the objective factors that are used to measure power (size, population, resources, and industrial and technological capacity), but also from the Indian elite's perception that it inherited the Britsher's strategic and political legacy, including the strategic unity that Britain had imposed on the subcontinent. [4]

One of the main difficulties of approaching the theme of India's position as an emerging major power is that it is difficult to measure its power with any degree of precision. Methods of ranking, such as the one based on economic resources and military hardware, the reputational method, and a 'class analysis' which measures a state's net power in relation to putative adversaries come up with conflicting results. The net outcome is a sense of fluidity with regard to India's rank as a power and the conclusion that India belongs to the class of countries that are always emerging but never quite arriving. [5]

The increase in defence allocation during Sino-Indian war period, and increased military co-operation with the West saw the beginning of a greater security consciousness. It is the most powerful SAARC member both militarily and economically, causing many smaller SAARC members to feel apprehensive about Indian hegemony. India has a large Muslim minority (over 13 percent) but, despite the country's religious, ethnic and linguistic diversity, its democratic system ensures a relative degree of political stability.

India is a leader so far as agricultural products are concerned. Wheat production is more than 3 times than that of its second, the Pakistan. Rice production of India is 4 times higher than that of Bangladesh. Other countries of South Asia are agriculturally poor. In the production of other cereals like maize, barley, millets etc, India is ahead of other South Asian countries. With all states set on the path of economic liberalisation, market forces are overtaking the state as an arbiter of intra-South Asian economic relations.

The enormous potential of intra-regional trade and the increasing importance of regional economic blocs in global trading, private enterprise and business associations are setting the pace in transforming regional relationships and establishing an institutional framework for regional co-operation and networking. India signed the South Asia Free-Trade Agreement (SAFTA) with six other South Asian countries in January 2004 (Bangladesh, Bhutan, the Maldives, Nepal, Pakistan and Sri Lanka).

It came into force in January 2006, and commits member countries to a phased trade-liberalisation programme that began in July 2006. To promote trade among member countries of the SAARC, India had unilaterally removed all quantitative restrictions on the import of around 2,300 items from the other SAARC countries (Bangladesh, Bhutan, the Maldives, Nepal, Pakistan and Sri Lanka) in 1998. [6]

At the economic level, India is Bhutan's and Nepal's major export and import partner and Bangladesh's and the Maldives' main import partner. However, all these partners are among the world's least developed countries, so the volume of their trade with India is not significant. The statistics for intra-SAARC trade could rise only if India and Pakistan conducted significant trade with one another. [7] Today India provides the second largest consumer market in the world. When South Asian Free Trade Area is fully realised, the region will be the largest market in the world. It will enormously increase India's own importance and potential. [8]

Acting as a Family Member with other Countries

India's improvement of relations with her neighbour has always been one of the pillars of India's foreign policy. The three major rivers like Indus, Ganga and Brahmaputra divided between India, Pakistan, Nepal and Bangladesh have resulted in dispute over water sharing. India's successful intervention in Bangladesh is a major landmark in Indian diplomacy. It result a more practical and power oriented policy on world affairs. Indo-Bangladesh relations have been opened with the signing of the historic agreement on the sharing of the Ganga Water.

India is the warrant of stability in the chronically unstable South Asian region. Its relationship with Pakistan is evolving positively and the 'composite dialogue' launched in early 2004 has clearly decreased tension; however, it remains a central element of uncertainty. India's relationships with Nepal, Bangladesh and Sri Lanka are closely linked to the domestic situation in these countries as they affect India's own security. The process of integration, SAARC is hampered by bilateral disputes but remains a potentially important framework of cooperation. [9]

The core issue of dispute between India and Pakistan is not Kashmir as such but a more fundamental difference on the nature of state in India and Pakistan. The two country rivalry revolved around three long standing issues: Kashmir, communal tensions and the military. On May 11, 1998 Indian nuclear tests passed a wave of panic in the region. As India already held an advantage in conventional weaponry, to restore the strategic balance to South Asia, Pakistan was obliged to respond to India's May 1998 nuclear blasts. Pakistan's nuclear tests were undertaken in self-defence. By achieving mutual deterrence both the states served the interest of the peace and stability in South Asia. [10]

This counter-move invited severe criticism from US and her allies imposed an embargo on Pakistan. Both the nuclear armed states of South Asia have reached at a stage where war is no more option for resolving perennial dispute over Kashmir. Indian and Pakistani policymakers and strategic analysts see nuclear weapons as essential to maintaining state security and ensuring state survival. The major factor bedevilling India-Pakistan relations is more fundamental and relates to the lack of congruence between the two countries' political elites in terms of how they view their respective roles in South Asia. [11]

Furthermore, India had actively worked for the establishment of a friendly Afghan government in order to outflank Pakistan on her Western frontier, and to establish an acceptable buffer between the Soviet Union and South Asia. [12] Relations with Bhutan are close and India is associated with the planned development of the country. India helped Bhutan to become a member of the United Nations. And also in 1988, India encouraged to preserve the integrity of Maldives by coming to the assistance of that country and preventing an attempted takeover by armed forces. From the beginning, India has been a highly desired market for the Sri Lankans and an important source of supply of primary products at a lower cost. Sri Lanka is not economically dependent on India; there are many areas in which both countries can forge a vibrant economic co-operation.

India is the only country that is either close to, or has a large coastal line with all other South Asian countries. The fact is that there is no other country, equally big in size and sufficiently close by, to counter the predominant Indian position. Land locked countries like Nepal and Bhutan, for example, can hardly survive economically without India's co-operation. Most of what they produce in India and most of what they consume comes from India, not to speak of the fact that nothing can ingress to or regress from there to other countries without India's approval.

Theoretically all states under the operative international state system are considered as sovereign and equal but realistic view clearly indicates that the states are neither equal nor enjoy absolute sovereignty. [13] It is an Indo-centric region implying that India is the dominant power. Indian policy objectives have not only been to strengthen themselves militarily in order to assert their dominant position but also to prevent outsiders from encouraging the regional powers to challenge India's authority and to limit their involvement in the region. [14] The victory against Pakistan in 1971 resulting in creation of Bangladesh, nuclear test explosion at Pokhran in 1974 and achievement of self-sufficiency in food production resulted India's credibility and image in international politics. So the year 1971 was a turning point for South Asia and for India's role in the region. [15]

India has strong political and economic linkages with most other SAARC members. Since its independence on 15 August 1947, these have been embodied most clearly in its security treaties with the landlocked states of Bhutan and Nepal, its role in the creation of Bangladesh in 1971, its role in aborting a coup d'état attempt in the Maldives in 1989 and its continued interest in Sri Lanka's Sinhalese-Tamil conflict. India's leadership of the region is not accepted unequivocally. While India considers herself to be status-quoits, the neighbours think of India as the 'big brother'. [16]

Leadership does not reflect only one country's national interest; it reflects the common interest of a group of states in the global order. Though India is not a part of any major military alliance, it has close strategic and military relationship with most of the major power.

India as a Regional Hegemon

Two aspects of India's foreign policy based on its national interest are often misunderstood by the South Asian neighbours and especially by Pakistan. First, India is concerned about its autonomous status in the region. Autonomy for India requires that the whole South Asian region be free from outside influences. Thus, India has always opposed outside intervention or roles in South Asian affairs. Second, contrary to her neighbour's perception, India has a vital interest in the territorial integrity, sovereignty, and independence of all the South Asian countries. They see India's varying military (and other) interventions with and in neighbouring countries in terms of 'the outward projection' and demonstration of military might. [17]

Apart from smaller nations such as Bhutan and the Maldives, perhaps the one country in the region where India's involvement has not played against it to date is Afghanistan. India expects that the South Asian countries should also respect India's unity and territorial integrity. [18] Differences in political systems also make regional cooperation difficult. Except for India, none of SAARC's members have a stable and secular democracy. The economic potential and military capabilities of India have made the country a primary regional force in South Asia. India was referred to as the "key to the development and progress of SAARC". Its responsibility in shaping and directing the cooperation drive was recognized by extra-regional powers. [19]

Indian policies with regard to the liberation movement in Bangladesh in 1971, the ethnic crisis in Sri Lanka in 1987 and the attempted military coup in Maldives in 1988 are cited as illustrations of India's hegemonic authority in region. The most important result of the 1971 crisis on regional perceptions has been the demonstrated ability of India to alter the geo-political landscape of South Asia. Though 1971 can be claimed by India to be an exceptional case, it exists as a tangible evidence of India's over-bearing presence in the region.

The Bangladeshi Government has rejected the proposal of an American Company to supply gas from Sylhet to New Delhi through pipelines. Despite being aware of the obvious economic advantages of the proposal, Bangladesh has rejected this World Bank recommended project on grounds that it is not in the interest of Bangladesh. The fear rather than the existence of Indian hegemon makes the South Asian states apathetic to pursuing mutually beneficial economic policies. [20]

The linkage between security politics in the region and domestic insecurities continued with on-again tensions between India on the one hand and Nepal (borders, trade and transit agreements, migrants, water), Sri Lanka (Tamil politics) and Bangladesh (water allocations, migrants, insurgency spillovers) on the other. As regards Indo-Pakistani relations, the traditional pattern of hostility has not only continued but has also significantly escalated. [21]

The South Asian countries were not enthusiastic about South Asian Preferential Trading Agreement (SAPTA) because they felt that the impact of their unfavourable trade balance with India would be accentuated if liberalization is encouraged in regional context. Countries in the region also fear that if market forces are allowed to guide the intraregional trade India would emerge as the dominating factor leading to the political dependence of these states on India. India favours a bilateral dialogue for addressing these concerns, while the neighbours demand a multilateral regional approach. India fears that the neighbours would gang-up against her and demand unrealistic concessions in a multilateral milieu, while the neighbours suspect that India seeks to take undue advantage of the weak bargaining capacity of each state in a bilateral dialogue.

After 1971, the balance of power in South Asia was altered significantly with the defeat of Pakistan in 1971, and the emergence of Bangladesh, and the 'peaceful nuclear explosion' of 1974 which gave yet another indication of an 'Indira Doctrine', which visualised India as the hegemonic power of South Asia. [22] The origins of the Doctrine are traced to the Sri Lankan crisis of 1988 and laid down that India would consider the presence or influence of an external power in the region as adverse to its interests.

India's justification for the policy was an attempt to insulate the region from the adverse effects of the Cold War, but the neighbours viewed it as a policy to abolish any challenge to India's regional position. Altaf Gauhar, leading Pakistani columnist commented that, "The Gujral Doctrine is not a doctrine of good neighbourly relations but a Bharti Plan to seize the neighbour peacefully". [23] In November 1988, the Indian military in response to a request by the de jure government of Maldives helped to crush an attempted coup on the Island. It provided for the apprehensions about India's politico-military clout in South Asia.

In recent times, however, the problem has to some extent changed because on the one hand India has toned down its rhetoric, and on the other democracy has begun to put down roots in SAARC countries such as Pakistan, Bangladesh, Bhutan, Maldives and Nepal, while Sri Lanka is actively encouraging its Tamil minorities to participate in the democratic process. India has been using rhetoric to undo the harm caused by her policies in the region. Gujral Doctrine best illustrates this reality. It is a standard practice in international relations for the bigger states to grant concessions to the smaller countries. [24]

India's membership in ARF and Pakistan's exclusion from this forum demonstrates India's successful implementation of the Gujral doctrine to break out of its shackles in the South Asian region. Assuming the role of a mature and responsible Asian power with nuclear capabilities, India has been able to represent itself as possessing self restraint despite provocation and border incursions along its border regions. [25]

India's military capability would most likely enhance its standing much more in the Asian zone of conflict than at the global level, where thinking remains dominated by more economic, post-modern values. Indian diplomacy was a combination of generous big brother behaviour giving aid, seeking common good, and pressing them to fall in line on issues where India's national interests were at the risk, relations with Pakistan, on the other hand have been consistently antagonistic. The India-Pakistan relationship is a classic example of the "security dilemma," in which an increase in one state's capabilities enhances the vulnerability of the other, thus creating an unending spiral of insecurity.

The divergence between India and Pakistan has also been evident in their respective positions on Afghanistan. [26] India signed an agreement with Iran creating a railway service that will connect Iran, Afghanistan and India delivering oil and natural gas, as well as steel needed for a continuation of development efforts that India continues to be at the forefront in Afghanistan. India has engaged in a whirlwind of diplomatic activity.

It all began with the *Afghan-India security and development pact*, as well as the declaration of Pakistan granting India *most favoured nation trade status*. This from the outset foreshadowed a peaceful trajectory for India and its neighbours. [27] According to Pervaiz Iqbal Cheema, the most important impediment on the road to collective self reliance is not the incumbent asymmetry and the overwhelming stature of India but how other members perceive India's intentions with reservations and apprehensions. [28]

The insecurity of smaller countries engenders demand for external intervention in South Asian conflicts. South Asia's strategic location in the middle of Southeast, Central and West Asia, and at the centre of the Indian Ocean, ensures an adequate supply of such intervention. South Asia is slowly moving towards the curious regional structure of what might be called 'contested hegemony', in which the peace and war pattern between India and its neighbours remains much the same, but power differentials steadily lift India into prominence as an Asian great power. [29]

Many countries consider India as "a factor for the stability and protection of democracies and human rights in the South Asian region". Trade and bilateral economic cooperation have become the cornerstones of India's relations with the world. Its economic performance is simultaneously a very successful international calling card for a nation wishing to stake a claim as a meaningful power. It is hard to escape the impression that market interests and democratic principles are uneasily aligned in India today.

Therefore, conscious efforts at the political level and demonstration of political will by the South Asian leaders are absolutely necessary for the growth of regional economic cooperation in South Asia. India's policies of demanding certain concessions can be classified as arrogant but not outright hegemonic. At the same time India's neighbours are unable to distinguish between the guidance and domination traits of India's policies.

Conclusion

India's foreign policy is caught between New Delhi's aspirations for regional security management and its inability to legitimize those aspirations on the basis of a region-wide consensus. India considers those aspirations an essential prerequisite for it to be able to play a role within the international system commensurate with its actual and potential capabilities. India's participation in the SAARC underscores this contradiction. India remains the biggest power in South Asia, and its significance in terms of how India sees itself and how others see it, is a key consideration for regional politics. India's large growing economy, strategic location and friendly foreign policy have won it more allies than enemies.

It is now emerging as the swing state in the global balance of power. India, therefore, considered suspicion of her neighbours that she might harbour hegemonic ambitions and misuse the SAARC to further her objectives, as unjustified. It was extremely sensitive to the intrusion of great powers in the

South Asian region and wanted to keep their influence at bay to preserve its ideology of Non-Alignment. India's size, resources and power potential makes it implicitly predominant in the asymmetrical power structure in South Asia.

Issues such as cross-border terrorism and incidents of anti-India activities from terrorists of our neighbouring countries have impacted on the process of regional economic engagement, connectivity and people-to-people contacts. In short, the extreme power differential coupled with divisive political, ethnic and historical factors have engendered intense distrust within SAARC. The most serious impediment to greater cooperation in South Asia is the lack of consensus about the future shaped of the region. The political problems in South Asia are basically a reflection of the absence of a regional consensus on the role of the pivotal power- India on security issues.

This lack of consensus, in turn, results from the disparity between India's objectively determined pre-eminence in the region and its inability to translate this pre-eminence into a managerial role in the subcontinent in such a way that its legitimacy is not challenged either within or outside South Asia. And also the sense of insecurity among India's neighbours has been impelling them to bring an extra-regional power to countervail India's influence.

India has witnessed rapid economic growth in the past decade, and it has now become one of the emerging economies in Asia. India has increasingly asserted itself on the international stage, seeking greater presence in multilateral institutions, for example through its campaign for a permanent seat in the UN Security Council. And also political and strategic dialogue with the US on bilateral and regional issues is a new feature of India's foreign policy.

The US-India Summit of July 2005 attracted strong international attention, notably through their agreement to boost civil nuclear cooperation. So it is the only SAARC country that can viably afford unilateral measures. This is true not only because of its large economy, but also because of the multiple levels on which it operates. [30] India has become a more self-confident player with a potential to induce systemic-level transformations not just in its own region but also elsewhere. India assumes a natural leadership role in the region by virtue of its size, location and economic potential.

However, the over bearing presence of a neighbour with aspirations for global leadership has also been a source of discernments for other south Asian countries. India is not acting as a Hegemon but due to their own sense of insecurity, most of the South Asian countries regard her as a regional bully, out to finish them. India's rise is not a threat to her neighbours, but can have positive consequences depending upon how leaders of these neighbours view this as a threat or as an opportunity. India is trying to adopt the formula of living in harmony with neighbours. India no longer looks for reciprocity from them and offer generous aid packages to poor neighbouring countries and addresses their concerns with sincerity.

India's efforts in SAARC are feeble and had improved its policy towards South Asian neighbours. Restoration of responsible governments and economic development are necessary with institutionalised arrangements for conflict resolution. The enlightened and self confident leadership in all South Asian countries will fulfil the future realisation of interlinked region. India should also adopt sublime attitude and should follow the phrase "keep your friends close and your enemies closer". Of course, India will be a great power but certainly not a superpower. By adopting a policy of passive dissociation rather than diplomatic innovativeness with regard to the crisis in the regional states India has surrendered its leadership role in the region. For the SAARC countries deepening the regional integration process through a definite and time-bound policy measures is not only necessary but is imperative.

End Notes

1. Bhabani Sen Gupta (1984), "The Big Brother Syndrome", *India*

Today, 30th April, p. 122.

2. Suman Sharma (2001), *India and SAARC,* Delhi: Gyan Publications, p. 22.

3. C. Raja Mohan (2006), "India and the Balance of Power", *Foreign Affairs,* July/August.

4. Mohammed Ayoob (1990), "India in South Asia: The Quest for Regional Predominance", *World Policy Journal,* Vol. 7, No. 1 (Winter, 1989/1990), p. 109.

5. Stepheri Cohen (2001), *India: Emerging Power,* (New Delhi: Oxford University Press), pp. 25-31.

6. India: Country Commerce 2011, The Economist Intelligence Unit Limited 2011, p. 20.

7. Alyson, J.K. Bailes, John Gooneratne, Mavara Inayat, Jamshed Ayaz Khan and Swaran Singh, "Regionalism in South Asian Diplomacy" *Stockholm International Peace Research Institute,* Policy Paper No. 15, p. 18.

8. Vatsala Shukla (2005), *India's Foreign Policy in the New Millennium,* Delhi: Atlantic Publishers, p. 206.

9. India, Country Strategy Paper 2007-2013, pp. 1-4.

10. Rizwan Naseer and Musarat Amin (2011), "Dynamics of Balance of Power in South Asia: Implications for Regional Peace", *Berkeley Journal of Social Sciences,* Vol. 1, No. 1, January, p. 10.

11. Mohammed Ayoob, (1990) p. 119.

12. Harish Kapur (1993), *India's Foreign Policy-1947-92: Shadows and Substance,* Delhi: Sage Publications, pp. 90-91.

13. Pervaiz Iqbal Cheema (2007), "Indian Hegemonic tendencies", *Pakistan Observer,* June 12.

14. Ibid.

15. Ramesh Trivedi (2008), *India's Relations with her Neighbours,* Delhi: Isha Books, pp. 34-37.

16. Ummu Salma Bava (2007), "New Powers for Global Change-India's Role in the Emerging World Order", *FES Briefing Paper,* No. 4, March, p. 3.

17. Rohan Mukharjee and David M. Malone (2011), "Indian Foreign Policy and Contemporary Security Challenges", *International Affairs,* Vol. 87, No. 1, p. 98.

18. Kishore C. Dash (1996), "The Political Economy of Regional Cooperation in South Asia", *Pacific Affairs,* Vol. 69, No. 2, (Summer), p. 4.

19. Madhavi Bhasin, (2008) "India's Role in South Asia—Perceived Hegemony or Reluctant Leadership" Indian Foreign Affairs Journal, Vol. 3, No. 4, October-December, p. 10.
20. Ibid., p. 14.
21. Barry Buzan (2002), "South Asia Moving Towards Transformation: Emergence of India as a Great Power", *International Studies,* Vol. 39. No.1, p. 8.
22. Subrata K. Mitra (2003), "The Reluctant Hegemon: India's Self Perception and the South Asian Strategic Environment", *Contemporary South Asia*, Vol. 12, No. 3, September, p. 405.
23. *Times of India*, 15th June, 1997.
24. Madhavi Bhasin (2008), p. 18.
25. Faisal Yahya (2004), "Pakistan, SAARC and ASEAN Relations", *Contemporary Southeast Asia*, Vol. 26, No. 2 August, p. 365.
26. M.K. Bhadrakumar (2009), 'Challenges for Indian Foreign Policy', *The Hindu*, 6 March.
27. David Wolfe (2011), India's Whirlwind Diplomacy: Balanced Approach or Unrealistic Goals, November 10.
28. Pervaiz Iqbal Cheema, (2007).
29. Barry Buzan, (2002), p. 22.
30. Vikas Kumar (2010), Why is SAARC Gridlocked and how can it be Revitalised?, December 16, available at, http://www.clingendael.nl/publications/2010/20101217saarc.pdf.

13

Af-Pak Region: A Major Challenge to Peace in South Asia

Yaqoob Ul Hassan

It is more than one a decade since 9/11 and subsequently the war on terror in Afghanistan, that the world community in general and US in particular, although have succeeded in bringing Afghanistan around the international security community, but have failed to stabilize the state, especially the Af-Pak region; where the terrorists still enjoy the safe haven and support. The growing militant commotion in Af-Pak border pose the number of key regional threats; the increase in major attacks against the coalition forces in Afghanistan, it will further destabilise the Pakistan, and it will add encumbrance to any political solution of the Afghanistan.

The Deputy Secretary of State Negroponte warned in late 2008, "the United States and our allies face near-term challenges from Pakistan's reluctance and inability to roll back terrorist sanctuaries in the tribal region". [1] Any terrorist activity in the world, the clue leads to the western border of the Pakistan. The Af-Pak portion of the border has a broad implication for the international terrorism, as was revealed from the State Department's, "Country Reports on Terrorism 2007 (released in April 2008).

The United States remained concerned that the Federally Administered Tribal Areas (FATA) of Pakistan were being used as a safe haven for Al Qaeda terrorists, Afghan insurgents, and other extremists…Extremists led by Baitullah Mehsud and other Al-Qaeda-related extremists re-exerted their hold in areas of South Waziristan. Extremists have also gained footholds in the settled areas bordering the FATA. P [2]

The primary objectives of the US war in Afghanistan have been to destroy the safe haven from which Al-Qaeda planned and directed the 9/11 attacks. According to the Pentagon, the existence of militant sanctuaries inside Pakistan's FATA represents "the greatest challenge to long-term security within Afghanistan". [3] This was further revealed by General David McKiernan, the US commander, who asserted that tribal regions provide the main pool for recruiting insurgents who fight in Afghanistan, and that infiltration has caused a 30 percent increase in number of militant attacks in eastern Afghanistan over the past year. Another report stated that the militant infiltration from Pakistan now accounts for about one third of the attacks on coalition troops in Afghanistan. [4]

The portion of Pakistan-Afghanistan border continues to be home of the deadliest terrorists. The Pakistani failure to target Taliban after the *Operation Enduring Freedom*, when the Taliban leadership and top echelons fled to Pakistani tribal areas, had several deleterious consequences for years to come. After the 9/11 attacks, the US succeeded in changing the behaviour or attitude of Islamabad towards Taliban, but was not succeeded enough to change its interest vis-à-vis Taliban in Afghanistan. Since Al-Qaeda's retreat from Afghanistan, the tribal areas of Pakistan gave them the sanctuary and these tribal areas have become a small scale copy of Taliban-controlled Afghanistan, where Islamist militants can recover and plan fresh operations while, gradually imposing their will on the secluded region. The violence also proliferated from tribal areas to mainland. [5]

Terrorism posed a grave threat to the stability of Pakistan, but the military has still pick and choose approach to counter terrorism, it kills or captures the foreign militants, but provides the sanctuary to the Afghan Taliban for the "Strategic Depth" in Afghanistan. The doctrine which now stands for denying India a foothold in Afghanistan; which became possible only after the dismantling of Taliban regime, and now there is growing influence of India in Afghanistan, which is investing both in economic and social sectors. Providing the sanctuary to Taliban in FATA, has permitted Taliban to nurture their indigenous bases of support within southern and eastern Afghanistan itself, "whence they can slowly evolve into a timorous state within a state". [6]

It also breeds the violent jihadi culture (*Wahabism and Sulifism*) that eroded Pakistan's South Asian identity of (*Sufism*) while promoting an "*Arabist Shift*". [7] The emergence and affiliation of Pakistani Taliban or TTP with Afghan Taliban and Al-Qaeda are committed to wage a holy war against the Pakistan in order to establish complete *Sharia* laws. As Arshi Saleem has meticulously revealed it, "The inherent danger posed by the Islamic groups is that there has been a fundamental shift in their agenda. Simply, there is now a distinction between what can be termed 'Old' and 'New' Islamists in Pakistan. New Islamists (Pakistani Taliban, jihadi organizations, Islamists), who were initially inspired by Maududi's Islamic liberation theology and latter developed their own interpretations are generally protagonists of Political Islam, that is, they seek transform politics through religion and religion through politics.

They are unlike Old Islamists (traditional Islamic Madaris/Ulemas/Pirs/Sufis and manly Baralvi religious parties) who were accommodated by the secular elites, and thus, avoided political confrontation. Islamists organizations are based manly in the economically marginalized and socially traditional regions of Pakistan. The new Islamists in Pakistan were to attempt to capture civil society institutions with a view to eventually capture the state." [8]

According to one estimate, there are fifteen to twenty small, local militant groups in South Wazirstan agency and twelve in North Wazirstan, who are not only closely coordinating their operations, but have committed themselves to come to each other's rescue if needed, and are highly inspired by Taliban. [9]

However, right from the beginning, the Pakistani army

adopted the selective approach. It targeted the foreign fighters; mostly from Arab, Chechnya and Uzbekistan, linked to Al-Qaeda, not the Taliban, whom the military establishment still views as the potentially valuable asset for projecting Pakistani influence into Afghanistan. Musharraf considered strategic depth as "the new alliance that was based on politics of mutual vulnerability and leverage, which if carefully and craftily managed could be highly advantageous to his regime and Pakistan". [10]

The Bush administration treated Pakistan more as a part of solution to Afghan security than as a part of problem. However, the Obama administration on March 27, 2009, officially released its White Paper of the Interagency Policy Group's Report on US policy towards Afghanistan and Pakistan. The new strategy emphasised five objectives focusing on security and governance for both Afghanistan and Pakistan as well as a role for the international community: [11]

1. Disrupting terrorist networks in Afghanistan and especially Pakistan to degrade any ability they have to plan and launch international terrorist attacks.

2. Promoting more capable, accountable, and effective government in Afghanistan that serves the Afghan people and can eventually function, especially regarding internal security, with limited international support.

3. Developing increasingly self-reliant Afghan security forces that can lead the counterinsurgency and counterterrorism fight with reduced US assistance.

4. Assisting efforts to enhance civilian control and stable constitutional government in Pakistan and a vibrant economy that provides opportunity for the people of Pakistan.

5. Involving the international community to actively assist in addressing these objectives for Afghanistan and Pakistan, with an important leadership role for the UN.

Defence Undersecretary, Michele Flournoy, identified the critical aspects of this new strategy as "the recognition that

Afghanistan and Pakistan are two countries but that they compromise a single theatre for our efforts and for diplomacy". [12] The ungoverned porous border have bent safe havens and proved conducive to narcotics smuggling.

Any US strategy vis-à-vis Pakistan requires addressing the veracity that the US has a limited leverage to influence policy and operations in Pakistan, despite the huge military and economic aid. Moreover, media reports indicate that "many Pakistanis–including opposition parliamentarians–see the rise of violent Islamist militancy not as Pakistan's problem but as a by product of Washington's war in Afghanistan. They believe the problem would be solved by the departure of the US forces and their allies from the region". [13]

To the great dismay, the cooperation between Pakistan-US has not been able to stabilize the Afghanistan and dismantle and destruction of Taliban and Al-Qaeda. Now questions are raised about the sincerity and dedication of Pakistan in the war on terror, as Colonel Scott R. Taylor has put it:

"Not surprisingly, doubts are rising (again) in Washington about the post-9/11 relationship with Pakistan and its reliability as a security partner. Much distrust, however, lingers on both sides resulting from the last period of strategic cooperation (1980-1988) when the US and Pakistan armed the Afghan mujahideen to fight the Soviet occupation". [14]

Militant Groups Operating on the Pak-Afghan Border

Al-Qaeda: With the death of Osama-bin-Laden, who was killed in Abbottabad in a Pakistani garrison town near Islamabad, not in tribal areas and with the growing success in decapitating the other highhanded terrorists by the aerial drones, the Al-Qaeda has dispersed in tribal areas of Pakistan. Some US government officials believe that the future threat from Al-Qaeda will come from Yemen and Somalia rather than from the tribal areas of Pakistan.

Some were of the view that Al-Qaeda is no more relevant, "basically, we are winning dramatically, and you have an organisation which is a shadow of its former self. We have got to the point where the real danger is from lone wolves who decide by themselves to turn violent". [15]

However, with the decentralisation of Al-Qaeda, it has become more dangerous, as there is no central hub that can be decapitated. [16]

According to reports from Jane's Terrorism and Insurgency Centre, there are at least sixteen active terrorist groups headquartered in Pakistan, with many more groups from Asia, Middle East, Europe, North America and Africa cycling recruits through Pakistani training camps. [17]

It has developed a relationship with other terrorist organisations in Pakistan. As Seth G. Jones has observed, "Al-Qaeda provides several types of assistance to local militant groups in return for sanctuary. One is coordination. It has helped establish Shuras (councils) to coordinate strategic priorities, operational campaigns and tactics against Western allied forces". [18]

He has divided the Al-Qaeda into five tiers: firstly, central Al-Qaeda; which consists of leaders of the organisation based in Pakistan, the second tier consisted of those groups who are affiliated or are benefited from central Al-Qaeda's financial assistance and inspiration, receive guidance, training, arms, money or other support. The third group are those who have established a direct relationship with Al-Qaeda, but have not become formal members, they remain independent and pursue their own goals, but work with Al-Qaeda for specific operations. Fourth involves small dispersed, who enjoy some direct connection with Al-Qaeda, they are unstructured but often self-organised, a group that radicalise, congregate, and plan attacks informally. Finally, individuals who are inspired by Al-Qaeda and are outraged by perceived oppressions in Iraq, Afghanistan, Chechnya and Palestine.

Lashkar-e-Taiba and other Pakistani Militant Groups: Lashkar-e-Taiba (LeT), the only major Wahabi/Ahl-e-Hadith Jihadi outfits, which was created during 1989-90 in

Afghanistan's Kunar province. It has become increasingly recognized for its attack in India. [19]

At present this is the most organised and lethal terrorist group in Pakistan. Its relationship with Al-Qaeda was revealed by David Coleman Headly, an American citizen of Pakistani origin. Leshkar-e-Taiba (LeT) has remained very loyal to ISI. It operates exclusively outside of Pakistan and does not target the state. LeT has also been careful in attacking or conspiring attack in US homeland, knowing that it would provoke US retaliation. [20]

However, the Pakistani diaspora in Europe remain main source of recruitment and financial support to LeT. Pakistan Salafist Jihadists have ethnic links with the Afghan Taliban and popularly represent the TTP. While they sympathize with the Afghan Taliban and consider Mullah Omar as their primary leader, they operate mainly in Pakistan in the areas bordering Afghanistan. There are other three main Sunni Deobandi Jihadi groups operating in the rest of Pakistan; with heavy concentrations in Punjab and Sindh. The three groups are: Sipah-e-Sahaba Pakistan (SSP), Lashkar-e-Jhangvi (LeJ), and Jaish-e-Moohmmad (JeM).

Nevertheless, none of the above categorization is necessarily mutually exclusive, they often overlap in membership, communicate, help and come each other's rescue when need is felt. Later, it was Abu Ali Tunisi, an Al-Qaeda linked jihadi hailing from Tunis, who have managed to bring the rebels of four militant groups–Harkatul-Jihad-ul-Islam, Harkat-ul-Mujahideen, Jaish-e-Mohammad, and, Lashkar-e-Jhangvi–under the fold of Al-Qaeda. [21]

Haqqani Network: Haqqani Network has close links with Al-Qaeda and Taliban, and its nexus with Pakistan's ISI has allowed the network to survive and thrive in its fortress stronghold of North Wazirstan. The network operates primarily in the Afghan province of Khost, Paktika, and also has an extensive presence in Kabul, Logar, Wardak, Ghazni, Zabul, Kandahar and Kunduz.

The group is one of Afghanistan's most experienced and sophisticated insurgent organisations and one of the biggest threats to NATO and United States forces. The Haqqani network has been implicated in some of the biggest terror attacks in the Afghan capital of Kabul, including the January 2008 suicide assault on the Serena Hotel, the February 2009 assault on Afghan ministers, and the July 2008 and October 2009 suicide attacks against the Indian embassy.

These cross border extremist movements present a serious threat to both Afghanistan and Pakistan. Both are at the risk from a combination of violent insurgency, loss of public confidence and economic crisis. These militant networks across the borders are reinforced by economic components of "network war", which relies on transnational links of communications, funding, recruitment, and armament, rather than a territorial base. The Af-Pak region had already turned into a land bridge for the drugs and transit trade economies of the region, "trafficking in drugs, arms, and other items, including people, is an important element of network war, and smuggling is the classic livelihood of the borderlands; both of the major frontier ethnic groups–Pashtuns and Baluch–gain much of their income from it". [22]

However, the growing capabilities of Al-Qaeda and other terrorist groups can be effectively addressed only when the sanctuaries in Pakistan are shutdown, while, Pakistan can be able to address the growing internal anti-state elements in FATA, KP, and Baluchistan or significantly expand economic development only when there is stable and friendly Afghanistan. [23]

Pakistan-India in the End Game of Afghanistan

While India commands trust in Afghanistan precisely because it has no territorial or cultural claims in Afghanistan, it has invested in both economic and social sectors in Afghanistan. India has a huge stake in Afghanistan; it has built roads, transmission grids, schools, hospitals, and the parliament. Raja Mohan, the South Asian security expert, explains how India defines its strategic space, arguing that India's grand strategy divides the world into three concentric circles. In the first, which encompasses the immediate neighbourhood, India has sought primacy and a veto over the actions of outside powers. In the second, which encompasses the so-called extended neighbourhood stretching across Asia and the Indian Ocean littoral, India has sought to balance the influence of other powers and prevent them from undercutting its interest. In the third, which includes the entire global stage, India has tried to take its place as one of the great powers, a key player in international peace and security. [24]

India's Interests in Afghanistan

1. Develop a diplomatic relations with Southwest, Central and Southeast Asia, Afghanistan is an important corridor through which India can project itself well beyond Afghanistan.
2. Securing and retaining Afghanistan as a friendly state from which it has the capacity to monitor Pakistan. To cultivate assets to influence activities in Pakistan.
3. Militant groups present in Pakistan-Afghanistan border pose threat to domestic fabric of Indian internal security. [25]

Historically, Pak-Afghan relations have never been smooth and had the elements of recurring mutual suspicion. The most irritant factor between Pakistan and Afghanistan has been the unresolved issue of Durand Line; difference in their levels of socio-economic development, social and political structures and their proclivity to meddle in each other's internal affairs have also strained their bilateral ties.

Pakistan's Interests

1. To have completely secure western borders.
2. To have peaceful environment in Pakistan in general and its two provinces, i.e. Baluchistan and KP in particular.

3. To get a reliable and alternative source of gas supply from Central Asia as its existing reservoir are depleting.

Pakistan is concerned over the growing presence and influence of India in Afghanistan. Pakistan also believes that Afghanistan is a willing partner in India's purportedly anti-Pakistan designs. The Wiki leaks revelation about Afghanistan's harbouring of Baloch rebels, "President Karzai admitted in January 2007, to sheltering more than 200 Baloch nationalists and their families who had fled Pakistan. However, Karzai denied that India is keeping them a claim Pakistan rejects". [26] Pakistan has been led to respond to this supposed Indian encirclement by wielding its strategic assets chiefly-extremist elements engaged in Afghanistan and Kashmir/India. Through its silent backing of the Taliban it hopes for pro-Islamabad regime to take shape in Kabul.

Both India and Pakistan are always in 'blame game' as one Pakistani scholar revealed:

"Given that India and Pakistan are conflictual states, both are bound to rely on their comparative advantage at any given point to frustrate the other. India wants to capitalize on its increasing ability to interest the world, Pakistan would on its ability to worry the world, Pakistan fear that India is simultaneously marshalling the world against Pakistan; Islamabad claims too that it is covertly leveraging groups against it, evidence of which has been shared with both New Delhi and Washington. In theory, the policy of covert ops offers plausible deniability and India can, to its great advantage use the same groups that have now turned on Pakistan. A smart strategy this, but there is nothing cooperative and Lockean from this angle". [27]

Meanwhile, as the US tries to move forward in Afghanistan its efforts might be thwarted less by Taliban, directly than by the relations between India and Pakistan. Pakistan is concerned that India is troubling it from the west, as one analyst put it, "India which has invested in development in Afghanistan right down to the district level, is loath to lower its salience just because Pakistan wants it to do that. The US is in no position to ask India to step aside just because it [US] needs Pakistan to help it stabilize Afghanistan and yet, the US does need Pakistan". [28]

There is a web of competing interests in the region and stabilizing Afghanistan requires not just efforts within that country but also around it for those efforts to succeed to any degree. If Afghanistan becomes the contested zone for Pakistan and India, we can be sure that the country would return to the nineties and this time with more vengeance. Any new steps therefore would require the US to do an even tougher job alleviating Pakistan's concern vis-à-vis India in Afghanistan. United States endorse of talks with Taliban publicly if succeeds, India's marginalization seems only to increase.

Nonetheless, Pakistani establishment is convinced that the US will not wish to reduce India's influence in post-2014 Afghanistan and that to contrary, the US would wish to see India exercise a dominant role in the future of Afghanistan that is conjunction with America's strategic pact with India. [29] However, there is a shift in Pakistan's policy elite and military analysts in their judgment of 'strategic depth' and complete controlling of Afghanistan by Taliban. As the former Pakistani diplomat observed that, the establishment believes that Taliban cannot again capture the Kabul and North. Pakistani military establishment do not want the Taliban to capture the whole of Afghanistan, "because they would be free to turn on Pakistan by giving their support to their Pashtun brothers who are in revolt against Pakistan as part of the Pakistani Taliban (TTP)". [30]

Thus, it is imperative for Pakistan and India to cooperate if they are to tackle the threat posed by the Taliban and Al-Qaeda combined. Yet Karzai remains suspicious of Pakistan. And with the belief that India is creating trouble in Baluchistan and in the tribal areas, it is unlikely that the Pakistani army would abandon the militant group it has relied on to fight as proxies in Afghanistan and in Kashmir.

Post-2014

US Defense Secretary Leon Panetta recently revealed that United States could wrap up combat operations in Afghanistan by the end of 2013, well before the longstanding 2014 deadline when full control is to be ceded to Kabul. Troops would remain in Afghanistan until at least 2014 and perhaps even later.

Despite several years of attempts to engage Taliban in the political process, nothing concrete has been achieved so far, the main reason being the communication gap between the adversaries and the hesitation of the United States to include the Taliban in any peace process without achieving some success against them on the battlefield. However, Taliban is opening their political office in Qatar, gives us the perception that the US and the world community has accepted them as a political force, necessary for the US exit strategy form Afghanistan. Till now US believed in the strategy of destroy, build and talk and it did not work, Taliban are still keeping their links with Al-Qaeda.

There is a more scepticism that US will stabilize the region and construct a capable Afghan Army. This of course, leaves a question: will Afghanistan become a base for Al-Qaeda or follow-on transnational Jihadist groups in the event of a US withdrawal? The US will want a coalition government in which Taliban elements take cabinet positions in the current structure of the Karzai regime. The Taliban will want an entirely new government in which elements of the existing power structure might have a position but that would be an altogether new regime. But once US withdraw after a "decent interval", will result in a Taliban dominated regime. [31]

The US does not trust either Taliban or Pakistan. According to George Friedman US also knows two things: [32]

1. That the future of Afghanistan is of fundamental interest to

Pakistan. Instability or Indian or Iranian influence in Afghanistan is not in Pakistan's interest. Therefore, the Pakistanis will play a leading role in Afghanistan as they did after the end of the Soviet occupation.

2. The United States knows that India remains Pakistan's major adversary.

The army-mullah-terrorist nexus is a reality in Pakistan; the Obama administration's Pak-Af policy cannot break the military-mullah-terrorist alliance, as the US treats the army as the solution rather than a part of problem. For India its consequence are negative. In early phase of war on terror in Afghanistan, Washington has tended to turn a blind eye to these links. Just as the Pakistani military sees value in keeping alive its old jihadi assets, the US military presumably does not want to squander six decades of investment it has made in the Pakistani armed forces. That is why the Pentagon and the State Department have avoided applying the kind of pressure Pakistan sorely needs in order for it to rid itself of military control once for all.

Conclusion

Thus, it is more than one decade of US involvement in Afghanistan; it has failed to understand the cultural incompetence. The challenge for US security interest in South Asia is thus, at its centre, not a social problem, or a religious problem, or a generic "tribal" problem. It is a unique cultural problem, which is especially problematic for a country whose ethos and foreign policymaking paradigm is the national sublimation of culture in favour of assimilation through democracy.

Meanwhile, if reconciliation process brings a modicum of peace to Afghanistan, the American interests in the region, particularly in Pakistan, where struggle against extremism and terrorism will continue for the years to come. For the United States, short-term solution lies in bringing the Pashtun lands back from the radical brink is to strengthen and rebuild the structures from the inside rather from outside and to avoid exerting more pressure. The US have to understand that all Taliban are Pashtun, but not all Pashtuns are Talibans. Taliban is more a Pashtun problem. The US has to accommodate Pashtunwali- the Pashtun code of conduct millennia old that rests all on honour, hospitality and revenge.

The United States and other external powers that seek to support the new order in Afghanistan and stabilize both Pakistan and Afghanistan should encourage a multidimensional process of dialogue and peace building focused on the problems of the border region.

The end game in Afghanistan needs a regional framework and number of national and regional approaches. First at the national level, among the Taliban and other ethnic stakeholders in Afghanistan for evolving a power sharing formula, consensus and a trust-building process on other national issues.

Second, at the regional level between U.S. Taliban, Kabul and Pakistan, in order to address the issue of Al-Qaeda between Taliban and US, non-interference treaty between Pakistan and Kabul including commitments against supporting each-others non-state actors. There should be dialogue between Pakistan and India, on peaceful coexistence in Afghanistan. The saner voice should prevail that there is ample opportunity for the two to co-exist, especially in the development sector. Some progress towards a resolution of the Kashmir conflict could induce Pakistan to scale down its military behemoth. It could potentially reduce the attractiveness of using militancy as an instrument of foreign policy.

End Notes

1. K. Alan Kronstadt and Kenneth Katzman (2008), "Islamist Militancy in the Pakistan-Afghanistan Border Region and US Policy", *Congressional Research Service (CRS) Report for Congress*, November 21, p. 1.
2. Quoted in Ibid., pp. 1-2.
3. Ibid., p. 3.

4. *U.S Department of Defence,* (2008), "Report on Progress towards Security and Stability in Afghanistan", June.

5. Barnett R. Rubin and Abubakar Siddique, (2006), "Resolving the Pakistan-Afghanistan Stalemate", *United States Institute of Peace*, Special Report 176, October, p. 3.

6. Ashley J. Tellis, (2008), "Pakistan and the War on Terror: Conflicted Goals, Compromised Performance", *Carnegie Endowment for International Peace*, p. 22.

7. Suroosh Irfani, (2009), "Pakistan: Reclaiming the Founding Moment" in "The Islamization of Pakistan, 1997-2009", View Points from, *The Middle East Institute Washington*, p. 16.

8. Arshi Saleem Hashmi (2009), "Pakistan Politics, Religion and Extremism", *Institute of Peace and Conflict Studies* (IPCS) Research Papers, No. 21, May, p. 11.

9. *International Crisis Group, Asian Report*, (2006) No. 125, "Pakistan's Tribal Areas: Appeasing The Militants", December, p. 21.

10. Amin Saikal (2009), "Musharraf and Pakistan's Crisis", in Rajshree Jetly (ed.), *Pakistan In Regional and Global Politics*, Routledge, New Delhi, p. 8.

11. "White Paper of the Interagency Policy Group's Report on US Policy towards Afghanistan and Pakistan", available at, http://www.whitehousegov/assets/documets/Afghanistan-Pakistan_White_Paper.pdf.

12. Quoted in Melissa Chadbourne, (2009), "US Policy towards Afghanistan and Pakistan: Implications for the US and its Allies", *Johns Hopkins-SAIS*, p. 24.

13. Ibid., p. 25.

14. Colonel Scott R. Taylor, "Stabilizing US-Pakistan Relations: A Forward", United Sates Army, USAWC Class of 2008, U.S Army War College Callisle Barracks, p. 3.

15. Alex Spillius, Is Al-Qaeda On the Run?, Telegraph, 3rd July 2011.

16. Seth G. Jones (2011), "The Terrorist Threat from Pakistan, Survival, Vol. 53, No. 4, August-September, p. 70.

17. Ibid., p. 70.

18. Ibid., p. 71.

19. Ayesha Siddiqa, (2011), "JihadismIn Pakistan: The Expanding Frontier", *Journal Of International Affairs*, Vol. 63, No. 1 (Fall/Winter 2009), pp. 63-64. And also see, C. Christine Fair,

"Lashkar-e-Tayiba and the Pakistani State", *Survival*, Vol. 53, No. 4, August-September, pp. 29-52.

20. C. Christine Fair, (2011) "Lashker-e-Taiba and the Pakistani State", *Survival*, Vol. 53, No. 4, August-September, p. 44.

21. Syed Mazar Abbas Zaidi, (2009) "Organizational Profiling of Suicide Terrorism: A Pakistani Case Study", *Defense Studies*, Vol. 9, No. 3, September, p. 429.

22. Barnett R. Rubin and Abubakar Siddique (2006), "Resolving the Pakistan-Afghanistan Stalemate", *United States Institute of Peace*, Special Report 176, October, p. 11.

23. "The Next Chapter: The United States and Pakistan", *A Report of Pakistan Policy Working Group*, September, 2008, p. 21.

24. C. Raja Mohan, (2006), "India and the Balance of Power", *Foreign Affairs*, Vol. 85, No. 4, July-August, pp. 17-34.

25. C. Christine Fair, (2011), "Under the Shrinking US Security Umbrella: India's End Game in Afghanistan?" *The Washington Quarterly*, Vol. 34, No. 2, Spring, pp.180-181.

26. C. Christine Fair (2011), Under the Shrinking US Security Umbrella: India's End Game in Afghanistan, The Washington Quarterly, Vol. 34, No. 2, Spring, p. 184.

27. Ejaz Haider, (2010), "Not So Beautiful From This Angle", *The Hindu,* 12, November.

28. Ejaz Haider, (2010), "A Web of Competing Interests", *The Friday Times*, (February 5-11, Vol. XXX1, No. 51.

29. Khalid Aziz, (2011), "Unsatisfactory Endgame", *The Dawn*, 9th December.

30. Anatol Lieven, (2012), "Afghanistan: The Best Way to Peace", *The New York Review*, February 9, p. 30.

31. George Friedman (2012), "Afghanistan: Moving towards a Distant Endgame", *Stratfor,* February 7, available at: http://www.stratfor.com/weekly/afghanistan-moving-toward-distant-endgame?utm_source=freelist.

32. Ibid.

Index

Index

Y

Z